Oracle SQL*Loader
The Definitive Guide

Oracle SQL*Loader
The Definitive Guide

Jonathan Gennick and Sanjay Mishra

Beijing · Cambridge · Farnham · Köln · Paris · Sebastopol · Taipei · Tokyo

Oracle SQL*Loader: The Definitive Guide
by Jonathan Gennick and Sanjay Mishra

Published by O'Reilly & Associates, Inc., 101 Morris Street, Sebastopol, CA 95472.

Editor: Deborah Russell

Production Editor: Colleen Gorman

Cover Designer: Ellie Volckhausen

Printing History:

> April 2001:   First Edition.

ISBN: 1-56592-948-9
[M]

*To my mother, who nurtured my curiosity
and love for learning.*

—Jonathan Gennick

I dedicate this book to my wife, Sudipti.

—Sanjay Mishra

Table of Contents

Preface

SQL*Loader is an Oracle utility that's been around almost as long as the Oracle database software itself. The utility's purpose originally was—and still is—to provide an efficient and flexible tool that you can use to load large amounts of data into an Oracle database. To put it as succinctly as possible, SQL*Loader reads data from flat files and inserts that data into one or more database tables.

When SQL*Loader was first written, relational databases were not the norm for storing business data, as they are today. At that time, COBOL was in wide use, and much of the data that people wanted to load came from COBOL-generated data files. You can see that early COBOL influence as you study the nuances of the various datatypes that SQL*Loader supports.

Another reflection on its heritage is the fact that SQL*Loader is a command-line-based utility. You invoke SQL*Loader from the command prompt, and then you use command-like clauses to describe the data that you are loading. No GUI-dependent users need apply! If you want to use SQL*Loader, you'll need to get comfortable with the command line.

In spite of its age, and the fact that it's not as easy to use as many might wish, SQL*Loader remains a very capable utility. Oracle has maintained SQL*Loader over the years, and has made improvements where they really count. When it comes to reading data from a file, SQL*Loader can deal with just about any type of record format. Given a file of data to load, chances are that SQL*Loader can do the job for you. You're not limited to COBOL datatypes and record formats. Oracle has continually enhanced SQL*Loader over the years, and it now includes support for variable-length fields, comma-delimited data, and even large objects (LOBs).

SQL*Loader is also a high-performance utility. Much of Oracle's SQL*Loader development effort over the past few years has gone towards enhancing the performance of this venerable tool. The addition of support for direct path loads, and especially parallel direct path loads, is perhaps Oracle's crowning achievement in this arena. If you need to load data fast, SQL*Loader can do the job.

Why We Wrote This Book

In our experience, SQL*Loader has proven to be an extremely flexible and high-performing tool. Yet it's also a difficult tool for many people to learn. We are both database administrators, and remember well the many times we sat staring at the *Oracle Utilities* manual, trying to puzzle out some aspect of SQL*Loader's behavior. The syntax of the various clauses in the LOAD statement, which controls almost all aspects of SQL*Loader behavior, is complex and at times difficult to understand. It's also difficult to explain. Even the authors of Oracle's own manuals seem to have difficulty explaining some aspects of SQL*Loader behavior.

When we learn a utility, we try to leverage it for all it's worth. SQL*Loader is capable of many things that save hours of work, but we had to work hard to acquire that knowledge. In this book, we've tried to save you a lot of time and effort by clearly explaining how SQL*Loader works and how you can apply its many features to your specific data-loading situations. We hope you'll learn new things about SQL*Loader in this book and come away with a new appreciation of the power and flexibility of this classic utility.

Audience for This Book

The audience for this book is anyone who uses SQL*Loader to load data into an Oracle database. In our experience, that primarily equates to Oracle database administrators. Oracle is a complex product and one that's difficult to understand. DBAs are expected to know everything about it. So when someone has data to load, his or her first step is usually to visit the DBA. If you're an Oracle DBA, and you want to be prepared for that visit, this book should help.

The use of SQL*Loader is not restricted to Oracle DBAs, however. If you are a developer or an end user who occasionally needs to load data into Oracle, we hope that this book will open your eyes to what you can accomplish with SQL*Loader, and all without writing any code yourself.

Platform and Version

We wrote this book using Oracle8*i* as the basis for all the examples and syntax. Oracle8*i* has been around for some time now, and as we go to press, Oracle9*i* is around the corner. We were lucky enough to get some advance information about SQL*Loader changes for Oracle9*i*, and we've included that information in the book. We didn't want to spend a lot of time researching older releases of SQL*Loader, because the number of users running those older releases is on a steady decline.

Even though this book is based primarily on the Oracle8*i* releases of SQL*Loader, much of what you read applies to earlier releases as well. As you go back to older releases, however, you'll find that some datatypes aren't supported. You'll also find that you need at least an Oracle8*i* release of SQL*Loader in order to load data into object tables, nested tables, and VARRAYs (varying arrays). Generally, you'll find that new features have been added to SQL*Loader over the years to keep it current with the database software. For example, when partitioning features were added to the Oracle database, support for loading partitions was added to SQL*Loader.

Structure of This Book

This book is divided into 12 chapters:

- Chapter 1, *Introduction to SQL*Loader*, introduces SQL*Loader and the sample data used for most of the examples in this book. You'll also find an example, based on a simple scenario, of how SQL*Loader is used to load data into a database table. Finally, you'll learn about the different SQL*Loader command-line options.

- Chapter 2, *The Mysterious Control File*, introduces you to the SQL*Loader control file. The SQL*Loader control file, which differs from the database control file, describes the input data, and controls almost every aspect of SQL*Loader's behavior.

- Chapter 3, *Fields and Datatypes*, describes the different datatypes that SQL*Loader supports. Here you'll learn the difference between portable and non-portable datatypes, and appreciate some of SQL*Loader's COBOL heritage.

- Chapter 4, *Loading from Fixed-Width Files*, shows you how to use SQL*Loader to load columnar data. You'll also learn about some of the issues encountered when loading this type of data.

- Chapter 5, *Loading Delimited Data*, talks about some of the issues associated with the loading of delimited data and shows you how to leverage SQL*Loader to load such data.

- Chapter 6, *Recovering from Failure*, explains your options for recovery when a load fails. You'll learn how to determine how much data actually was loaded and how to restart a load from the point of failure.

- Chapter 7, *Validating and Selectively Loading Data,* explains the use of the bad file and the discard file, and shows you how SQL*Loader can be used to selectively load data from your input files.

- Chapter 8, *Transforming Data During a Load,* is one of our favorite chapters. You don't have to take your data as it comes. You can put SQL*Loader to work for you to validate and transform data as it is loaded. This chapter shows you how.

- Chapter 9, *Transaction Size and Performance Issues,* shows you a number of settings that you can adjust in order to get the maximum performance from SQL*Loader.

- Chapter 10, *Direct Path Loads,* explains the direct path load, which is possibly the single most important performance-enhancing SQL*Loader feature that you need to know about.

- Chapter 11, *Loading Large Objects,* shows several different ways to load large object (LOB) columns using SQL*Loader.

- Chapter 12, *Loading Objects and Collections,* discusses the issues involved when you use SQL*Loader in an environment that takes advantage of Oracle's new object-oriented features.

Conventions Used in This Book

The following typographical conventions are used in this book:

Italic
> Used for file names, directory names, table names, field names, and URLs. It is also used for emphasis and for the first use of a technical term.

`Constant width`
> Used for examples and to show the contents of files and the output of commands.

`Constant width italic`
> Used in syntax descriptions to indicate user-defined items.

`Constant width bold`
> Indicates user input in examples showing an interaction.

UPPERCASE
> In syntax descriptions, usually indicates keywords.

lowercase
> In syntax descriptions, usually indicates user-defined items such as variables.

[ ]
> In syntax descriptions, square brackets enclose optional items or sets of items from which you may choose only one.

{ }

In syntax descriptions, curly brackets enclose a set of items from which you must choose only one.

|

In syntax descriptions, a vertical bar separates the items enclosed in curly or square brackets, as in {TRUE | FALSE}.

...

In syntax descriptions, ellipses indicate repeating elements.

Indicates a tip, suggestion, or general note. For example, we'll tell you if a certain setting is version-specific.

Indicates a warning or caution. For example, we'll tell you if a certain setting has some kind of negative impact on the system.

Comments and Questions

We have tested and verified the information in this book to the best of our ability, but you may find that features have changed or that we have made mistakes. If so, please notify us by writing to:

O'Reilly & Associates
101 Morris Street
Sebastopol, CA 95472
(800) 998-9938 (in the United States or Canada)
(707) 829-0515 (international or local)
(707) 829-0104 (fax)

There is a web page for this book, which lists errata, examples, or any additional information. You can access this page at:

http://www.oreilly.com/catalog/orsqlloader

To comment or ask technical questions about this book, send email to:

bookquestions@oreilly.com

For more information about books, conferences, software, Resource Centers, and the O'Reilly Network, see the O'Reilly web site at:

http://www.oreilly.com

Acknowledgments

An extraordinarily large number of people had a hand in helping us develop and write this book—more so than in any other book that we've ever written. We extend our heartfelt thanks to the following people:

Deborah Russell

For editing this book with her usual deft hand.

Stephen Andert, Ellen Batbouta, Jay Davison, Chris Gait, John Kalogeropoulos,
  Cindy Lim, Kurt Look, Daryn Lund, Ray Pfau, Rich Phillips, Paul Reilly, Mike
  Sakayeda, Jim Stenoish, and Joseph Testa

For taking the time to read a draft copy of our book in order to perform a technical review of our work. Their suggestions and comments have made this a much better book.

David Dreyer

For generously expending the time and effort to write a C program to convert the text feature name data used throughout this book into various platform-specific datatypes. This allowed us to verify various aspects of SQL*Loader's behavior. Some of David's work appears as downloadable examples on this book's web site.

Daniel Jacot

For his help in explaining the characters used to represent positive and negative values in COBOL's numeric display and packed-decimal datatypes. Daniel also reviewed all the COBOL-related sidebars for accuracy.

Michael Mattias

For pointing us to his excellent, and rather fun, graphic and text tutorial on COBOL datatype representations.

Steve Comstock

For reminding us that in COBOL you use dashes, and not underscores, to separate words in variable names.

Ken Jacobs

For taking an interest in this book. Ken was the original product manager for SQL*Loader and is now the Vice President of Server Technologies for Oracle Corporation. Ken was instrumental in arranging for key Oracle developers to review this book.

From Jonathan

In addition to the many people who help directly with a book, there are always those who help in indirect ways. To my wife Donna, I express my heartfelt thanks for her continued support of my writing endeavors. I owe her big time, because our household would fall apart if she weren't running things while I write.

To my son Jeff, my daughter Jenny, and their friends Heather and John Grubbs, I say thanks for all the distractions. If you guys didn't traipse down to my office every once in a while and pull me away to go skiing, ice climbing, snowshoeing, waterfalling, or whatever, I'd turn into a workaholic for sure. Thanks for providing some balance in my life.

From Sanjay

Many thanks to Jonathan Gennick for providing me with the opportunity to be his coauthor. Thanks to my coworkers at i2 Technologies for always encouraging me to write my next book. Thanks to readers of my first book, *Oracle Parallel Processing*, who provided valuable feedback, and in turn encouraged me to write this second book. Thanks to my friends and family members for always being there for me.

Thanks to my wife, Sudipti, for her incredible patience and understanding. Much of the time I spent researching and writing this book would otherwise have been spent with her. I could never have written this book but for her constant support and encouragement.

1

*Introduction to SQL*Loader*

SQL*Loader is an Oracle-supplied utility that allows you to load data from a flat file into one or more database tables. That's it. That's the sole reason for SQL*Loader's existence.

The basis for almost everything you do with SQL*Loader is a file known as the *control file*. The SQL*Loader control file is a text file into which you place a description of the data to be loaded. You also use the control file to tell SQL*Loader which database tables and columns should receive the data that you are loading.

Do not confuse SQL*Loader control files with database control files. In a way, it's unfortunate that the same term is used in both cases. Database control files are binary files containing information about the physical structure of your database. They have nothing to do with SQL*Loader. SQL*Loader control files, on the other hand, are text files containing commands that control SQL*Loader's operation.

Once you have a data file to load and a control file describing the data contained in that data file, you are ready to begin the load process. You do this by invoking the SQL*Loader executable and pointing it to the control file that you have written. SQL*Loader reads the control file to get a description of the data to be loaded. Then it reads the input file and loads the input data into the database.

SQL*Loader is a very flexible utility, and this short description doesn't begin to do it justice. The rest of this chapter provides a more detailed description of the SQL*Loader environment and a summary of SQL*Loader's many capabilities.

The SQL*Loader Environment

When we speak of the SQL*Loader environment, we are referring to the database, the SQL*Loader executable, and all the different files that you need to be concerned with when using SQL*Loader. These are shown in Figure 1-1.

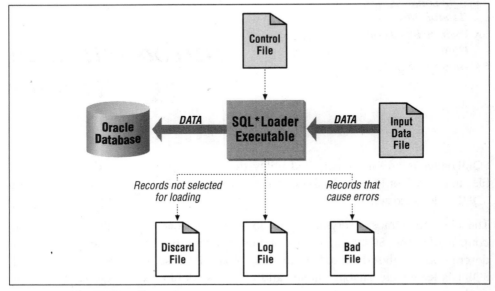

Figure 1-1. The SQL*Loader environment

The functions of the SQL*Loader executable, the database, and the input data file are rather obvious. The SQL*Loader executable does the work of reading the input file and loading the data. The input file contains the data to be loaded, and the database receives the data.

Although Figure 1-1 doesn't show it, SQL*Loader is capable of loading from multiple files in one session. You'll read more about this in Chapter 2, *The Mysterious Control File*. When multiple input files are used, SQL*Loader will generate multiple bad files and discard files—one set for each input file.

The SQL*Loader Control File

The SQL*Loader control file is the key to any load process. The control file provides the following information to SQL*Loader:

- The name and location of the input data file
- The format of the records in the input data file
- The name of the table or tables to be loaded

- The correspondence between the fields in the input record and the columns in the database tables being loaded

- Selection criteria defining which records from the input file contain data to be inserted into the destination database tables.

- The names and locations of the bad file and the discard file

Some of the items shown in this list may also be passed to SQL*Loader as command-line parameters. The name and location of the input file, for example, may be passed on the command line instead of in the control file. The same goes for the names and locations of the bad files and the discard files.

It's also possible for the control file to contain the actual data to be loaded. This is sometimes done when small amounts of data need to be distributed to many sites, because it reduces (to just one file) the number of files that need to be passed around. If the data to be loaded is contained in the control file, then there is no need for a separate data file.

The Log File

The *log file* is a record of SQL*Loader's activities during a load session. It contains information such as the following:

- The names of the control file, log file, bad file, discard file, and data file

- The values of several command-line parameters

- A detailed breakdown of the fields and datatypes in the data file that was loaded

- Error messages for records that cause errors

- Messages indicating when records have been discarded

- A summary of the load that includes the number of logical records read from the data file, the number of rows rejected because of errors, the number of rows discarded because of selection criteria, and the elapsed time of the load

Always review the log file after a load to be sure that no errors occurred, or at least that no unexpected errors occurred. This type of information is written to the log file, but is not displayed on the terminal screen.

The Bad File and the Discard File

Whenever you insert data into a database, you run the risk of that insert failing because of some type of error. Integrity constraint violations undoubtedly represent the most common type of error. However, other problems, such as the lack of free space in a tablespace, can also cause insert operations to fail. Whenever SQL*Loader encounters a database error while trying to load a record, it writes that record to a file known as the *bad file*.

Discard files, on the other hand, are used to hold records that do not meet selection criteria specified in the SQL*Loader control file. By default, SQL*Loader will attempt to load all the records contained in the input file. You have the option, though, in your control file, of specifying selection criteria that a record must meet before it is loaded. Records that do not meet the specified criteria are not loaded, and are instead written to a file known as the *discard file*.

Discard files are optional. You will only get a discard file if you've specified a discard file name, and if at least one record is actually discarded during the load. Bad files are not optional. The only way to avoid having a bad file generated is to run a load that results in no errors. If even one error occurs, SQL*Loader will create a bad file and write the offending input record (or records) to that file.

The format of your bad files and discard files will exactly match the format of your input files. That's because SQL*Loader writes the exact records that cause errors, or that are discarded, to those files. If you are running a load with multiple input files, you will get a distinct set of bad files and discard files for each input file.

You'll read more about bad files and discard files, and how to use them, in Chapter 7, *Validating and Selectively Loading Data*.

A Short SQL*Loader Example

This section contains a short example showing how SQL*Loader is used. For this example, we'll be loading a file of geographic place names taken from the United States Geological Survey's (USGS) Geographic Name Information System (GNIS).

Learn more about GNIS data or download it for yourself by visiting *http://mapping.usgs.gov/www/gnis/*. The specific data file used for this example is also available from *http://www.oreilly.com/catalog/orsqlloader* and *http://gennick.com/sqlldr*.

The Data

The particular file used for this example contains the feature name listing for the State of Michigan. It's a delimited text file containing the official names of the many thousands of lakes, streams, waterfalls, and other geographic features in the state. The following example shows three records from that file. The lines wrap on the printed page in this book, but in the file each name is on its own line:

```
"MI","Agate Falls","falls","Ontonagon","26","131","462851N","0890527W",
"46.48083","-89.09083","","","","","","","Trout Creek"

"MI","Agate Harbor","bay","Keweenaw","26","083","472815N","0880329W",
"47.47083","-88.05806","","","","","","","Delaware"

"MI","Agate Point","cape","Keweenaw","26","083","472820N","0880241W",
"47.47222","-88.04472","","","","","","","Delaware"
```

As you can see, the data in the file is comma-delimited, and each field is enclosed within double quotes. Table 1-1 shows the contents and maximum length of each field.

Table 1-1. Fields in the GNIS Feature Names File

Field Number	Maximum Length	Contents
1	2	Alphanumeric state code
2	60	Feature name
3	9	Feature type
4	35	County name
5	2	FIPS state code
6	3	FIPS county code
7	7	Primary latitude in degrees, minutes, and seconds
8	8	Primary longitude in degrees, minutes, and seconds
9	8	Primary latitude in decimal degrees
10	8	Primary longitude in decimal degrees
11	7	Source latitude in degrees, minutes, and seconds
12	8	Source longitude in degrees, minutes, and seconds
13	8	Source latitude in decimal degrees
14	8	Source longitude in decimal degrees
15	5	Elevation (feet above sea level)
16	10	Estimated population
17	30	The name of the USGS 7.5 minute series map on which the feature can be found

We used the following SQL statement to create the table into which all this data will be loaded:

```
CREATE TABLE gfn_gnis_feature_names (
    gfn_state_abbr CHAR(2),
    gfn_feature_name VARCHAR2(60),
    gfn_feature_type VARCHAR2(9),
```

```
    gfn_county_name VARCHAR2(35),
    gfn_primary_latitude_dms CHAR(7),
    gfn_primary_longitude_dms CHAR(8),
    gfn_elevation NUMBER(7,2),
    gfn_population NUMBER(10),
    gfn_cell_name VARCHAR2(30)
    ) TABLESPACE gnis_data;
```

As you can see, not all fields in the data file are to be loaded into the table. The source latitude and longitude fields will not be loaded, nor will the decimal versions of the primary latitude and longitude. The FIPS coding will also be omitted.

The Control File

The following control file will be used to load the feature name data for the State of Michigan:

```
LOAD DATA
    APPEND INTO TABLE gfn_gnis_feature_names
    (
    gfn_state_abbr CHAR TERMINATED BY "," ENCLOSED BY '"',
    gfn_feature_name CHAR TERMINATED BY "," ENCLOSED BY '"',
    gfn_feature_type CHAR TERMINATED BY "," ENCLOSED BY '"',
    gfn_county_name CHAR TERMINATED BY "," ENCLOSED BY '"',
    gfn_fips_state_code FILLER INTEGER EXTERNAL
        TERMINATED BY "," ENCLOSED BY '"',
    gfn_fips_county_code FILLER INTEGER EXTERNAL
        TERMINATED BY "," ENCLOSED BY '"',
    gfn_primary_latitude_dms CHAR TERMINATED BY "," ENCLOSED BY '"',
    gfn_primary_longitude_dms CHAR TERMINATED BY "," ENCLOSED BY '"',
    gfn_primary_latitude_dec FILLER DECIMAL EXTERNAL
        TERMINATED BY "," ENCLOSED BY '"',
    gfn_primary_longitude_dec FILLER DECIMAL EXTERNAL
        TERMINATED BY "," ENCLOSED BY '"',
    gfn_source_latitude_dms FILLER CHAR
        TERMINATED BY "," ENCLOSED BY '"',
    gfn_source_longitude_dms FILLER CHAR
        TERMINATED BY "," ENCLOSED BY '"',
    gfn_source_latitude_dec FILLER DECIMAL EXTERNAL
        TERMINATED BY "," ENCLOSED BY '"',
    gfn_source_longitude_dec FILLER DECIMAL EXTERNAL
        TERMINATED BY "," ENCLOSED BY '"',
    gfn_elevation DECIMAL EXTERNAL
        TERMINATED BY "," ENCLOSED BY '"',
    gfn_population INTEGER EXTERNAL
        TERMINATED BY "," ENCLOSED BY '"',
    gfn_cell_name CHAR TERMINATED BY "," ENCLOSED BY '"'
    )
```

Some explanations are in order. The LOAD DATA command tells SQL*Loader that you are going to load data from an operating system file into a database table.

Everything else that you see in this particular control file represents a clause of the LOAD DATA command.

The destination table is identified by the following INTO TABLE clause:

```
APPEND INTO TABLE gfn_gnis_feature_names
```

The APPEND keyword tells SQL*Loader to preserve any preexisting data in the table. Other options allow you to delete preexisting data, or to fail with an error if the table is not empty to begin with.

The field definitions are all contained within parentheses, and are separated from each other by commas. The fields in the data file are delimited by commas, and are also enclosed by double quotes. The following clause is used at the end of each field definition to pass this delimiter and enclosure information to SQL*Loader:

```
TERMINATED BY "," ENCLOSED BY '"'
```

The following three datatypes are used in this control file. They have no bearing on, or relationship to, the database datatypes of the columns being loaded. The purpose of the datatypes in the control file is to describe the data being loaded from the input data file:

CHAR

Tells SQL*Loader that a field is a text field.

INTEGER EXTERNAL

Tells SQL*Loader that a field is an integer represented using the text digits "0" through "9".

DECIMAL EXTERNAL

Tells SQL*Loader that a field is a decimal value represented using the text digits "0" through "9" and an optional decimal point (".").

Each field is given a name that is meaningful to SQL*Loader. For the nine fields being loaded into the table, the SQL*Loader name must match the corresponding column name in the table. The keyword FILLER identifies the eight fields that are not being loaded into the database. Their names do not matter, but the same naming convention has been followed as for all the rest of the fields.

FILLER fields are a new feature in Oracle8*i*. If you are using a release prior to the Oracle8*i* release, SQL*Loader will not recognize the FILLER keyword.

The Command Line

The command used to initiate this load needs to invoke SQL*Loader and point it to the control file describing the data. In this case, since the input file name is not provided in the control file, that name needs to be passed in on the command line as well. The following *sqlldr* command will do the job:

```
sqlldr gnis/gnis@donna control=gnis log=gnis_michigan data=mi_deci.
```

There are four parameters for this command:

gnis/gnis@donna

> The first parameter consists of a username, password, and net service name. SQL*Loader uses this information to open a connection to the database. The "gnis" user owns the table to be loaded.

control = gnis

> The second parameter tells SQL*Loader that the control file name is *gnis.ctl*. The default control file extension is *.ctl*, so the parameter needs to specify only the file name in this case.

log = gnis_michigan

> The third parameter specifies a log file name of *gnis_michigan.log*. The default log file extension is *.log*, so it's not specified explicitly in the parameter setting.

data = mi_deci.

> The fourth parameter specifies an input file name of *mi_deci.* This name ends with an explicit period, because the file name has no extension. Without the period on the end, SQL*Loader would assume the default extension of *.dat*.

By not including the input file name in the control file, but instead passing it as a command-line parameter, we've made it easy to use the same control file to load feature name data for all 50 states. All we need to do is change the value of the DATA and LOG parameters on the command line. Here's what it looks like to issue this *sqlldr* command and load the data:

```
$ sqlldr gnis/gnis@donna control=gnis log=gnis_michigan data=mi_deci.

SQL*Loader: Release 8.1.5.0.0 - Production on Wed Apr 5 13:35:53 2000

(c) Copyright 1999 Oracle Corporation.  All rights reserved.

Commit point reached - logical record count 28
Commit point reached - logical record count 56
Commit point reached - logical record count 84
...
Commit point reached - logical record count 32001
Commit point reached - logical record count 32029
Commit point reached - logical record count 32056
```

Pretty much all you see on the screen when you run SQL*Loader are these "Commit point" messages. If nothing else, they provide some reassurance that the load is progressing, and that your session is not hung. All other information regarding the load is written to the log file.

The Log File

The log file resulting from the load of Michigan's feature name data begins with the SQL*Loader banner. It goes on to list the names of the files involved in the load, and also the values of some important command-line parameters. For example:

```
SQL*Loader: Release 8.1.5.0.0 - Production on Wed Apr 5 13:35:53 2000

(c) Copyright 1999 Oracle Corporation.  All rights reserved.

Control File:   gnis.ctl
Data File:      mi_deci.
  Bad File:     mi_deci.bad
  Discard File: none specified

 (Allow all discards)

Number to load: ALL
Number to skip: 0
Errors allowed: 50
Bind array:     64 rows, maximum of 65536 bytes
Continuation:   none specified
Path used:      Conventional
```

You can see that the names of the control file, bad file, and data file are recorded in the log. This information is invaluable if you ever have problems with a load, or if you ever need to backtrack in order to understand what you really did. The log also displays the number of records to be loaded, the number to be skipped, the number of errors to allow before aborting the load, the size of the bind array, and the data path. The data path is an important piece of information. The load in this example is a *conventional path load*, which means that SQL*Loader loads the data into the database using INSERT statements. There is another type of load called a *direct path load*, which has the potential for far better performance than a conventional path load. Direct path loads are discussed in Chapter 10, *Direct Path Loads*.

The next part of the log file identifies the table being loaded, indicates whether or not preexisting data was preserved, and lists the field definitions from the control file:

```
Table GFN_GNIS_FEATURE_NAMES, loaded from every logical record.
Insert option in effect for this table: APPEND

   Column Name            Position   Len  Term Encl Datatype
------------------------------ ---------- ----- ---- ---- ------------
GFN_STATE_ABBR                   FIRST      *    ,    "   CHARACTER
GFN_FEATURE_NAME                 NEXT       *    ,    "   CHARACTER
```

```
GFN_FEATURE_TYPE                 NEXT      *    ,    "   CHARACTER
GFN_COUNTY_NAME                  NEXT      *    ,    "   CHARACTER
GFN_FIPS_STATE_CODE              NEXT      *    ,    "   CHARACTER
    (FILLER FIELD)
GFN_FIPS_COUNTY_CODE             NEXT      *    ,    "   CHARACTER
    (FILLER FIELD)
GFN_PRIMARY_LATITUDE_DMS         NEXT      *    ,    "   CHARACTER
GFN_PRIMARY_LONGITUDE_DMS        NEXT      *    ,    "   CHARACTER
GFN_PRIMARY_LATITUDE_DEC         NEXT      *    ,    "   CHARACTER
    (FILLER FIELD)
GFN_PRIMARY_LONGITUDE_DEC        NEXT      *    ,    "   CHARACTER
    (FILLER FIELD)
GFN_SOURCE_LATITUDE_DMS          NEXT      *    ,    "   CHARACTER
    (FILLER FIELD)
GFN_SOURCE_LONGITUDE_DMS         NEXT      *    ,    "   CHARACTER
    (FILLER FIELD)
GFN_SOURCE_LATITUDE_DEC          NEXT      *    ,    "   CHARACTER
    (FILLER FIELD)
GFN_SOURCE_LONGITUDE_DEC         NEXT      *    ,    "   CHARACTER
    (FILLER FIELD)
GFN_ELEVATION                    NEXT      *    ,    "   CHARACTER
GFN_POPULATION                   NEXT      *    ,    "   CHARACTER
GFN_CELL_NAME                    NEXT      *    ,    "   CHARACTER
```

The last part of the log file contains summary information about the load. If there were any errors, or any discarded records, you would see messages for those before the summary. The summary tells you how many rows were loaded, how many had errors, how many were discarded, and so forth. It looks like this:

```
Table GFN_GNIS_FEATURE_NAMES:
  32056 Rows successfully loaded.
  0 Rows not loaded due to data errors.
  0 Rows not loaded because all WHEN clauses were failed.
  0 Rows not loaded because all fields were null.


Space allocated for bind array:                  65016 bytes(28 rows)
Space allocated for memory besides bind array:       0 bytes

Total logical records skipped:          0
Total logical records read:         32056
Total logical records rejected:         0
Total logical records discarded:        0

Run began on Wed Apr 05 13:35:53 2000
Run ended on Wed Apr 05 13:36:34 2000

Elapsed time was:     00:00:41.22
CPU time was:         00:00:03.81
```

You can see from this summary that 32,056 feature names were loaded into the *gfn_gnis_feature_names* table for the state of Michigan. There were no errors, and no records were discarded. The elapsed time for the load was a bit over 41 seconds.

SQL*Loader's Capabilities

SQL*Loader is very flexible, and the example in the previous section shows only a small amount of what can be done using the utility. Here are the major SQL*Loader capabilities that you should be aware of:

*   SQL*Loader can read from multiple input files in a single load session.

*   SQL*Loader can handle files with fixed-length records, variable-length records, and stream-oriented data.

*   SQL*Loader supports a number of different datatypes, including text, numeric, zoned decimal, packed decimal, and various machine-specific binary types.

*   Not only can SQL*Loader read from multiple input files, but it can load that data into several different database tables, all in the same load session.

*   SQL*Loader allows you to use Oracle's built-in SQL functions to manipulate the data being read from the input file.

*   SQL*Loader includes functionality for dealing with whitespace, delimiters, and null data.

*   In addition to standard relational tables, SQL*Loader can load data into object tables, varying arrays (VARRAYs), and nested tables.

*   SQL*Loader can load data into large object (LOB) columns.

*   SQL*Loader can handle character set translation between the input data file and the database.

The capabilities in this list describe the types of data that SQL*Loader can handle, and what SQL*Loader can do to with that data. SQL*Loader also implements some strong, performance-related features. SQL*Loader can do direct path loads, which bypass normal SQL statement processing, and which may yield handsome performance benefits. SQL*Loader can also do parallel loads and even direct-path parallel loads; direct path parallel loads allow you to maximize throughput on multiple CPU systems. You'll read more about these performance-related features in Chapter 9, *Transaction Size and Performance Issues*, and in Chapter 10.

Issues when Loading Data

There are a number of issues that you need to be concerned about whenever you use SQL*Loader to load data into your database—indeed, you need to be concerned about these whenever you load data, period. First, there's the ever-present possibility that the load will fail in some way before it is complete. If that happens, you'll be left with some data loaded, and some data not loaded, and you'll need a way to back out and try again. Other SQL*Loader issues include transaction size, data validation (including referential integrity), and data transformation. Transaction size is partly a performance issue, but it also has an impact on how much data you need to reload in the event that a load fails. Data validation and referential integrity both relate to the need for clean, reliable data.

Recovery from Failure

There are really only two fundamental ways that you can recover from a failed load. One approach is to delete all the data that was loaded before the failure occurred, and simply start over again. Of course, you need to fix whatever caused the failure to occur before you restart the load. The other approach is to determine how many records were loaded successfully, and to restart the load from that point forward. Regardless of which method you choose, you need to think things through *before* you start a load.

Deleting data and restarting a load from scratch really doesn't require any special functionality on the part of SQL*Loader. The important thing is that you have a reliable way to identify the data that needs to be deleted. SQL*Loader does, however, provide support for continuing an interrupted load from the point where a failure occurred. Using the SKIP command-line parameter, or the SKIP clause in the control file, you can tell SQL*Loader to skip over records that were already processed in order to have the load pick up from where it left off previously. Chapter 6, *Recovering from Failure*, describes the process for continuing a load in detail, and some of the issues you'll encounter. It's a chapter worth reading, because there are some caveats and gotchas, and you'll want to learn about those before you have a failure, not afterwards.

Transaction Size

Transaction size is an issue related somewhat to performance, and somewhat to recovery from failure. In a conventional load, SQL*Loader allows you to specify the number of rows that will be loaded between commits. The number of rows that you specify has a direct impact on the size of the bind array that SQL*Loader uses, and consequently on the amount of memory required for the load. The *bind array* is an area in memory where SQL*Loader stores data for rows to be inserted into the database. When the bind array fills, SQL*Loader inserts the data into the table being loaded, and then executes a COMMIT.

The larger the transaction size, the more data you'll need to reprocess if you have to restart the load after a failure. However, that's usually not a significant issue unless your bind array size is quite large. Transaction size can also affect performance. Generally, the more data loaded in one chunk the better. So a larger bind array size typically will lead to better performance. However, it will also lead to fewer commits, resulting in the use of more rollback segment space. Chapter 9 describes these issues in detail.

Data Validation

Data validation is always a concern when loading data. SQL*Loader doesn't provide a lot of support in this area, but there are some features at your disposal that can help you ensure that only good data is loaded into your database.

The one thing that SQL*Loader does do for you is ensure that the data being loaded into a column is valid given the column's datatype. Text data will not be loaded into NUMBER fields, and numbers will not be loaded into DATE fields. This much, at least, you can count on. Records containing data that doesn't convert to the destination datatype are rejected and written to the bad file.

SQL*Loader allows you to selectively load data. Using the WHEN clause in your SQL*Loader control file, you can specify conditions under which a record will be accepted. Records not meeting those conditions are not loaded, and are instead written to the discard file.

Finally, you can take advantage of the referential integrity features built into your database. SQL*Loader won't be able to load data that violates any type of primary key, unique key, foreign key, or check constraint. Chapter 7, *Validating and Selectively Loading Data*, discusses using SQL*Loader and Oracle features to ensure that only good data gets loaded.

You don't always have to rely on SQL*Loader's features for data validation. It's entirely feasible to load data into a staging table, run one or more external programs to weed out any rows that are invalid, and then transfer that data to a production table.

Data Transformation

Wouldn't it be great if the data we loaded was always in a convenient format? Unfortunately, it frequently is not. In the real world, you may deal with data from a variety of sources and systems, and the format of that data may not match the format that you are using in your database. Dates, for example, are represented using a wide variety of formats. The date 1/2/2000 means one thing in the United States and quite another in Europe.

For dates and numbers, you can often use Oracle's built-in TO_DATE and TO_NUMBER functions to convert a character-based representation to a value that can be loaded into a database DATE or NUMBER column. In fact, for date fields, you can embed the date format into your control file as part of the field definition.

SQL*Loader allows you access to Oracle's entire library of built-in SQL functions. You aren't limited to just TO_DATE, TO_NUMBER, and TO_CHAR. Not only can you access all the built-in SQL functions, you can also write PL/SQL code to manipulate the data being loaded. This opens up a world of possibilities, which are discussed in Chapter 8, *Transforming Data During a Load.*

Invoking SQL*Loader

On Unix systems, the command used to invoke SQL*Loader is *sqlldr*. On Windows systems running Oracle8*i*, release 8.1 or higher, the command is also *sqlldr*. Prior to release 8.1, the SQL*Loader command on Windows systems included the first two digits of the Oracle release number. Thus you had *sqlldr80* (Oracle8, release 8.0), *sqlldr73* (Oracle7, release 7.3), and so forth.

SQL*Loader can be invoked in one of three ways:

```
sqlldr

sqlldr keyword=value [keyword=value ...]

sqlldr value [value ...]
```

Issuing the *sqlldr* command by itself results in a list of valid command-line parameters being displayed. Command-line parameters are usually keyword/value pairs, and may be any combination of the following:

```
USERID={username[/password][@net_service_name]|/}
CONTROL=control_file_name
LOG=path_file_name
BAD=path_file_name
DATA=path_file_name
DISCARD=path_file_name
DISCARDMAX=logical_record_count
SKIP=logical_record_count
SKIP_INDEX_MAINTENANCE={TRUE | FALSE}
SKIP_UNUSABLE_INDEXES={TRUE | FALSE}
LOAD=logical_record_count
ERRORS=insert_error_count
ROWS=rows_in_bind_array
BINDSIZE=bytes_in_bind_array
SILENT=[(]keyword[,keyword...][)]
DIRECT={TRUE | FALSE}
PARFILE=path_file_name
PARALLEL={TRUE | FALSE}
READSIZE=bytes_in_read_buffer
FILE=database_datafile_name
```

Command-line parameters may be passed by position instead of by keyword. The rules for doing this are described at the end of the next section.

Command-Line Parameters

The SQL*Loader parameter descriptions are as follows:

USERID = {username[/password] [@net_service_name] | /}

Specifies the username and password to use when connecting to the database. The *net_service_name* parameter optionally allows you to connect to a remote database. Use a forward-slash character (/) to connect to a local database using operating system authentication. On Unix systems, you may want to omit the password and allow SQL*Loader to prompt you for it. If you omit both the username and the password, SQL*Loader will prompt you for both.

On Unix systems you should generally avoid placing a password on the command line, because that password will be displayed whenever other users issue a command, such as *ps −ef,* that displays a list of current processes running on the system. Either let SQL*Loader prompt you for your password, or use operating system authentication. (If you don't know what operating system authentication is, ask your DBA.)

CONTROL = control_file_name

Specifies the name, which may include the path, of the control file. The default extension is *.ctl.*

LOG = path_file_name

Specifies the name of the log file to generate for a load session. You may include a path as well. By default, the log file takes on the name of the control file, but with a *.log* extension, and is written to the same directory as the control file. If you specify a different name, the default extension is still *.log.* However, if you use the LOG parameter to specify a name for the log file, it will no longer be written automatically to the directory that contains the control file.

BAD = path_file_name

Specifies the name of the bad file. You may include a path as part of the name. By default, the bad file takes the name of the control file, but with a *.bad* extension, and is written to the same directory as the control file. If you specify a different name, the default extension is still *.bad.* However, if you use the BAD parameter to specify a bad file name, the default directory becomes your current working directory. If you are loading data from multiple files, then this bad file name only gets associated with the first file being loaded.

DATA = path_file_name

Specifies the name of the file containing the data to load. You may include a path as part of the name. By default, the name of the control file is used, but with the *.dat* extension. If you specify a different name, the default extension is still *.dat*. If you are loading from multiple files, you can only specify the first file name using this parameter. Place the names of the other files in their respective INFILE clauses in the control file.

DISCARD = path_file_name

Specifies the name of the discard file. You may include a path as part of the name. By default, the discard file takes the name of the control file, but it has a *.dis* extension. If you specify a different name, the default extension is still *.dis*. If you are loading data from multiple files, then this discard file name only gets associated with the first file being loaded.

DISCARDMAX = logical_record_count

Sets an upper limit on the number of logical records that can be discarded before a load will terminate. The limit is actually one less than the value specified for DISCARDMAX. When the number of discarded records becomes equal to the value specified for DISCARDMAX, the load will terminate. The default is to allow an unlimited number of discards. However, since DISCARDMAX only accepts numeric values, it is not possible to explicitly specify the default behavior.

 There is also an undocumented parameter named DISCARDS that functions the same as DISCARDMAX. The use of DISCARDMAX is preferred, but you may occasionally encounter references to DISCARDS.

SKIP = logical_record_count

Allows you to continue an interrupted load by skipping the specified number of logical records. If you are continuing a multiple table direct path load, you may need to use the CONTINUE_LOAD clause in the control file rather than the SKIP parameter on the command line. CONTINUE_LOAD allows you to specify a different number of rows to skip for each table that you are loading.

SKIP_INDEX_MAINTENANCE = {TRUE | FALSE}

Controls whether or not index maintenance is done for a direct path load. This parameter does not apply to conventional path loads. A value of TRUE causes index maintenance to be skipped. Any index segments (partitions) that should have been updated will be marked as unusable. A value of FALSE causes indexes to be maintained as they normally would be. The default is FALSE.

SKIP_UNUSABLE_INDEXES = {TRUE | FALSE}

Controls the manner in which a load is done when a table being loaded has indexes in an unusable state. A value of TRUE causes SQL*Loader to load data into tables even when those tables have indexes marked as unusable. The indexes will remain unusable at the end of the load. One caveat is that if a UNIQUE index is marked as unusable, the load will not be allowed to proceed.

A value of FALSE causes SQL*Loader not to insert records when those records need to be recorded in an index marked as unusable. For a conventional path load, this means that any records that require an unusable index to be updated will be rejected as errors. For a direct path load, this means that the load will be aborted the first time such a record is encountered. The default is FALSE.

LOAD = logical_record_count

Specifies a limit on the number of logical records to load. The default is to load all records. Since LOAD only accepts numeric values, it is not possible to explicitly specify the default behavior.

ERRORS = insert_error_count

Specifies a limit on the number of errors to tolerate before the load is aborted. The default is to abort a load when the error count exceeds 50. There is no way to allow an unlimited number of errors. The best you can do is to specify a very high number for this parameter.

ROWS = rows_in_bind_array

The precise meaning of this parameter depends on whether you are doing a direct path load or a conventional load. If you are doing a conventional load, then you can use this parameter to control the number of rows in the bind array. This represents the number of rows that SQL*Loader loads with each INSERT statement, and also represents the commit frequency. The default is 64 rows.

If you are doing a direct path load, then ROWS specifies the number of rows to read from the input file before saving the data to the database. SQL*Loader will round up the ROWS value to coincide with an even number of database blocks. A data save in a direct path load is analogous to a commit in a conventional path load. The default, when a direct path load is done, is to do one save at the end of the load.

The BINDSIZE and ROWS parameters *both* affect the size of the bind array. Chapter 9 discusses this topic in greater detail.

BINDSIZE = bytes_in_bind_array

Specifies the maximum size, in bytes, of the bind array. This parameter overrides any bind array size computed as a result of using the ROWS parameter. The default bind array size is 65,536 bytes, or 64K.

SILENT = [(]keyword [, keyword…][)]

Allows you to suppress various header and feedback messages that SQL*Loader normally displays during a load session. Table 1-2 describes the effect of each of the keywords.

Table 1-2. Keywords for Use with the SILENT Parameter

Keyword	Effect
ALL	Is the same as specifying all the other keywords.
DISCARDS	Suppresses the message that is normally written to the log file each time a record is discarded.
ERRORS	Suppresses the error messages that are normally written to the log file when a record generates an Oracle error.
FEEDBACK	Suppresses the "commit point reached" messages that are normally displayed each time SQL*Loader executes a commit or a save.
HEADER	Suppresses the messages that SQL*Loader displays on the screen when you first launch the executable. Note, however, that the header messages are always written to the log file.
PARTITIONS	Suppresses the per-partition statistics that are normally written to the log file when doing a direct path load of a partitioned table.

There are two ways you can specify values for the SILENT parameter. If you have only one keyword, you can supply it following the equals sign (=), as follows:

```
SILENT = ALL
```

If you have several keywords to use, you can place them in a comma-delimited list. You may optionally place that list inside parentheses. For example:

```
SILENT = (DISCARDS,ERRORS)
```

DIRECT = {TRUE | FALSE}

Determines the data path used for the load. A value of FALSE results in a conventional path load. A value of TRUE results in a direct path load. The default is FALSE.

PARFILE = path_file_name

Tells SQL*Loader to read command-line parameter values from a text file. This text file is referred to as a *parameter file*, and contains keyword/value pairs. Usually, the keyword/value pairs are separated by line breaks. Use of the PARFILE parameter can save a lot of typing if you need to perform the same load several times, because you won't need to retype all the command-line parameters each time. There is no default extension for parameter files.

PARALLEL = {TRUE | FALSE}

>Indicates whether or not you are doing a direct path parallel load. If you are loading the same object from multiple direct path load sessions, then set this to TRUE. Otherwise, set it to FALSE. The default is FALSE.

READSIZE = bytes_in_read_buffer

>Specifies the size of the buffer used by SQL*Loader when reading data from the input file. The default value is 65,536 bytes, or 64K. The values of the READSIZE and BINDSIZE parameters should match. If you supply values for these two parameters that do not match, SQL*Loader will adjust them.

FILE = database_datafile_name

>Specifies the database data file from which to allocate extents. Use this parameter when doing parallel loads, to ensure that each load session is using a different disk. If you are not doing a direct path load, this parameter will be ignored.

In addition to being passed by keyword, parameters may also be passed by position. To do this, you simply list the values after the *sqlldr* command in the correct order. For example, the following two SQL*Loader commands yield identical results:

```
sqlldr system/manager profile.ctl profile.log
sqlldr userid=system/manager control=profile.ctl log=profile.log
```

You can even mix the positional and keyword methods of passing command-line parameters. The one rule when doing this is that all positional parameters must come first. Once you start using keywords, you must continue to do so. For example:

```
sqlldr system/manager control=profile.ctl log=profile.ctl
```

When you pass parameters positionally, you must not skip any. Also, be sure to get the order right. You must supply parameter values in the order shown earlier in this section. Given the fact that you typically will use only a few parameters out of the many that are possible, it's usually easier to pass those parameters as keyword/value pairs than it is to pass them positionally. Using keyword/value pairs also makes long SQL*Loader commands somewhat self-documenting. The one exception to this rule is that you might wish to pass the username and password positionally, since they come first, and then pass in the rest of the parameters by name.

Command-Line Syntax Rules

There are several syntax rules to be aware of when writing SQL*Loader commands. These rules fall into the following areas:

- Case-sensitivity
- Separation of parameters
- Special characters in the command line

SQL*Loader itself is not case-sensitive. Keywords on the command line may be in either upper- or lowercase—it doesn't matter. However, some operating systems, notably Unix, are case-sensitive. When running SQL*Loader on a case-sensitive operating system, you do need to be careful of the case used in file names. You also need to pay attention to the case used for the command to invoke SQL*Loader. On Unix and other case-sensitive operating systems, the SQL*Loader executable name is usually lowercase. So on Unix, Linux, and so forth, use *sqlldr*. Under Windows, and other operating systems where case doesn't matter, you can use *SQLLDR* or *sqlldr* as you prefer.

Parameters on the command line may be separated by spaces, by commas, or by both spaces and commas. All three of the following commands for example, are legitimate:

```
sqlldr system/manager,control=product.ctl,log=product.log
sqlldr system/manager, control=product.ctl, log=product.log
sqlldr system/manager control=product.ctl log=product.log
```

Spaces are acceptable as well, on either side of the equals sign (=), in keyword/value pairs.

Special characters are rarely needed on the command line, but when you do use them in an option value, you must enclose that value within quotes. For example, beginning with release 8.1.7, if you connect as the user SYS, you also need to specify "AS SYSDBA" as part of your connect string. Because of the spaces, you'll need to enclose your entire connect string within quotes. For example, for Windows:

```
sqlldr 'sys/password AS SYSDBA' control=product.ctl    (Windows)
```

And for Unix:

```
sqlldr \'sys/password AS SYSDBA\' control=product.ctl (Unix)
```

The backslash characters that you see in the second command are there because some Unix operating systems require that quotes on the command line be escaped. In this example, the backslash was used as the escape character.

Parameter Precedence

The term "command-line" notwithstanding, most SQL*Loader command-line parameters can actually be specified in three different places:

- On the command line
- In a parameter file, which is then referenced using the PARFILE parameter
- In the control file

Parameters on the command line, including those read in from a parameter file, will always override values specified in the control file. In the case of the bad and discard file names, though, the control file syntax allows for each distinct input file to have its own bad file and discard files. The command line syntax does not allow for this, so bad file and discard file names specified on the command line only apply to the first input file. For any other input files, you need to specify these bad and discard file names in the control file or accept the defaults.

The FILE parameter adds a bit of confusion to the rules stated in the previous paragraph. As with the bad file and discard file names, you can have multiple FILE values in the control file. However, when you specify the FILE parameter on the command line, it does override any and all FILE values specified in the control file.

Parameters read from a parameter file as a result of using the PARFILE parameter may override those specified on the command line. Whether or not that happens depends on the position of the PARFILE parameter with respect to the others. SQL*Loader processes parameters from left to right, and the last setting for a given parameter is the one that SQL*Loader uses.

2

In this chapter:
- *Syntax Rules*
- *The LOAD Statement*
- *Command-Line Parameters in the Control File*
- *Placing Data in the Control File*

The Mysterious Control File

The control file is the key to SQL*Loader. Understanding the control file is like having the keys to the kingdom. You'll not only be able to get work done, you'll be able to leverage all of SQL*Loader's built-in capabilities. As a result, you'll work less, and SQL*Loader will work more.

This chapter describes the three parts of the control file:

- The LOAD statement

- Command-line parameters (the OPTIONS command)

- Data

The LOAD statement is present in any SQL*Loader control file. Command-line parameters and data are optional.

Syntax Rules

Before getting into the details of the LOAD, it's worth taking the time to understand some things about control file syntax. There are various issues with respect to formatting, case sensitivity, special characters, and reserved words that you should at least be aware of. Usually you don't need to think much about any of these issues, but sooner or later you will find all this information to be helpful.

Free Format

Control file syntax is free format in the sense that you can insert any amount of whitespace between any two syntax elements. A syntax element could be, for instance, a keyword, or it could be a value that you supply. Carriage returns, line feeds, and tabs, as well as space characters, are all considered whitespace. Thus, the following two LOAD statements are considered identical even though they are formatted differently:

```
LOAD DATA
INFILE 'mi_deci.'
BADFILE 'mn_deci.bad' DISCARDFILE 'mn_deci.dis'
TRUNCATE INTO TABLE gfn_gnis_feature_names
WHEN gfn_feature_type='lake' (
gfn_state_abbr CHAR TERMINATED BY "," ENCLOSED BY '"',
gfn_feature_name CHAR TERMINATED BY "," ENCLOSED BY '"',
gfn_feature_type CHAR TERMINATED BY "," ENCLOSED BY '"')

LOAD DATA
INFILE 'mi_deci.'
    BADFILE 'mn_deci.bad'
    DISCARDFILE 'mn_deci.dis'
TRUNCATE
INTO TABLE gfn_gnis_feature_names
    WHEN gfn_feature_type='lake' (
    gfn_state_abbr CHAR TERMINATED BY "," ENCLOSED BY '"',
    gfn_feature_name CHAR TERMINATED BY "," ENCLOSED BY '"',
    gfn_feature_type CHAR TERMINATED BY "," ENCLOSED BY '"'
    )
```

The second LOAD statement is obviously easier to follow. When writing control files, it's best to use whitespace and indentation as tools to make your control files readable. In this example, the INFILE and INTO TABLE clauses are both subordinate to LOAD DATA, and they appear flush-left underneath those keywords. The BADFILE and DISCARDFILE clauses are related to the input file, and thus have been indented underneath INFILE. Similarly, the WHEN clause is part of the INTO TABLE clause, and has been indented accordingly.

In general, when we are writing control files, we try to use the following formatting conventions:

- Place the LOAD keyword, or the CONTINUE_LOAD keyword, on a line by itself.

- If UNRECOVERABLE or RECOVERABLE is being used, put that keyword on the same line as LOAD.

- Begin each INFILE clause on a new line, and indent subordinate clauses.

- Begin each INTO TABLE clause on a new line, and indent subordinate clauses.

- Begin each field description on a new line.

While you shouldn't get too caught up in the arcane details of formatting your control files, some judicious attention to indentation and whitespace will make your work much more understandable, not only for you, but for the person who comes after you.

Case Sensitivity

For the most part, control file syntax is case-insensitive. Keywords are always case-insensitive; thus, both of the following examples represent valid and equivalent LOAD statements:

```
LOAD DATA
   INFILE 'mi_deci.'
   TRUNCATE INTO TABLE gfn_gnis_feature_names
   ...

load data
   infile 'mi_deci.'
   truncate into table gfn_gnis_feature_names
   ...
```

Table names, column names, and file names may or may not be case-sensitive, depending on your operating system and whether or not those elements are enclosed within quotes.

Table and column names

Table names, column names, and the names of other database objects are never case-sensitive unless enclosed within double quotes. The following two clauses, for example, have the same meaning:

```
INTO TABLE gfn_gnis_feature_names

INTO TABLE GFN_GNIS_FEATURE_NAMES
```

In both cases, the table name will be converted to uppercase by SQL*Loader, and the *GFN_GNIS_FEATURE_NAMES* table will be loaded. If, for some reason, you have a table name that is mixed case or lowercase, you must use double quotes around the name when you reference it in your control file. For example:

```
INTO TABLE "gfn_gnis_feature_names"
```

When you place double quotes around a table name or a column name, SQL*Loader uses it just as it is. If you want to qualify a table name with a user name, each name must be quoted separately. For example:

```
INTO TABLE "gnis"."gfn_gnis_feature_names"
```

It is acceptable to quote some parts of an identifier without quoting others. For example:

```
INTO TABLE GNIS."gfn_gnis_feature_names"
```

However, you must not attempt to place the quotes such that the dot separating a user and table name, or table and column name, is enclosed within the quotes. The following will not work:

```
INTO TABLE "gnis.gfn_gnis_feature_names"
```

Also remember that double quotes, not single quotes, must be used when quoting table names, column names, and other identifiers that have meaning in SQL. This is the same rule that you follow when writing SQL statements in general. Identifiers are quoted using double quotes. Single quotes are reserved for string constants.

 It's rare that you need to quote a table name or column name in an Oracle environment. The need to do so is often the result of having previously created a table using a third-party tool, such as Microsoft Access, that allows for spaces and lowercase characters in table and column names.

Filenames

Whether filenames are case-sensitive or not depends on the operating system under which you are running SQL*Loader. On Unix and Linux systems, filenames are case-sensitive. On Windows-based systems (Windows 2000, Windows NT, Windows 98, and so forth), filenames are not case-sensitive.

Comments

Use the double dash (−−) to indicate the beginning of a comment. Comments extend from the double dash to the end of the line. For example:

```
--This control file loads geographic place names
--for the following states: MI, MN, IA, AK, AL, OH.
LOAD DATA
INFILE 'e:\gnis\mn_deci.' --Minnesota
INFILE 'e:\gnis\ia_deci.' --Iowa
INFILE 'e:\gnis\ak_deci.' --Alaska
INFILE 'e:\gnis\al_deci.' --Alabama
INFILE 'e:\gnis\mi_deci.' --Michigan
INFILE 'e:\gnis\oh_deci.' --Ohio
TRUNCATE
INTO TABLE GNIS."GFN_GNIS_FEATURE_NAMES" (
...
```

Comments may appear anywhere in the control file where whitespace is allowed. However, they must not appear in the data itself. If you use the BEGINDATA keyword in your control file, and follow that with data, do not attempt to place comments in the data.

Special Characters

Occasionally you will deal with table names, column names, filenames, or other identifiers that include special characters. You can deal with these names by quoting them. In some cases, you may also need to take advantage of SQL*Loader's escape character.

Table and column names

When it comes to table and column names, SQL*Loader respects standard SQL syntax and allows the following characters:

- The letters A–Z and a–z
- The digits 0–9
- The dollar sign ($), pound sign (#), and underscore (_).

All of the characters listed here may be used in an identifier name without having to quote the name. If you need to use any other characters as part of a SQL identifier, you must enclose that identifier within double quotes. For example:

```
INTO TABLE GNIS."GFN%GNIS%FEATURE%NAMES"
```

Filenames

Filenames consisting of just a name and an extension may usually be specified without using quotes. This is true on Unix, Linux, and Windows systems. For example:

```
INFILE mi_deci.dat
```

To specify a path with your filename, you must enclose the entire reference in quotes. Either single or double quotes may be used. For example:

```
INFILE "e:\gnis\mi_deci.dat"  --Windows

INFILE '/home/oracle/gnis/mi_deci.dat'  --Unix
```

The escape character

On some operating systems, notably Unix and Linux, the backslash (\) character functions as an escape character. You can use the escape character to embed backslash (\), single-quote (') or double-quote (") characters into a string.

Table 2-1 provides some examples by showing different INFILE clauses together with the filenames that SQL*Loader will actually look for.

*Table 2-1. SQL*Loader Escape Character Examples*

INFILE Clause	Actual Filename
INFILE 'mi_\'deci'	mi_'deci
INFILE "mi_\"deci'	mi_"deci
INFILE "mi_\\deci'	mi_\deci

Where supported, escape characters can be applied to any string in the SQL*Loader control file. This includes strings that specify table names, column names, delimiter characters, enclosure characters, and SQL code.

The use of the escape character is not supported on Windows platforms. When embedded in a string under Windows, the backslash is treated just like any other character. While this may appear to be a limitation, it does make it easier to specify fully-qualified path names and filenames when running SQL*Loader under Windows.

Reserved Words

A final issue to be aware of with respect to writing control files is that SQL*Loader reserved words must be quoted whenever they appear as part of a filename, table name, column name, or other identifier. Suppose that you are developing a system to manage game preserves, and that your system includes a table named *PRESERVE*. Because PRESERVE is also a SQL*Loader reserved word, you would need to quote the table name as follows:

```
LOAD DATA
INFILE ...
INTO TABLE "PRESERVE"
...
```

Table 2-2 presents a list of all SQL*Loader reserved words. Use double quotes around any SQL identifier that matches one of these words. Use either single or double quotes around any filename that matches a reserved word.

*Table 2-2. SQL*Loader Reserved Words*

AND	DOUBLE	NULLIF	SORTNUM
APPEND	ENCLOSED	OBJECT	SQL/DS
BADDN	EOF	OID	STORAGE
BADFILE	EXCEPTIONS	OPTIONALLY	STREAM
BEGINDATA	EXTERNAL	OPTIONS	SUBPARTITION

Table 2-2. SQL*Loader Reserved Words (continued)

BFILE	FIELDS	PART	SYSDATE
BLANKS	FILLER	PARTITION	TABLE
BLOCKSIZE	FIXED	PIECED	TERMINATED
BY	FLOAT	POSITION	THIS
BYTEINT	FORMAT	PRESERVE	TRAILING
BYTEORDER	GENERATED	RAW	TRUNCATE
CHAR	GRAPHIC	READBUFFERS	UNLOAD
CHARACTERSET	INDDN	READSIZE	UNRECOVERABLE
COLUMN	INDEXES	RECLEN	USING
CONCATENATE	INFILE	RECNUM	VARCHAR
CONSTANT	INSERT	RECORD	VARCHARC
CONTINUEIF	INTEGER	RECOVERABLE	VARGRAPHIC
CONTINUE_LOAD	INTO	REENABLE	VARIABLE
COUNT	LAST	REF	VARRAW
DATA	LOAD	REPLACE	VARRAWC
DATE	LOBFILE	RESUME	VARRAY
DECIMAL	LOG	SDF	WHEN
DEFAULTIF	LONG	SEQUENCE	WHITESPACE
DELETE	MAX	SID	WORKDDN
DISABLED_CONSTRAINTS	MLSLABEL	SINGLEROW	YES
DISCARDDN	NESTED	SKIP	ZONED
DISCARDFILE	NEXT	SMALLINT	
DISCARDMAX	NO	SORTDEVT	
DISCARDS	NULLCOLS	SORTED	

The LOAD Statement

When you run SQL*Loader, it's ultimately the LOAD statement that tells SQL*Loader what data to load, where to get it from, where to put it, and how to interpret it. You saw a simple example of the LOAD statement in Chapter 1, *Introduction to SQL*Loader*. However, LOAD statements can be much longer and more complex than what you've seen so far.

LOAD statements are made up of the following components:

- The LOAD keyword that begins the statement
- One or more INFILE clauses to identify the input data files
- One or more INTO TABLE clauses to identify the target database tables

- Optionally, a CONCATENATE clause to specify the rules for concatenating multiple physical records into one logical record

- Other miscellaneous clauses

In the sections that follow, you'll learn how to write the clauses that specify input files and target tables for the data that you want to load. Chapter 3, *Fields and Datatypes*, shows you how to describe the data in your input files. Subsequent chapters cover other clauses that are used for validation, data transformation, continuation, and other SQL*Loader features.

LOAD DATA Syntax

The following diagram shows the basic syntax of the LOAD statement:

```
[UNRECOVERABLE | RECOVERABLE] {LOAD | CONTINUE_LOAD} [DATA]
    [CHARACTERSET character_set] [BYTEORDER]
    [INFILE clause [INFILE clause...]]
    [MAXRECORDSIZE bytes
    [READBUFFERS integer]
    [INSERT | APPEND | REPLACE | TRUNCATE]
    [concatenate_rules]
    [PRESERVE BLANKS]
    INTO TABLE clause [INTO TABLE clause...]
    [BEGINDATA]
```

The elements in the syntax are as follows:

UNRECOVERABLE

Specifies that the load not be recorded in the database redo log. This improves performance, but requires you to reload the data in the event that any affected database files are lost and subsequently restored and recovered. This option is only applicable to direct path loads. See Chapter 9, *Transaction Size and Performance Issues*, for more details on unrecoverable loads.

RECOVERABLE

Specifies that the load be recorded in the database redo log. This option is applicable only to direct path loads, and it represents the default behavior.

LOAD [DATA]

Marks the beginning of a LOAD statement. The DATA keyword is optional. Either LOAD or LOAD DATA may be used.

CONTINUE_LOAD [DATA]

Replaces LOAD when you have a direct path load that has failed and that you want to restart from the point of failure. Read Chapter 6, *Recovering from Failure*, for detailed information on recovering from a failed load.

CHARACTERSET character_set

Specifies the character set used for the input data. See Chapter 8, *Transforming Data During a Load*, for information on character set conversions.

BYTEORDER

Indicates that binary integers, including those used in VARCHAR-type fields to specify field length, were generated on a machine with a byte order opposite to the one on which SQL*Loader is currently running. This keyword is only available in the Oracle9*i* release of SQL*Loader.

INFILE clause

A clause identifying a file containing data that you want to load. See the section "Specifying Input Files," later in this chapter, for details on this clause.

MAXRECORDSIZE bytes

Specifies the maximum logical record size in bytes.

READBUFFERS integer

Specifies the number of buffers to use during a direct path load. The default value is 4. You should only increase the number of buffers in response to an ORA-02374 error.

[INSERT | APPEND | REPLACE | TRUNCATE]

Specifies at a global level what is to be done to any existing data in the tables that you are loading. Generally, you'll find it better to specify these options at the table level (using the INFILE clause) rather than globally. The default setting is INSERT. Descriptions of possible settings follow:

INSERT

Requires that all tables being loaded be empty to begin with. If any table is not empty, SQL*Loader will abort the load with an error.

APPEND

Preserves any existing data in the tables being loaded.

REPLACE

Uses a SQL DELETE statement to delete all existing data from the tables being loaded.

TRUNCATE

Uses a SQL TRUNCATE statement to delete all existing data from the tables being loaded.

concatenate_rules

Specifies the manner in which multiple physical records are concatenated into one logical record. Concatenation is discussed in Chapter 4, *Loading from Fixed-Width Files*, and in Chapter 5, *Loading Delimited Data*.

PRESERVE BLANKS

Tells SQL*Loader to preserve leading and trailing blanks in the input record fields. The manner in which SQL*Loader handles whitespace depends on whether you are loading fixed-width or delimited data. Chapters 4 and 5, respectively, cover this topic.

INTO TABLE clause

Identifies a table that you are loading. You may specify multiple occurrences of the INTO TABLE clause if you need to distribute the data that you are loading over multiple tables. See the section "Specifying the Target Tables," later in this chapter, for details on this clause.

BEGINDATA

Marks the end of a LOAD command when you are including data in the control file. The data then begins with the line immediately following the BEGINDATA keyword.

The number of keywords and clauses for the LOAD statement may seem intimidating at first. This becomes even more true as you delve into the syntax for each of the individual clauses. But don't be put off by this apparent complexity. Many keywords and clauses are optional. Generally, to reduce complexity, you should allow optional clauses to remain at their default settings. Only specify clauses and keywords that you understand and need.

Only one LOAD statement is allowed in a control file.

Specifying Input Files

To load data, you need a source. Usually that source will be a file other than the control file. Use the LOAD statement's INFILE clause to specify one or more operating system files as the source of the data to be loaded. The syntax is as follows:

```
{INFILE | INDDN} {filename|*} [os_specific_options]
   [{BADFILE | BADDN} badfile_name]
   [{DISCARDFILE | DISCARDDN} discardfile_name]
   [{DISCARDS | DISCARDMAX} discardmax]
```

The keywords INDDN, BADDN, and DISCARDDN exist to provide compatibility with IBM DB2, and are rarely used.

The elements in the syntax are as follows:

filename

   The name of the file containing the data to load. You may optionally specify a
   path and extension as part of the file name. On most systems, the extension
   defaults to *.dat*.

   On some systems, notably Linux, there is no default extension.

---

*

   Indicates that data is to be loaded from the control file. See the section "Placing Data in the Control File," later in this chapter.

os_specific_options

   A quoted string containing operating system–specific file options. The valid
   options for Sun Solaris, Windows NT, Linux, AIX, HP-UX, and Digital Unix are
   as follows:

   " "

      A null string, or no option string at all, causes SQL*Loader to use a stream
      record format in which each line is terminated by a newline character.
      This is usually appropriate when loading text files.

   "FIX rec_len"

      Causes SQL*Loader to use a fixed-length record format in which each
      record is exactly *rec_len* bytes long.

   "VAR len_bytes"

      Causes SQL*Loader to use a variable-length record format in which each
      record is prefixed by a number that gives the length of the record in
      bytes. The default prefix size is 5 bytes. Use the *len_bytes* value to specify
      a different prefix length.

badfile_name

   The name of the file into which you want SQL*Loader to write records that
   could not be loaded because of database errors or problems with the data.
   The default bad file name is the datafile name, but with the extension *.bad*.

discardfile_name

   The name of the file into which you want SQL*Loader to write records that
   were discarded because they failed to meet the conditions of the WHEN
   clauses specified for any of the tables being loaded. The default discard file
   name is the datafile name, but with the extension *.dis*.

discardmax

> The maximum number of records to discard before terminating the load process. Use this to have SQL*Loader do a sanity check on the number of records being discarded. If the number of discards exceeds the limit you specify, then the load is aborted. The default is to allow all discards.

> If you specify *discardmax* without specifying a discard file name, and SQL*Loader discards a record, it will automatically create a discard file using the default name.

Specifying a bad file name or a discard file name is optional. If you omit a bad file name, and a record fails to load because of an error, SQL*Loader will create a bad file using the default name. If you omit a discard file name, SQL*Loader will not create a discard file, and any discarded records will not be recorded. Chapter 7, *Validating and Selectively Loading Data,* talks in detail about the use of these files.

Loading from one input file

If you are loading from only one input file, then use only one INFILE clause. The following example shows a control file that you can use to load geographic feature names for the State of Michigan:

```
LOAD DATA
INFILE 'mi_deci.'
TRUNCATE
INTO TABLE GNIS."GFN_GNIS_FEATURE_NAMES"
   (
   gfn_state_abbr CHAR
      TERMINATED BY "," ENCLOSED BY '"',
   gfn_feature_name CHAR
      TERMINATED BY "," ENCLOSED BY '"',
   gfn_feature_type CHAR
      TERMINATED BY "," ENCLOSED BY '"',
   gfn_county_name
      CHAR TERMINATED BY "," ENCLOSED BY '"'
   )
```

In this example, the input file name is *mi_deci*. The trailing period in the name tells SQL*Loader that there is no extension. A name was not specified for the bad file, so the default name of *mi_deci.bad* will be used. No name was specified for the discard file either, so none will be generated.

Loading from multiple input files

Use multiple INFILE clauses to load data from multiple files. For example:

```
LOAD DATA
INFILE 'mi_deci.'
```

```
INFILE 'mn_deci.'
INFILE 'ak_deci.'
TRUNCATE
INTO TABLE GNIS.GFN_GNIS_FEATURE_NAMES
   (
   gfn_state_abbr CHAR
      TERMINATED BY "," ENCLOSED BY '"',
   gfn_feature_name CHAR
      TERMINATED BY "," ENCLOSED BY '"',
   gfn_feature_type CHAR
      TERMINATED BY "," ENCLOSED BY '"',
   gfn_county_name
      CHAR TERMINATED BY "," ENCLOSED BY '"'
   )
```

When you load data from multiple files, the data format in each file must be the same. SQL*Loader opens each file in the order listed, reads through it, loads the data, and moves on to the next file. In essence, SQL*Loader concatenates all the input files to create one large, logical file.

Discard file and bad file names are specific to each input file. In the previous example, SQL*Loader will create three bad files using the default names *mi_deci. bad*, *mn_deci.bad*, and *ak_deci.bad*. No discard files will be created, because no discard file names were specified. You can, however, specify these filenames as in this example:

```
LOAD DATA
INFILE 'mi_deci.'
   BADFILE 'mi_deci.bad'
   DISCARDFILE 'mi_deci.dis
INFILE 'mn_deci.'
   BADFILE 'mn_deci.bad'
   DISCARDFILE 'mn_deci.dis
INFILE 'ak_deci.'
   BADFILE 'ak_deci.bad'
   DISCARDFILE 'ak_deci.dis
TRUNCATE INTO TABLE GNIS.GFN_GNIS_FEATURE_NAMES
   . . .
```

As you can see, for purposes of specifying bad file and discard file names, you treat each INFILE clause independently.

Do not specify the same discard file name, or bad file name, for two or more INFILE clauses. SQL*Loader creates bad and discard files anew for each INFILE clause. Any existing data, even from other input files processed during the same SQL*Loader run, will be lost.

Trick of the Trade

This tip comes from Stephen Andert, one of our technical reviewers. He once had a situation where he had many tables to load many times over. By writing a short shell script and taking advantage of SQL*Loader's naming defaults, he was able to save himself a lot of repetitious work. First of all, he created a control file for each table that he needed to load on a regular basis. In each control file, he specified an input file name made up of the table name plus the extension *.dat*. For example, if he was loading a table named FEATURES, his control file specified *features.dat* as the input file. Then, he wrote the following Unix shell script:

```
echo $1 >> master.log
date >> master.log
sqlldr username/password control=$1.ctl log=$1.log
date >> master.log
echo $1 >> master.log
```

To load any given table, all he had to do was to invoke the script and pass in the table name as a parameter:

```
load.sh features &
```

The *echo* and *date* commands in the script recorded the start and end of each load in a master log file, enabling him to easily track the progress of multiple loads invoked using this mechanism.

Specifying the table loading method

The table loading method may be specified in the LOAD syntax between the INFILE clauses and the INTO TABLE clauses. The table loading method controls the following two aspects of SQL*Loader behavior:

- What data does SQL*Loader expect to be in the destination table(s) when the load begins?

- What should SQL*Loader do with that data?

By default, SQL*Loader expects to load an empty table. This is referred to as the *INSERT load method*, and an error will be returned if any of the tables being loaded contains data when the load starts. The INSERT load method is a rather unfortunate choice for a default, because it confuses many beginners. They go to load data into a table with existing data, and are greeted with an error such as the following:

```
SQL*Loader-601: For INSERT option, table must be empty.
Error on table GFN_GNIS_FEATURE_NAMES
```

All told, SQL*Loader supports the following four load methods:

INSERT

Requires that the table being loaded be empty.

APPEND

Allows you to load data into an existing table regardless of whether the table contains data or is empty.

REPLACE

Deletes existing data from the table being loaded.

TRUNCATE

Truncates the table being loaded. Also resets the table's high-water mark.

The INSERT method is the default and may be explicitly specified using the INSERT keyword. The following example uses APPEND, and shows where the load method keyword goes in relation to the INTO TABLE clause:

```
LOAD DATA
INFILE 'mi_deci.'
APPEND
INTO TABLE gfn_gnis_feature_names
```

The REPLACE and TRUNCATE methods both have the same underlying goal of deleting any existing data in the target table, or tables, before the load begins. The difference lies in how that goal is accomplished. Table 2-3 highlights the differences between REPLACE and TRUNCATE.

Table 2-3. REPLACE Versus TRUNCATE

REPLACE	TRUNCATE
SQL*Loader issues a SQL DELETE statement to delete existing data from the table.	SQL*Loader issues a SQL TRUNCATE statement to delete existing data from the table.
You must have the DELETE privilege on the table.	You must own the table in question, or you must have the DELETE ANY TABLE system privilege.
Oracle writes rollback information to rollback segments, requiring both time and disk space. This is where performance most suffers with respect to TRUNCATE.	No rollback information is written.
Redo log entries are generated for each block affected by the delete.	One redo log entry suffices to record the execution of the TRUNCATE statement.
Delete triggers defined on the table will fire.	Delete triggers will not fire.
Cascaded deletes are carried out for constraints defined using the ON DELETE CASCADE clause.	You must disable all referential integrity constraints referencing the table prior to your initiating the load, or an error will be returned.
Does not reset high-water mark.	Resets high-water mark.

In terms of performance, the TRUNCATE method is preferable to the REPLACE method. It's much faster to truncate a table than it is to issue a DELETE statement against it. If none of the considerations listed in Table 2-3 require you to use REPLACE, then use the TRUNCATE method. You will have better performance.

> When SQL*Loader issues the TRUNCATE statement to delete existing data from a table, it uses the REUSE STORAGE clause to preserve existing extents. If you've changed storage parameters and want to recreate extents, then you must issue the TRUNCATE TABLE statement manually from SQL*Plus.

Another benefit of using TRUNCATE is that truncating a table resets the table's high-water mark. This can impact the performance of subsequent queries against the table. If the new amount of data that you are loading results in a lower high-water mark than before, you have fewer blocks to be read in the event of a full table scan.

Specifying the Target Tables

You specify the target table(s) for a load using one or more INTO TABLE clauses. Here is the complete syntax for that clause:

```
INTO TABLE table_name
    [{PARTITION | SUBPARTITION} (partition_name)]
    {INSERT | REPLACE | TRUNCATE | APPEND}
    [SORTED [INDEXES] (index_list)] [SINGLEROW]
    [{INSERT | REPLACE | TRUNCATE | APPEND}]
    [OPTIONS (FILE=database_filename)]
    [REENABLE [DISABLED_CONSTRAINTS][EXCEPTIONS exception_table_name]]
    [WHEN field_conditions]
    [{OID(fieldname)|SID(fieldname)}]
    [FIELDS [delimiter_description]]
    [TRAILING [NULLCOLS]
    [SKIP skip_count]
    (field_list)
```

The elements in the syntax are as follows:

table_name

> The name of the table that you are loading. You may optionally specify an owner name using the *owner.table_name* format.

partition_name

> The name of a partition, or subpartition, of the table being loaded. Use the PARTITION clause if you are loading a partitioned table, and all the data goes into the same partition.

INSERT | REPLACE | TRUNCATE | APPEND

Specifies the load method on a table-specific basis. This overrides the load method specified for the load as a whole. Note that there are two possible locations in the INTO TABLE clause where these keywords may appear.

index_list

The name of one or more indexes that match the way in which the input data is sorted. If you specify more than one index name, use a comma-separated list. This option only applies to direct path loads, and is discussed in Chapter 9.

database_filename

The name of a datafile in the tablespace of the table or partition being loaded. This applies only to parallel, direct path loads. When such a load is performed, SQL*Loader will use the specified datafile for any temporary segments that it creates during the load. This allows you to have multiple parallel loads against the same table (or partition), but using separate datafiles. Chapter 9 discusses parallel loads in more detail.

REENABLE [DISABLED_CONSTRAINTS]

Causes SQL*Loader to reenable any disabled constraints at the end of a direct path load. This clause applies only to direct path loads. Chapter 9 discusses this functionality in detail.

exception_table_name

The name of a table to hold rows that violate constraints that have been reenabled as a result of your use of the REENABLE clause. This table name is used in the SQL statement that SQL*Loader executes in order to enable constraints. This applies only to direct path loads.

field_conditions

The conditions that an input data record must meet in order to be loaded. Field conditions are specified in a manner similar to the WHERE clause of a SQL SELECT statement. See Chapter 7 for details on how to selectively load data.

OID(fieldname)

Identifies the field in the input file that contains a 32-digit Oracle system-generated object identifier in hexadecimal format. This clause is used only when loading object tables. Prior to Oracle9*i*, this clause could only be used in conventional path loads. Beginning with Oracle9*i*, this clause can also be used in direct path loads.

SID(fieldname)

Identifies the field in the input file that contains the set identifier that is for a nested table.

delimiter_description

Identifies the delimiters and enclosing characters used for delimited data. This clause functions at the table level, and should only be used when the same delimiters and enclosing characters apply to all fields in the input file. See Chapter 5 for information on loading delimited data.

TRAILING [NULLCOLS]

Applies when delimited data is being loaded, and tells SQL*Loader to treat missing fields at the end of a record as nulls.

skip_count

The number of logical records to skip before beginning the load. The SKIP clause is used to continue a load that has previously failed. See Chapter 6 for information on resuming a failed load.

field_list

A list of fields in the input data record that includes datatypes and lengths. Refer to Chapter 3 for a comprehensive discussion of field lists and datatypes.

The syntax for the INTO TABLE clause is obviously much more complex than that for the INFILE clause. This chapter discusses the most fundamental and most commonly used elements. Later chapters in the book will cover the other elements.

Loading one table

If you have been following along in this chapter, you've already seen control file examples that load one database table. The following is another example, but this one loads county names for the State of Michigan into the *gc_gnis_county* table. The two filler fields are not loaded:

```
LOAD DATA
INFILE 'mi_deci.'
INTO TABLE gc_gnis_county
   APPEND
   (
   gc_state_abbr CHAR
      TERMINATED BY "," ENCLOSED BY '"',
   gc_feature_name FILLER CHAR
      TERMINATED BY "," ENCLOSED BY '"',
   gc_feature_type FILLER CHAR
      TERMINATED BY "," ENCLOSED BY '"',
   gc_county_name
      CHAR TERMINATED BY "," ENCLOSED BY '"'
   )
```

Notice that in this example, the APPEND keyword follows INTO TABLE. That makes the load method table-specific. Since only one table is being loaded, the load method could just as easily have been specified globally. For example:

```
LOAD DATA
INFILE 'mi_deci.'
```

```
APPEND
INTO TABLE gc_gnis_county
   (
   gc_state_abbr CHAR
      TERMINATED BY "," ENCLOSED BY '"',
   gc_feature_name FILLER CHAR
      TERMINATED BY "," ENCLOSED BY '"',
   gc_feature_type FILLER CHAR
      TERMINATED BY "," ENCLOSED BY '"',
   gc_county_name
      CHAR TERMINATED BY "," ENCLOSED BY '"'
   )
```

This time, because APPEND appears prior to the first INTO TABLE clause, it applies globally to all tables being loaded.

Loading delimited data into multiple tables

If the data you are loading needs to be spread across two or more tables, you can accomplish that by writing an INTO TABLE clause for each table that you want to load. Whether the data is delimited or not has an effect on how you write those clauses. The following example builds on the single-table load example shown previously. It loads county names into the *gc_gnis_county* table, and it loads feature names into the *gfn_gnis_feature_names* table. The load method—REPLACE, this time—is specified globally and applies to both tables:

```
LOAD DATA
INFILE 'mi_deci.'
REPLACE
INTO TABLE gc_gnis_county
   (
   gc_state_abbr CHAR
      TERMINATED BY "," ENCLOSED BY '"',
   gc_feature_name FILLER CHAR
      TERMINATED BY "," ENCLOSED BY '"',
   gc_feature_type FILLER CHAR
      TERMINATED BY "," ENCLOSED BY '"',
   gc_county_name
      CHAR TERMINATED BY "," ENCLOSED BY '"'
   )
INTO TABLE gfn_gnis_feature_names
   (
   gfn_state_abbr POSITION(1) CHAR
      TERMINATED BY "," ENCLOSED BY '"',
   gfn_feature_name CHAR
      TERMINATED BY "," ENCLOSED BY '"',
   gfn_feature_type CHAR
      TERMINATED BY "," ENCLOSED BY '"',
   gfn_county_name
      CHAR TERMINATED BY "," ENCLOSED BY '"'
   )
```

Based on this control file, SQL*Loader will read records from the input file *mi_ deci*. From each record it will extract county information and insert a new row into the *gc_gnis_county* table. Again, the two filler fields in the first INTO TABLE clause are not loaded. SQL*Loader will then extract feature name information and insert a new row with that information into the *gfn_gnis_feature_names* table.

Notice the use of POSITION(1) in the *gfn_state_abbr* field description in the second INTO TABLE clause. That's very important. When SQL*Loader processes delimited data, it takes fields from the input record in the order in which they occur. This order transcends INTO TABLE clauses. Thus, without POSITION(1) in this example, SQL*Loader would expect a second state abbreviation to follow the county name. That's not intuitive behavior, and usually is not what you want, either. You can use the POSITION clause in any field description to reset SQL*Loader to a specific character position in the record. In this case, POSITION(1) was used to send SQL*Loader back to the first character position so that it could pick up the state abbreviation and county name for the row to be inserted into *gfn_gnis_feature_names*.

Loading fixed-width data into multiple tables

It's actually a bit simpler to load fixed-width, columnar data into multiple tables than it is to load delimited data. Since the data is columnar in nature, you are specifying the positions of each column to begin with. There's no need to reset the position back to 1 in each new INTO TABLE clause. For example:

```
LOAD DATA
INFILE 'michigan.'
INTO TABLE gc_gnis_county
   TRUNCATE
   (
   gc_state_abbr POSITION(1:2) CHAR,
   gc_county_name POSITION(65:80) CHAR
   )
INTO TABLE gfn_gnis_feature_names
   TRUNCATE
   (
   gfn_state_abbr POSITION(1:2) CHAR,
   gfn_feature_name POSITION(4:54) CHAR,
   gfn_feature_type POSITION(55:64) CHAR,
   gfn_county_name POSITION(65:80) CHAR
   )
```

In this example, notice that the load method has been specified separately for each table. In this case, the TRUNCATE method was used for both, but there's no reason why you can't use a different load method for each table when your requirements call for that.

Eliminating Duplicate Rows

The *mi_deci* file (and the *michigan* file as well) contains more than one record per county, so you ultimately need some way to avoid or eliminate duplicate rows in the *gc_gnis_county* table. This is a common problem when using detail data to load what is, in essence, a master table. It's best if you can eliminate duplicates prior to the load using an operating system utility or perhaps a custom program to do the job. But if you must deal with duplicates during the load process, there are a couple of approaches you can take.

One approach would be to define a primary or unique key constraint on the combination of state and county name. For example:

```
CREATE TABLE gc_gnis_county (
   gc_state_abbr CHAR(2),
   gc_county_name VARCHAR2(60),
   CONSTRAINT pk_gc
      PRIMARY KEY (gc_state_abbr, gc_county_name)
   )
   TABLESPACE gnis_data;
```

With such a constraint in place, duplicate records fail to load, and instead are written to the bad file. While this works, it is a brute force method that may perform very poorly. It takes time to attempt an insert only to have it fail due to a constraint violation. It then takes even more time to undo that insert. The greater the percentage of duplicates in the input file, the worse this method will perform.

Another approach to the same problem is to insert all the records into a temporary work table, and then use a statement such as the following to select only unique rows for insertion into the permanent table:

```
INSERT INTO gc_gnis_county
   SELECT DISTINCT gc_state_abbr, gc_county_name
   FROM temp_gnis_county;
```

This second method requires the use of a second, albeit temporary, table, but will perform significantly better than the first method when the percentage of distinct rows is low with respect to the total number of rows.

Loading a table partition

If you are loading data into a partitioned table, you have the option of specifying the specific partition that you wish to load. Do this using the PARTITION keyword following the name of the table that you are loading. You can also use the SUBPARTITION keyword to load a specific subpartition. For example, if you were loading county names for the State of Michigan, you might write a LOAD statement such as the following:

```
LOAD DATA
INFILE 'mi_deci.'
REPLACE
INTO TABLE gc_gnis_county PARTITION (gc_gnis_county_mi)
...
```

In this example, the specific partition being loaded is named *gc_gnis_county_mi*. When you are loading a specific partition, keep the following points in mind:

- The table loading method (APPEND, INSERT, TRUNCATE, or REPLACE) applies only to the partition you are loading. Data in other partitions remains intact.

- Input data records that do not belong in the specified partition will not be loaded. Instead, these records will generate errors, and a record of those errors will be written to the log file.

The fact that the table loading method is partition-specific can be turned to your advantage. You can completely reload one partition while leaving the others untouched. The only way to reload an unpartitioned table is to reload all of it.

Data not belonging to the partition you are loading will be rejected. So if you have a file with data for several partitions, you can filter out the data for any one partition simply by specifying that partition in your INTO TABLE clause. While this may occasionally be convenient, you take a bit of a performance hit when you rely on the database to reject records that don't belong to the partition you are loading. If you have a large number of rejects, it's more efficient to filter them out using SQL*Loader's WHEN clause. This is especially true if you are loading over a Net8 connection.

Command-Line Parameters in the Control File

In Chapter 1 you read about the SQL*Loader command and the parameters you can use with it. Certain command-line parameters may also be specified in the control file. You accomplish this using the OPTIONS command, which must precede your LOAD statement. The syntax for the OPTIONS command is:

```
OPTIONS (parameter=value[,parameter=value...])
```

The following parameters are valid with the OPTIONS command:

```
SKIP = logical_record_count
LOAD = logical_record_count
```

```
ERRORS = insert_error_count
ROWS = rows_in_bind_array
BINDSIZE = bytes_in_bind_array
SILENT = [(keyword[,keyword...][)]
DIRECT = {TRUE | FALSE}
PARALLEL = {TRUE | FALSE}
READSIZE = bytes_in_read_buffer
```

Valid keywords for the SILENT parameter include ALL, DISCARDS, ERRORS, FEED-BACK, HEADER, and PARTITIONS.

You can find a detailed description of these parameters in Chapter 1. Parameter/value pairs listed in the OPTIONS statement should be separated by commas. The OPTIONS command in the following control file specifies that a silent load be performed, and sets the maximum error count to 999,999:

```
OPTIONS (SILENT=ALL, ERRORS=999999)
LOAD DATA
INFILE 'mi_deci.'
TRUNCATE
INTO TABLE GNIS.GFN_GNIS_FEATURE_NAMES
   (
   gfn_state_abbr CHAR
      TERMINATED BY "," ENCLOSED BY '"',
   gfn_feature_name CHAR
      TERMINATED BY "," ENCLOSED BY '"',
   gfn_feature_type CHAR
      TERMINATED BY "," ENCLOSED BY '"',
   gfn_county_name
      CHAR TERMINATED BY "," ENCLOSED BY '"'
   )
```

Not all parameters may be set using the OPTIONS command. Strangely enough, however, you can specify a value for any valid command-line parameter in the OPTIONS command, and SQL*Loader will not generate an error. For example, you could write the following OPTIONS command:

```
OPTIONS (SILENT=ALL, ERRORS=999999, BAD=mybad.bad)
```

The BAD parameter is not in the list of those supported by the OPTIONS command, but rather than generate an error, SQL*Loader will simply ignore it. The effect is the same as if you had not specified **BAD=mybad.bad** at all. Specify a command-line parameter that is completely invalid, however, and SQL*Loader will return an error.

Parameters specified on the SQL*Loader command line almost always override those specified using the OPTIONS command in the control file. The lone exception to the rule is the SILENT parameter. The effects of SILENT are cumulative. Any SILENT options you specify on the command line are combined with those you specify in the control file.

Placing Data in the Control File

SQL*Loader gives you the option of placing the data to be loaded into the control file. This is sometimes useful when you have data to distribute to multiple sites, because it minimizes the number of files that you need to pass around. Instead of sending separate data and control files, you can place everything into one control file and send that.

We prefer to keep data in its own file, separate from the control file. In our experience, that ultimately provides for more flexibility.

In order to place data into your control file, you must do the following:

• Place the BEGINDATA keyword at the end of your LOAD statement.

• Start your data on the line following BEGINDATA.

• Use INFILE * to tell SQL*Loader to read data from the control file.

The BEGINDATA keyword marks the end of your LOAD statement in cases where you place data into the control file. The first line following BEGINDATA then becomes the first input data record. To tell SQL*Loader to look in the control file as opposed to an external file, use an asterisk as the file name in your INFILE clause. For example:

```
LOAD DATA
INFILE *
TRUNCATE
INTO TABLE GFN_GNIS_FEATURE_NAMES
  (
  gfn_state_abbr CHAR
     TERMINATED BY "," ENCLOSED BY '"',
  gfn_feature_name CHAR
     TERMINATED BY "," ENCLOSED BY '"',
  gfn_feature_type CHAR
     TERMINATED BY "," ENCLOSED BY '"',
```

```
        gfn_county_name
            CHAR TERMINATED BY "," ENCLOSED BY '"'
        )
BEGINDATA
"MI","2 Lake","lake","Marquette"
"MI","3 Lake","lake","Marquette"
"MI","8 Lake","lake","Marquette"
```

When your data is in the control file, the default file names for the bad and discard files are derived from the control file name. Your bad file name will be the control file name, but with the extension *.bad*. Your discard file name will be the control file name, but with the extension *.dis*. If you specify a path for your control file name because the control file is in a different directory, that same path will be used for the bad and discard files.

When you are loading from multiple files, one of those files may be the control file. If that's the case, the control file must be the first file to be loaded. For example:

```
LOAD DATA
INFILE *
INFILE 'mi_deci.'
TRUNCATE
INTO TABLE GFN_GNIS_FEATURE_NAMES
...
```

In this example, SQL*Loader will first read all the data from the control file, and then it will move on to the file named *mi_deci*. The control file, if it is used, must always be the first file in a multi-file load.

 If you use BEGINDATA in your control file, but do not use INFILE *
for your first INFILE clause, SQL*Loader will return an error.

3

Fields and Datatypes

The subject of fields and datatypes cuts to the very core of SQL*Loader's capabilities. The whole purpose of the tool is to extract information from a file and load it into a database. SQL*Loader's power comes from its ability to handle a wide range of datatypes, and also from its flexibility in describing and manipulating the different fields in an input record.

Field Specifications

A *field specification* is that portion of an INTO TABLE clause describing a field to be extracted from the input record. Syntactically, each INTO TABLE clause contains a comma-delimited list of field specifications in the manner shown here:

```
INTO TABLE table_name
   (
   field_specification,
   field_specification,
   field_specification,
   . . .
   )
```

This comma-delimited list of field specifications is always the last component of an INTO TABLE clause, and it's always enclosed within parentheses. Field specifications typically describe fields to be extracted from records in a data file, but they can also describe values that you want SQL*Loader to generate for you. SQL*Loader supports the following five field types:

• Scalar fields

• Filler fields

- Generated fields
- Collection fields
- Column object fields

Scalar fields are the type you deal with most often on a daily basis. Character strings and numbers are typical examples of scalar fields. Filler fields function somewhat as placeholders. They are fields that you define for use within SQL*Loader, but that are not ultimately loaded into the database. Generated fields represent values such as a record number that SQL*Loader can generate for you. You'll read about all these types in this chapter.

Collection and column object fields correspond to Oracle8*i*'s object features. Collection fields allow you to load nested tables and varying arrays. Column object fields allow you to load object columns. These more complex field types are big subjects in themselves, and are covered in Chapter 11, *Loading Large Objects.*

Scalar Fields

SQL*Loader scalar fields consist of numbers, dates, character strings, and large object (LOB) files. In most cases, a scalar field is read from an input record and loaded into a single database column. In the case of a LOB file, all the data in one operating system file is read and stored in a database column of type CLOB, BLOB, or BFILE. Information on loading LOB files can be found in Chapter 10, *Direct Path Loads.* This chapter concentrates on the more traditional scalar datatypes.

Scalar fields can have any or all of the following attributes:

- A defined position in the record
- A datatype, which may include a length, a delimiter, and enclosing characters
- Conditions under which the field should take on a null or zero value
- A SQL expression that uses the input data to compute a value that is then loaded into the database column

The syntax for describing a scalar field is as follows:

```
column_name [POSITION({start|*[+offset]}[{:|-}end])]
            [datatype] [PIECED]
            [NULLIF condition [AND condition...]]
            [DEFAULTIF condition [AND condition...]]
            ["sql_expression"]
```

Don't worry if this syntax appears complex. You don't need to learn it all at once. For now, focus on the POSITION and datatype clauses. The rest you'll learn about in other chapters. The elements in this syntax are as follows:

column_name

> The name of the database column into which you want data for the field to be loaded. This is only the column name. The INTO TABLE clause identifies the table.

start

> The starting position of the field in the input record. The first byte is position one, the second byte is position two, and so forth.

*

> Tells SQL*Loader that the first byte of the field immediately follows the last byte of the previous field. If you use * for the first field that you define, SQL*Loader will start with the first byte in the record.

The value of * only defaults to 1 for the first INTO TABLE clause in your control file. See the section, "Loading delimited data into multiple tables," in Chapter 2, *The Mysterious Control File*, for details.

---

offset

> An optional offset that you can have SQL*Loader add to the position represented by the * character.

end

> The position of the last byte of data in the field. This is optional. If you omit the ending position, SQL*Loader will determine it based on information that you supply in your datatype specification.

datatype

> A datatype specification for the field. This may include information about delimiters and enclosing characters. The "Datatypes" section later in this chapter shows the syntax for all datatypes supported by SQL*Loader.

PIECED

> An option that's relevant only when you're doing a direct-path load.

condition

> A Boolean condition in either the NULLIF or DEFAULTIF clauses. When the specified conditions are met, these clauses cause SQL*Loader to store null or zero into the database column instead of the value that the field actually contains.

Chapter 4, *Loading from Fixed-Width Files*, and Chapter 5, *Loading Delimited Data*, both describe aspects of specifying NULLIF and DEFAULTIF conditions.

sql_expression

A SQL expression, the result of which is stored in the database column. Usually, such an expression involves the field it's associated with, but that doesn't have to be the case. Chapter 8, *Transforming Data During a Load*, shows you how to write SQL expressions that leverage the power of Oracle SQL to transform your data.

Understanding Field Positions

You use the POSITION clause to specify the location of the fields in the records that you are loading. The clause is optional. Usually, you use it with fixed-width, columnar data, and usually you omit it when loading delimited data. There are exceptions to both rules, however. The POSITION clause is sometimes necessary with delimited data, and it is possible to omit it entirely in certain cases when loading fixed-width data.

Specifying the starting position of a field

There are two ways that you can specify the starting position of a field. You can specify an absolute position, which is always relative to the beginning of the record, or you can specify a relative position. You always count bytes, so if a field starts in the tenth byte of a record, your POSITION clause would be as follows:

```
POSITION(10)
```

Absolute positions are relative to the beginning of the record. You can also specify the starting position of one field with respect to the previous field in the list of field specifications. To do this, you use the asterisk (*) and an optional offset. Consider the following data:

```
Munising   49862 MI
Shingleton49884 MI
Seney      49883 MI
```

You can see that while the second field immediately follows the first, there is one space between fields two and three. The field specifications in the following LOAD statement could be used to load this data:

```
LOAD DATA
   INFILE 'zipcodes.dat'
   REPLACE INTO TABLE zipcodes (
      city_name POSITION(1) CHAR(10),
      zip_code POSITION(*) CHAR(5),
      state_abbr POSITION(*+1) CHAR(2)
      )
```

You see the * character being used here to specify the position of the ZIP Code and state abbreviation fields in relative terms. The POSITION clauses for the three fields function as follows:

POSITION(1)

Tells SQL*Loader that the city name field begins with the first byte of the record.

POSITION(*)

Tells SQL*Loader that the ZIP Code field follows immediately after the previous field in the list.

POSITION(+1)*

Tells SQL*Loader that the state abbreviation field is separated from the previous field by one byte. In other words, the value 1 is added to the position indicated by the *.

In this example, the datatype specifications for the three fields also specified the lengths. If you prefer, you can specify the ending position of each field, and let SQL*Loader derive a default length based on that.

Specifying the ending position of a field

To specify the ending position of a field, you simply add it to the POSITION clause following the starting position. Separate the two values using either a colon or a hyphen. For example:

```
city_name POSITION(1:10) CHAR(10),
```

When you specify both a starting and an ending position, SQL*Loader will use those values to calculate a default length for the field. Then you don't need to specify the same length redundantly in the datatype clause. For example, the following LOAD statement will load the same ZIP Code data shown earlier:

```
LOAD DATA
   INFILE 'zipcodes.dat'
   REPLACE INTO TABLE zipcodes (
      city_name POSITION(1:10) CHAR(10),
      zip_code POSITION(*:15) CHAR,
      state_abbr POSITION(17-18) CHAR
      )
```

Here, each POSITION clause specifies both the starting and ending positions of each field. Several different variations have been used in order to demonstrate the possibilities:

city_name POSITION(1:10) CHAR(10),

The city name begins at position 1 and goes through position 10. In this case, the length was specified redundantly in the datatype specification. A colon was used to separate the beginning and ending values.

zip_code POSITION(*:15) CHAR,

> The * indicates that the ZIP Code begins with the first byte following the city name. The ending position has been hardcoded as the 15th byte. A colon has been used to separate the two values. No length has been specified with the datatype, so SQL*Loader will compute the length as *ending – beginning + 1.*

state_abbr POSITION(17–18) CHAR

> The state abbreviation has been specified in absolute terms. This time, a hyphen has been used to separate the two values. Again, no length has been specified with the datatype, so SQL*Loader will derive the length based on the beginning and ending values.

The specification for the ZIP Code field is rather odd in that the * character is used to specify the beginning of the field relative to the previous field, but the ending position has been specified in absolute terms. SQL*Loader will allow you to do this, but we can't think of any situation where it possibly makes sense to mix absolute and relative positioning in one POSITION clause. If you're going to use relative positioning, you should allow SQL*Loader to calculate the end of the field based on a length that you supply in the datatype specification.

Advantages of relative positioning

The primary advantage of relative positioning is that you can change the size of one or more fields without needing to recalculate each field's beginning and ending positions in the record. Consider the following LOAD statement:

```
LOAD DATA
    INFILE 'zipcodes.dat'
    REPLACE INTO TABLE zipcodes (
        city_name POSITION(1) CHAR(10),
        zip_code POSITION(*) CHAR(5),
        state_abbr POSITION(*+1) CHAR(2)
        )
```

The first field has been set to begin in position 1. The remaining fields are all positioned relative to the preceding field. This LOAD statement can be used with the following data:

```
Munising  49862 MI
Shingleton49884 MI
Seney     49883 MI
```

If you later changed the format of your datafile to allow ZIP+4 values, your data might appear as follows:

```
Munising  49862-1234 MI
Shingleton49884-1234 MI
Seney     49883-1234 MI
```

Because you used relative positioning in your control file, the only change you would need to make is to the size of the ZIP Code field. You would expand the size from five characters to ten. For example:

```
zip_code POSITION(*) CHAR(10),
```

You would not need to recalculate any beginning and ending byte positions. Relative positioning ensures that the byte positions for all subsequent fields are adjusted to compensate for the additional five bytes.

Relative positioning is also helpful if you know your data in terms of the size of each field, but haven't been given a list of exact beginning and ending positions. This is the case, for example, if someone hands you a data file together with a COBOL record description. The following record description describes the five-digit ZIP Code data shown earlier:

```
01 ZIP-CODE-REC.
   05 CITY-NAME      PIC X(10).
   05 ZIP-CODE       PIC X(5).
   05 STATE-CODE     PIC XX.
```

COBOL record descriptions tell you only the size of each field. You could then manually calculate each field's starting and ending position, but it's much easier to use relative positioning, as seen in this section.

Filler Fields

Filler fields were introduced in Oracle release 8.1 and are a relatively new innovation. Filler fields are fields in the input file that are described in the control file, but that are not ultimately loaded into a database column.

 The term *filler* was undoubtedly borrowed from COBOL. In the COBOL language, FILLER is a special name given to fields that you need to define because of where they appear in a record, but that you do not want to use in your program.

The syntax for declaring a filler field is similar to that used for declaring a scalar field. The key difference is the use of the keyword FILLER immediately following the column name. In addition, some clauses, such as NULLIF and DEFAULTIF, do not apply to filler fields. The syntax for declaring a filler field is as follows:

```
field_name FILLER [POSITION({start | *[+offset]}[{: | -}end])]
           [datatype] [PIECED]
```

You can see that this syntax is a scaled-down version of the syntax used for scalar fields. The elements in this syntax are as follows:

field_name

The name that you want to use to refer to the filler field. This name is only valid in the SQL*Loader control file. It does not correspond to any database column.

FILLER

The keyword that tells SQL*Loader that the field is not one to be loaded into the destination database table.

start

The starting position of the field in the input record. The first byte is position 1, the second byte is position 2, and so forth.

*

Tells SQL*Loader that the first byte of the field immediately follows the last byte of the previous field. If you use * for the first field that you define, SQL*Loader will start with the first byte in the record.

offset

An optional offset that you can have SQL*Loader add to the position represented by the * character.

end

The position of the last byte of data in the field. This is optional. If you omit the ending position, SQL*Loader will determine it based on information that you supply in your datatype specification.

datatype

A datatype specification for the field. This may include information about delimiters and enclosing characters. The "Datatypes" section, later in this chapter, shows the syntax for all datatypes supported by SQL*Loader.

PIECED

An option that causes SQL*Loader to load a field one piece at a time. PIECED is only valid in direct path loads, and only for the last field in a record.

Using filler fields to skip data

One fairly obvious use for filler fields is to skip a column of delimited data that you don't want to load—something that was very difficult to do in earlier releases of Oracle. Consider the following geographic feature name data:

```
"MI","Germfask Cemetery","cemetery","Schoolcraft"
"MI","Germfask Church","church","Schoolcraft"
"MI","Germfask, Township of","civil","Schoolcraft"
```

Each of these records consists of four delimited fields containing the following information:

- Two-letter state code
- Feature name
- Feature type
- County

Assume that you don't care about the feature type, but that you want to load the other three fields. Prior to the introduction of FILLER fields in Oracle8*i*, this would have been very difficult to do. SQL*Loader never used to have a facility to skip a delimited field. With fixed-width data, this was never a problem, because you simply defined the fields that you wanted to load, along with their positions. Delimited fields, however, are typically positioned relative to the previous field, and skipping such a field simply wasn't possible prior to Oracle8*i*.

Now that filler fields are available, skipping a delimited field is as easy as defining it with the FILLER keyword. For example:

```
LOAD DATA
    INFILE 'filler_test.dat'
    REPLACE INTO TABLE filler_test (
        gfn_state_abbr CHAR
            TERMINATED BY "," ENCLOSED BY '"',
        gfn_feature_name CHAR
            TERMINATED BY "," ENCLOSED BY '"',
        feature_type FILLER CHAR
            TERMINATED BY "," ENCLOSED BY '"',
        gfn_county_name CHAR
            TERMINATED BY "," ENCLOSED BY '"'
        )
```

The *feature_type* field in this LOAD statement is defined similarly to the others, but with the addition of the FILLER keyword. That's all you need to do to skip the field. Because it's a filler field, SQL*Loader won't try to load it into the destination table.

Other uses for filler fields

Even though filler fields aren't loaded into the database, SQL*Loader does extract the values for filler fields from each record that it processes. These values are available to you and can be used in the following locations:

- In NULLIF and DEFAULTIF expressions for non-filler fields. You can set a field to null or zero depending on the value in a filler field.
- In the LOBFILE clause used for loading large object fields. In the LOBFILE clause, filler fields are used to hold the name of an operating system file to be loaded into a database LOB column.

- In WHEN clauses to determine whether or not an input record even gets loaded.

- In the SID, OID, and REF clauses used to load object tables and REF columns.

- In the BFILE clause, to identify an operating system file to be loaded.

One place you can't use FILLER fields that you might at first expect to be able to use them is in SQL expressions for fields that you are loading into the database. Filler fields cannot be used in SQL expressions. The reason for this limitation likely has to do with the fact that since filler fields aren't being loaded, they aren't part of the bind array transmitted from SQL*Loader to Oracle. Hence, the values aren't available on the server.

 Oracle9*i* includes a new type of FILLER field known as a BOUND FILLER. These BOUND FILLER fields are usable in SQL expressions.

Generated Fields

Generated fields are those that don't really exist in the input record. Instead, SQL*Loader generates a value for you. Some types of generated values only apply when loading object tables and BFILE columns. These are discussed in Chapters 10 and 11, respectively. The syntax for the more conventional generated fields is as follows:

```
column_name {RECNUM
            |SYSDATE
            |CONSTANT {string | "string"}
            |SEQUENCE [({COUNT | MAX|integer}[,increment])]
            }
```

The elements in the syntax are as follows:

column_name

> The name of the database column into which you want the generated data to be loaded. This is only the column name. The INTO TABLE clause identifies the table.

RECNUM

> Causes SQL*Loader to generate a sequentially increasing record number for each logical record that is read from the input file. The first record is number 1, the second is number 2, and so forth. Skipped, discarded, and error records are all counted.

SYSDATE

> Causes SQL*Loader to store the system date into the column being loaded. The destination column may be either a character column or a DATE column. If the destination is a character column (CHAR, VARCHAR2, etc.), the date will always be stored in "DD-MON-YY" format. The value stored in the database column is a date/time value that comes from Oracle's built-in SYSDATE function. For conventional path loads, a new date/time value is generated for each bind array (group of records) loaded. For direct path loads, a new date/time value is generated for each database block.

> Oddly enough, the instance's NLS_DATE_FORMAT setting has no effect on the format used by SQL*Loader to store SYSDATE constants in a character column.

CONSTANT

> Causes SQL*Loader to use the constant value that you specify for each row loaded into the destination table.

string | *"string"*

> The character string constant that you want loaded. Ideally, you should quote this string. However, you may be able to omit the quotes if the string contains letters, digits, no whitespace, no punctuation, and is not a reserved word.

SEQUENCE

> Causes SQL*Loader to generate a unique sequence number for each row that is loaded. This is similar to, but not quite the same as, RECNUM. Sequence numbers increment for each row that SQL*Loader attempts to load. This includes rows that fail to load because they generate an error (those written to the bad file). Sequence numbers do not increment for discarded or skipped rows. By default, sequence numbers begin with 1 and increment by 1. You can change that behavior using the following optional parameters:

COUNT

> Determine the current number of rows in the table, add the increment value, and use the result as the first sequence number.

MAX

> Determine the maximum value of the column being loaded, add the increment value, and use the result as the first sequence number.

integer

> Use the specified integer value as the first sequence number. You must specify either zero or a positive number.

increment

> Use the specified integer value for the increment. This allows you to set
> an increment of other than 1. Negative increments are not allowed. An
> increment of zero, strangely enough, is allowed; the result is that the same
> sequence number is used for all records.

The following LOAD statement contains two generated fields, and will load the
same geographic feature name data that you saw in the previous section:

```
LOAD DATA
    INFILE 'filler_test.dat'
    REPLACE INTO TABLE constant_test (
        gfn_state_abbr CHAR
            TERMINATED BY "," ENCLOSED BY '"',
        gfn_feature_name CHAR
            TERMINATED BY "," ENCLOSED BY '"',
        feature_type FILLER CHAR
            TERMINATED BY "," ENCLOSED BY '"',
        gfn_county_name CHAR
            TERMINATED BY "," ENCLOSED BY '"',
        gfn_data_source CONSTANT "United States Geological Survey",
        gfn_timestamp SYSDATE
        )
```

Of course, for this load to work, the destination table must contain a character column named *gfn_data_source* that is of the appropriate length. It must also contain a *gfn_timestamp* column of type DATE, CHAR, or VARCHAR2.

When using SEQUENCE to generate sequence numbers, be careful of the MAX
and COUNT options. Both result in a query being issued against the destination
table—either SELECT MAX(*column_name*) or SELECT COUNT(*), depending on
which option you choose. If you have a very large table, such a query may turn
out to be quite expensive in terms of time and disk I/O. You also must consider
that the table may be updated by other processes while the load takes place. For
example, using MAX with a column may cause SQL*Loader to begin the sequence
with 101, but you have no guarantee that some other process won't insert values
into the same column that conflict with the sequence numbers that SQL*Loader is
loading. This can result in problems, especially if your sequence column is part of
a primary key or unique key constraint.

> If you are loading a column where the value usually is derived from
> an Oracle database sequence, the SEQUENCE keyword won't help
> you. Instead, you can deal with this by writing a SQL expression.
> See Chapter 8 for an example.

Datatypes

SQL*Loader supports a wide variety of datatypes, some of them more useful than others. These datatypes are grouped into the following two families:

- Portable datatypes

- Nonportable datatypes

It's critical that you understand the distinction between portable and nonportable datatypes. The distinction is simple. Nonportable datatypes are hardware-specific: you typically must read a file from the same hardware on which it was generated. Portable datatypes are for use with textual data, which can usually be transferred from one machine to another without affecting the semantics, or meaning, of the data.

The other key thing to understand about SQL*Loader datatypes is that you use them to describe the fields in the data files that SQL*Loader reads. Their names do not correspond to the datatype names of the columns that you are loading. In fact, the SQL*Loader datatypes do not need to correspond at all to the database datatypes of the columns that you are loading. SQL*Loader interprets input data using the SQL*Loader datatypes you specify. It then converts each value to the appropriate database datatype. You never have to tell SQL*Loader the database datatype, because SQL*Loader derives that information directly from the Oracle data dictionary.

Portable Datatypes

While we can't point to any statistics to back up our claim, we think it's safe to say that SQL*Loader's portable datatypes are the most commonly used. In our experience, SQL*Loader is most often used to load data from a text file. This entails the use of the portable datatypes, which are listed in Table 3-1.

*Table 3-1. SQL*Loader Portable Datatypes*

Type	Comments
CHAR	Identifies character data in the data file. Typically, you use CHAR to describe data being loaded into a VARCHAR2 or CHAR database column.
DATE	Identifies character data that represents a date. Usually, you provide a date mask describing the exact representation used. The destination is typically a database DATE column.
INTEGER EXTERNAL	Identifies character data that represents an integer value.
FLOAT EXTERNAL	Identifies character data that represents a floating-point value.
DECIMAL EXTERNAL	Identifies character data that represents a decimal value.
ZONED EXTERNAL	Is synonymous with DECIMAL EXTERNAL.
GRAPHIC	Identifies double-byte character data that is to be loaded "as is," without any translation or conversion.

Table 3-1. SQL*Loader Portable Datatypes (continued)

Type	Comments
GRAPHIC EXTERNAL	Identifies GRAPHIC data that is enclosed by leading and trailing shift-in and shift-out characters.
RAW	Identifies binary data that is to be loaded "as is," without any conversion taking place.
VARCHARC	Identifies a character string preceded by a series of digits representing the length of the string.
VARRAWC	Identifies binary data preceded by a series of digits representing the length of the string.

GRAPHIC, GRAPHIC EXTERNAL, and RAW fields are only loaded "as is" when the datatype of the destination column is a binary type such as BLOB, RAW, or LONG RAW. See the section "GRAPHIC" later in this chapter for more information on this point.

CHAR

The CHAR field type is used to identify character data. For example, all of the fields in the following records would be considered character fields:

```
"MI","Munising Falls","falls","Alger"
"MI","Munising Falls Creek","stream","Alger"
"MI","Munising Junction","ppl","Alger"
"MI","Munising Sanitary Landfill","locale","Alger"
```

You should usually use CHAR if your destination database column is one of the following types:

> VARCHAR2
> CHAR
> NVARCHAR2
> NCHAR
> LONG

The syntax used to describe a CHAR field is as follows:

```
CHAR [(length)] [enclosure | termination [[OPTIONALLY] enclosure]]

enclosure := ENCLOSED [BY] [{'string' | X'hex_value'}]
             [AND {'string' | X'hex_value'}]

termination := TERMINATED [BY] {WHITESPACE|X'hex_value'
                              | 'string'}
```

The elements in the syntax are as follows:

length

> The length of the string in bytes. The default length is derived from the POSITION clause, and is 1 if no POSITION clause has been specified. This overrides the default.

enclosure

> An enclosure specification describing characters such as quotes that enclose the field.

termination

> A termination specification that tells SQL*Loader how to recognize the end of the field.

OPTIONALLY

> Indicates that the presence of the enclosing characters is optional.

string

> A character, or series of characters, that marks the end of a field, or that encloses a field.

hex_value

> The hexadecimal representation of one or more characters that terminate the field, or that enclose the field.

WHITESPACE

> A keyword denoting any type of whitespace. Whitespace includes space characters, tab characters, and newline characters.

Table 3-2 shows several possible character fields along with their appropriate descriptions.

Table 3-2. Sample CHAR Field Descriptions

Sample Data	CHAR Clause
Munising Falls xxx... Munising Junctionxxx...	CHAR(17)
Munising Falls,xxx,... Munising Junction,xxx,...	CHAR DELIMITED BY ','
"Munising Falls","xxx",... "Munising Junction","xxx",...	CHAR DELIMITED BY ',' ENCLOSED BY '"'
"Munising Falls","xxx",... Munising Junction,xxx,...	CHAR DELIMITED BY ',' OPTIONALLY ENCLOSED BY '"'

When SQL*Loader loads CHAR data, character set translation may be performed. If the character set of the data being loaded is different from that used in the destination database, then SQL*Loader will perform the necessary translation.

DATE

The DATE field type is used to identify character data that represents a date. When SQL*Loader reads such data, it ultimately converts it to Oracle's internal date representation. Use the DATE field type whenever you have data to load into an Oracle database column of type DATE.

The syntax used to describe a DATE field is as follows:

```
DATE [EXTERNAL] [(length)] ["mask"]
      [enclosure | termination [[OPTIONALLY] enclosure]]

enclosure := ENCLOSED [BY] [{'string' | X'hex_value'}]
              [AND {'string' | X'hex_value'}]

termination := TERMINATED [BY] {WHITESPACE | X'hex_value'
                                | 'string'}
```

The elements of the syntax are as follows:

length

> The length of the date string in bytes. The default length is initially derived from the number of characters in the date mask, if one is present. Any length derived from the POSITION clause, if it exists, then overrides the length derived from the mask. This length overrides both of those other values.

mask

> Tells SQL*Loader how to interpret the date. This mask ends up being used with Oracle's built-in TO_DATE function. Table 3-3 provides examples of some commonly used date masks. The default date mask is "DD-MON-YY" and is not affected by the NLS_DATE_FORMAT parameter or environment variable setting.

enclosure

> An enclosure specification that describes characters such as quotes that enclose the field.

termination

> A termination specification that tells SQL*Loader how to recognize the end of the field.

OPTIONALLY

> Indicates that the presence of the enclosing characters is optional.

string

> A character or series of characters that marks the end of a field, or that encloses a field.

hex_value

> The hexadecimal representation of one or more characters that terminate the field, or that enclose the field.

WHITESPACE

> A keyword denoting any type of whitespace. Whitespace includes space characters, tab characters, and newline characters.

Table 3-3 shows the syntax to use for several typical date formats.

Table 3-3. Sample DATE Field Descriptions

Sample Data	DATE Clause
11/15/1961	DATE "mm/dd/yyyy"
11/15/61	DATE "mm/dd/yy"
15-Nov-1961	DATE "dd-mon-yyyy"
"Nov 15, 1961",...	DATE "mon dd, yyyy" TERMINATED BY "," ENCLOSED BY QUOTES
19611115,...	DATE "yyyymmdd" TERMINATED BY ","

While the syntax allows you to specify a length for a DATE field, it's often not necessary. Instead, you may be able to allow SQL*Loader to derive the length from the date mask. For example, a mask of "dd-mon-yyyy" indicates that the date field is 11 characters long. It's important to know that SQL*Loader derives this length simply by counting the characters in the mask, without regard for their meaning. This can lead to problems if the representation of a date component in the mask does not contain *exactly* the same number of characters as are used to represent that component in the data. As an example of this problem, consider the date mask shown in the following field definition:

```
DATE "month dd, yyyy"
```

The date element, "month", in this example tells SQL*Loader to look for the full name of a month. English month names range from three characters (May) to nine characters (September) in length. SQL*Loader has no way to know this, and will simply expect the date field to be 14 characters—the number of characters in the mask—in length. In such a situation, you need to tell SQL*Loader the maximum length of the field. In this case, you should specify a length of 18 characters as follows:

```
DATE(18) "month dd, yyyy"
```

If you are using the POSITION clause to load fixed-width data, you can allow SQL*Loader to derive the length of a date field from that. Any length derived from the POSITION clause overrides the value derived from the date mask. In turn, an explicitly specified length overrides any value derived from the POSITION clause.

Blank Date Fields

Date fields that sometimes contain blanks can be a bit of a problem. You may encounter such date fields in a fixed-width data file. For example, the following set of records shows a date field that is sometimes blank:

```
05-Feb-2001Sand Point
            Tannery Falls
07-Feb-2001Valley Spur
...
```

With data like this, you should consider defining the date field with not only a date mask, but a NULLIF clause as well. For example:

```
LOAD DATA
INFILE 'visit_dates.dat'
REPLACE INTO TABLE feature_visits (
    visit_date DATE 'dd-mon-yyyy'
            NULLIF = blanks,
    feature_name char(1)
)
```

The date mask tells SQL*Loader how to interpret the date, but as a side effect you'll get errors whenever a record contains a blank date field. The NULLIF clause prevents those errors, and instead causes blank date fields to be set to null.

Note that beginning with release 8.1.7, SQL*Loader automatically loads blank DATE fields as null values.

INTEGER, FLOAT, DECIMAL, and ZONED EXTERNAL

The various numeric external datatypes are used to load numeric data that is represented in character form. All four types function identically. The different names only serve as an aid in making your control file somewhat self-documenting. Consider the following data:

```
123456     123456     123456     123456
123.456E+3 123.456E+3 123.456E+3 123.456E+3
123.456    123.456    123.456    123.456
-123.00    -123.00    -123.00    -123.00
-123       -123       -123       -123
123456E-3  123456E-3  123456E-3  123456E-3
```

Each of the four columns contains an integer value, a decimal value, and a floating-point value in scientific notation. In spite of the different numeric representations used, this data can be accurately loaded using the following LOAD statement:

```
LOAD DATA
    INSERT INTO TABLE numeric_external_test
    (
```

```
a POSITION (1:10) INTEGER EXTERNAL,
b POSITION (12:21) FLOAT EXTERNAL,
c POSITION (23:32) DECIMAL EXTERNAL,
d POSITION (34: 43) ZONED EXTERNAL
)
```

 When you're dealing with columnar numeric data that has an assumed decimal point, consider using the nonportable ZONED datatype. See the description for ZONED under "Nonportable Datatypes" later in this chapter.

The syntax used to describe numeric external fields is as follows:

```
{INTEGER | DECIMAL | FLOAT | ZONED} EXTERNAL[(length)]
    [enclosure | termination [[OPTIONALLY] enclosure]]

enclosure := ENCLOSED [BY] [{'string' | X'hex_value'}]
            [AND {'string' | X'hex_value'}]

termination := TERMINATED [BY] {WHITESPACE | X'hex_value'
                            | 'string'}
```

The elements of the syntax are as follows:

length

The length of the numeric field. This refers to the length of the character representation in the input data file, and has nothing to do with the precision of the destination column in the database. The default length is derived from the POSITION clause, and is 1 if no POSITION clause has been specified. This overrides the default.

enclosure

An enclosure specification that describes characters, such as quotes, that enclose the field.

termination

A termination specification that tells SQL*Loader how to recognize the end of the field.

OPTIONALLY

Indicates that the presence of the enclosing characters is optional.

string

A character or series of characters that mark the end of a field, or that enclose a field.

hex_value

The hexadecimal representation of one or more characters.

WHITESPACE

A keyword denoting any type of whitespace. Whitespace includes space characters, tab characters, and newline characters.

You can actually load human-readable numeric data using the CHAR datatype. As far as SQL*Loader is concerned, the data is just character data. The conversion to a numeric value comes about because the destination database column is defined as a NUMBER. The one difference between CHAR and the numeric external datatypes is the manner in which SQL*Loader implements the DEFAULTIF keyword. The default CHAR value is a null, while the default value for numeric external fields is zero.

 Any sign characters must be leading. Trailing sign characters will cause errors, resulting in rows being written to the bad file.

GRAPHIC

The GRAPHIC field type is used to load raw, double-byte characters into a RAW, LONG RAW, or BLOB database column. No character set translation is performed. The data is loaded "as is." As far as we can tell, GRAPHIC is equivalent to RAW, except for the way in which the length is specified.

The syntax used to describe a GRAPHIC field is as follows:

```
GRAPHIC [(length)]
```

The length for a GRAPHIC field is not expressed in terms of bytes, but rather in terms of double-byte characters. Thus a "length" of 2 would represent not 2 bytes, but 4 bytes (2 characters at 2 bytes each = 4 bytes). Regardless of this emphasis on "double-byte" characters, GRAPHIC data is simply treated as a stream of bytes to be loaded "as is."

The end of a GRAPHIC field can never be marked by a delimiter. You have to specify a length, or rely on the default length derived from the field's POSITION clause. A GRAPHIC field can be enclosed by a single character on either side, but rather than accomplishing that via the enclosure clause, you must use the GRAPHIC EXTERNAL type.

The default length of a GRAPHIC field is derived from the POSITION clause. Relying on the default happens to be the only way to define a GRAPHIC field with an odd number of bytes. Any explicit length you specify is multiplied by 2, which always yields an even number. A definition such as the following, however, can result in an odd number of bytes:

```
POSITION (1:3) GRAPHIC,
```

Here, the GRAPHIC field is defined to be in positions 1–3. The values in the POSITION clause always refer to bytes; hence, the length of the field will be three bytes. You're probably better off using the RAW field type, though, rather than relying on behavior such as this that's likely to be poorly understood.

GRAPHIC data should normally be loaded into a database column defined using a datatype that is designed to hold binary data. Such types include BLOB, RAW, and LONG RAW. When you load GRAPHIC data into such a column, the string of bytes is simply loaded "as is." Try to load GRAPHIC data into a character-based column such as LONG or VARCHAR2, however, and you'll get very unusual results. In such cases, Oracle will do an implicit conversion to convert the string of raw bytes to a character string composed of hexadecimal digits corresponding to the hexadecimal representation of the underlying raw data. Use GRAPHIC to load a value such as X'0102' (two bytes) into a VARCHAR2 column, and you'll end up with the string "0102" (four characters). The result is the same as if you took a raw value and used Oracle's built-in RAWTOHEX function to convert it to a character string.

Hexadecimal Notation

When representing a string of data using hexadecimal digits, it's common to enclose that string within single quotes (') and precede it with an X. This convention differentiates the string from a quoted text string—you know when you see X'...' enclosing a string of hexadecimal digits that each two digits represent one character. Thus, X'0102' represents a string of bytes where the first byte contains the value 1 and the second byte contains the value 2.

GRAPHIC EXTERNAL

The GRAPHIC EXTERNAL field type is used to load GRAPHIC data that is enclosed by shift-in and shift-out characters. For example, suppose you have data like this:

```
X'0083983456...00'
```

The beginning and end of this data is marked by the X'00' character. You don't want those beginning and ending characters to be loaded, but you do want to load the rest of the data. You can accomplish that by using GRAPHIC EXTERNAL, which arbitrarily throws away the first and last bytes.

The syntax for GRAPHIC EXTERNAL looks like this:

```
GRAPHIC EXTERNAL [(length)]
```

The length has the same semantics as for the GRAPHIC type. It represents the number of two-byte characters in the field. Do not include the enclosing bytes in the length. SQL*Loader assumes that they are in addition to whatever length you specify.

RAW

The RAW type is used to load binary data "as is" into a RAW, LONG RAW, or BLOB database column. The syntax for the RAW type is as follows:

```
RAW [(length)]
```

The default length is that derived from the POSITION clause, if there is one. Unlike the case with the two GRAPHIC types, the length you specify for a RAW field is always in terms of bytes.

As with the GRAPHIC type, if you load RAW data into a character column such as a VARCHAR2 or LONG column, Oracle will convert the data to a hexadecimal character string.

VARCHARC

The VARCHARC type is used to load variable-length strings that are preceded by a series of digits indicating their length. Take a look at the following set of data:

```
008Munising
013Iron Mountain
005Seney
008Germfask
011Blaney Park
```

This is a list of five cities. Each city name is prefaced by a three-digit number that gives the length of the city name. This is the type of data that the VARCHARC type allows you to load. The number of digits used for the length does not need to be three. You can specify any number of digits for the length.

The syntax for VARCHARC is as follows:

```
VARCHARC(length_bytes [,max_bytes])
```

The elements in the syntax are as follows:

length_bytes

> Specifies the number of digits used for the length of the string. This is required. You can't have a VARCHARC field without a length subfield.

max_bytes

> Specifies the maximum length of the string in bytes. SQL*Loader will reserve enough memory to handle the size string that you specify. The default maximum length is 4 KB.

To load the list of city names shown earlier, you would define the city field as VARCHARC(3). Ideally, you would also supply a more reasonable maximum length than the default 4 KB. VARCHARC fields may not be delimited, nor may they be enclosed. You can't include enclosure and termination clauses for this datatype.

VARRAWC

The VARRAWC field type is identical in every way but one to VARCHARC. That one difference is that VARRAWC is used to load data "as is" into RAW, LONG RAW, or BLOB database columns.

The syntax for VARRAWC is as follows:

```
VARRAWC(length_bytes [,max_bytes])
```

The elements in the syntax are as follows:

length_bytes

Specifies the number of digits used for the length of the string. Required.

max_bytes

Specifies the maximum length of the string in bytes. SQL*Loader will reserve enough memory to handle the size string that you specify. The default maximum length is 4 KB.

If you use the VARRAWC type, you should read the previous sections describing the GRAPHIC and RAW types. They explain how SQL*Loader treats raw data.

Nonportable Datatypes

SQL*Loader's nonportable datatypes allow you to load data from binary files. The reason they are called *nonportable* is that, for the most part, binary datatypes are hardware-specific. This is especially true of numeric values where you have to contend with such issues as the number of bits in an integer, whether the most or least significant bytes come first, and how the sign is represented. Table 3-4 lists all of SQL*Loader's nonportable datatypes.

*Table 3-4. SQL*Loader Nonportable Datatypes*

Type	Comments
INTEGER	Identifies a word integer value. This corresponds to the C LONG INT type.
SMALLINT	Identifies a half-word integer value. This corresponds to the C SMALLINT type.
FLOAT	Identifies a single-precision, floating-point value. This corresponds to the C FLOAT type.
DOUBLE	Identifies a double-precision, floating-point value. This corresponds to the C DOUBLE and LONG FLOAT types.
BYTEINT	Identifies a single-byte, unsigned, binary integer. This corresponds to the C UNSIGNED CHAR type.
ZONED	Identifies zoned decimal data. This corresponds to typical COBOL PIC 9 USAGE IS DISPLAY fields.

Table 3-4. SQL*Loader Nonportable Datatypes (continued)

Type	Comments
DECIMAL	Identifies packed-decimal data. This corresponds to COBOL packed-decimal fields. These are also referred to as COMP-3, COMPUTATIONAL-3, or binary-coded decimal (BCD) fields.
VARGRAPHIC	Identifies a variable-length, double-byte string.
VARCHAR	Identifies a variable-length character string.
VARRAW	Identifies a variable-length sequence of bytes that are loaded "as is."
LONG VARRAW	The same as VARRAW, but allows for a four-byte length value instead of a two-byte length value.

Many of the numeric types listed in Table 3-4 correspond directly to C datatypes. Some, such as ZONED and DECIMAL, are related to field types commonly encountered in data files generated by COBOL programs. The ZONED type can actually be helpful sometimes with straight character data that you might otherwise match up with a portable datatype. We frequently use ZONED when loading character-represented numeric data with an assumed decimal point.

INTEGER, SMALLINT, FLOAT, DOUBLE, and BYTEINT

The INTEGER, SMALLINT, FLOAT, DOUBLE, and BYTEINT types are used to load numeric values represented in hardware-specific formats. In all cases, the length of these fields is fixed for any given hardware platform. For example, on Intel-based systems, INTEGER values are always 32 bits. Since the representation used for these values varies from one hardware platform to the next, it's best to understand them in terms of their C equivalents. These are given in Table 3-4.

 The start and end values in a POSITION clause cannot be used to override the length of nonportable binary numbers. SQL*Loader will ignore any end values that you specify, and will use the correct lengths for your platform.

By default, INTEGER and SMALLINT identify signed values. Beginning with release 8.1.7, you can add the UNSIGNED keyword to these datatypes to identify unsigned values. For example, use INTEGER UNSIGNED to load unsigned integer data.

ZONED

The ZONED field type is used to load zoned decimal data. *Zoned decimal* data usually comes from a COBOL environment, and is simply numeric data in a character format. The decimal point is always assumed. The sign, if there is one, is represented by an overpunch in either the leading or the trailing character. The term *overpunch* comes from the days when data was stored on 80-column punch cards. To record a negative sign, two characters were actually punched into the same card column. First the digit was punched, and then holes for the sign were punched right on top of it. The result usually manifests itself as a letter. Table 3-5 shows some sample zoned decimal data, and indicates how it is interpreted using various COBOL declarations.

The term *zoned* has fallen out of use. Today, you'll typically hear this type of data described as USAGE IS DISPLAY—referring to the keywords used to declare such data.

Table 3-5. Zoned Decimal Examples

Data	COBOL Declaration	SQL*Loader Declaration	Value
12345	PIC 999V99	ZONED(5,2)	123.45
12345	PIC 99999	ZONED(5)	12345
12345	PIC S99999	ZONED(5)	12345
1234N	PIC S999V99	ZONED(5,2)	−123.45

The "1234N" value that you see in Table 3-5 is the likely representation of −12345 in the EBCDIC character set. In ASCII, you would be likely to see "1234U".

Many current versions of COBOL support both leading and trailing signs—the sign can be overpunched on either the first or the last character, as you choose. Trailing signs are always the default (for historic reasons), and they are the only ones supported by SQL*Loader.

The syntax to use for ZONED fields is as follows:

```
ZONED (precision[,scale])
```

The elements in the syntax are as follows:

precision

> The number of digits in the number. This corresponds directly to the total number of characters occupied by the field.

scale

> The number of digits that are assumed to be to the right of the decimal point. The default scale is 0, which results in integer values being loaded.

Using ZONED for External Numeric Data

Unless you are dealing with negative numbers, zoned decimal data is made up of the characters "0" through "9". If you are loading external numeric data that is all positive, you can just as easily use ZONED in place of an external type such as INTEGER EXTERNAL. Why would you want to do this? The answer is that ZONED allows you to specify an assumed decimal point. Consider the following book price data:

```
Oracle Essentials                 3495
SQL*Plus: The Definitive Guide    3995
Oracle PL/SQL Programming         4495
Oracle8 Design Tips               1495
```

You can readily see that there's an assumed decimal place, and that 3495 really means $34.95. One problem with SQL*Loader is that none of the external numeric datatypes can handle this situation. DECIMAL EXTERNAL will recognize a decimal point if it's there, but it won't assume one. There are three approaches you can take to load this data:

- You can manipulate the text file using an editor or other text manipulation program, and insert the decimal point into your numbers.

- You can write a SQL expression for SQL*Loader that causes every number to be divided by 100. Chapter 8 shows you how to do this.

- You can use the ZONED datatype.

The price data shown here could be described to SQL*Loader as ZONED(4,2). This tells SQL*Loader that there are four digits, with two to the right of the decimal point. The decimal point itself is assumed, and should never be present in the number. When we are loading positive numbers with an assumed decimal point, we find using ZONED much easier than either of the other two methods.

The one thing you have to be careful about is that ZONED will not correctly interpret the traditional "+" and "−" characters. If your data contains positive signs, negative signs, or decimal points, you must use one of the external numeric types.

Today, COBOL also allows USAGE IS DISPLAY data to be written with a separate leading or trailing sign character. If a separate sign character is used, you should use one of SQL*Loader's numeric external types. However, those do not support trailing sign characters.

DECIMAL

The DECIMAL field type is used to load packed decimal data. Sometimes, this is referred to as binary-coded decimal (BCD) data. Like zoned decimal, packed decimal also is typically found in COBOL environments. Packed decimal manages to cram two numeric digits into each byte. It does this by using one *nibble* (four bits) to represent each decimal digit. The sign is always trailing and always takes up one nibble. The decimal point is assumed. Table 3-6 shows examples of packed decimal data.

Table 3-6. Packed Decimal Examples

Data (Hex)	COBOL Declaration	SQL*Loader Declaration	Value
X'12345C'	PIC S9(3)V99 COMP-3	DECIMAL(5,2)	123.45
X'12345C'	PIC S9(3)V99 PACKED-DECIMAL	DECIMAL(5,2)	123.45
X'12345D'	PIC S9(3)V99 COMP-3	DECIMAL(5,2)	−123.45
X'12345F'	PIC 9(5) COMP-3	DECIMAL(5)	12345
X'01234C'	PIC S9(4) COMP-3	DECIMAL(4)	1234

Typically, the last nibble of a packed decimal value will be either a C, F, or D, depending on whether the value is positive, unsigned, or negative. Other values, however, are possible. The values C, A, F, and E (CAFE) always represent positive values, while B and D represent negative values. Unsigned numbers are considered positive.

The syntax to use for DECIMAL fields is as follows:

```
DECIMAL (precision[,scale])
```

The elements in the syntax are as follows:

precision
    The number of digits in the number.

scale
    The number of digits that are assumed to be to the right of the decimal point. The default scale is 0, which results in integer values being loaded.

The number of bytes occupied by a packed-decimal field will always be an even number. To compute it, take the precision, go up to the next even number to accommodate the sign, and divide by two. Table 3-7 shows two examples, one for an even number of digits, the other for an odd number of digits.

Table 3-7. Computing the Bytes Used to Represent a Number in Packed-Decimal Format

Step	Odd Number of Digits	Even Number of Digits
How many digits?	5	4
Advance to next highest even number.	6	6
Divide by 2.	3	3

From a practical standpoint, there's never an advantage to declaring a packed decimal value with an even number of digits. You can see from Table 3-7 that a 4- and 5-digit number will both take up three bytes.

VARGRAPHIC

The VARGRAPHIC field type is used to load variable-length, double-byte, binary data. The data to be loaded must be preceded by a subfield indicating the length of the data. The format of the length subfield is machine-specific and corresponds to the C SHORT INT type for your platform. Assuming a 1-byte SHORT INT value, the following hexadecimal value represents a 7-byte VARGRAPHIC value:

```
X'06333837313639'
```

The first byte has a value of 6, which tells SQL*Loader to load the next 6 bytes into the database column.

> The size of the length subfield is platform-specific and may not be one byte on your platform.

The following syntax is used to describe a VARGRAPHIC field:

```
VARGRAPHIC[(max_doublebytes)]
```

SQL*Loader determines the actual length of a VARGRAPHIC field by inspecting the SHORT INT length value that precedes it. By default, SQL*Loader allocates enough memory to handle a maximum of 8 KB (8 kilobytes = 4096 double-byte characters). If you use a POSITION clause and specify both starting and ending byte positions, the default maximum length will be based on that. You can override the default maximum length by supplying a *max_doublebytes* value. This value is in terms of two-byte characters, so a declaration of VARGRAPHIC(8096) allows for 8096 two-byte characters, or 16 KB.

SQL*Loader does not perform character set translation on VARGRAPHIC fields. The VARGRAPHIC type should normally be used to load binary database columns such as RAW, LONG RAW, and BLOB.

VARCHAR

The VARCHAR type is used to load variable-length character data. Just like with VARGRAPHIC, the data to be loaded must be preceded by a SHORT INT value containing the length. The following example shows the hexadecimal representation of "Munising Falls" in VARCHAR format on an Intel-based system:

```
0E 00 4D 75 6E 69 73 69 6E 67 20 46 61 6C 6C 73
```

Why Packed Decimal?

For those used to programming in C, or more recently in Java, packed decimal must seem like a strange, and perhaps inefficient, way to represent numbers. How did it come about? For that matter, how did zoned decimal come about?

Packed decimal and zoned decimal both have their origins in the 1950s, when the COBOL programming language was first designed. Back then, 80-column punch cards made of cardboard were the storage medium of choice. Numeric data was often represented as strings of character digits; this representation was almost always used when numeric data needed to be transferred between two computers. Human-readable characters were the lingua franca of that era. Hence the need for the zoned decimal type, which uses the characters "0" through "9" to represent numeric values.

Space was at a premium: those punch cards only held 80 columns. No one wanted to waste an entire column on a sign, so the convention of using an overpunch was developed. Each punch card column had a separate hole for each digit. If the digit in that column was an 8, the hole corresponding to 8 would be punched. In the case of negative numbers, the last digit was special. Two holes were punched for that: one to indicate the digit, and one to indicate that the number was negative.

Packed decimal came about as a more space-efficient way to represent numeric values. This type was mostly used where portability wasn't an issue. It achieved its efficiency by taking every group of two digits and treating that as a hexadecimal value—each nibble (a *nibble* is four bits or one hexadecimal digit) representing one decimal digit. An extra nibble was given over to the sign.

While you might think that arithmetic using zoned and packed decimal numbers would be inefficient, that wasn't the case. Hardware vendors—some of them, at least—implemented packed-decimal arithmetic in hardware. On such a system, packed-decimal arithmetic was not only blazingly fast, it was accurate. Decimal values could be calculated without the rounding errors inherent in floating-point arithmetic, and very large numbers could be represented with no loss of precision in the least-significant digits.

There's much more to the representation of COBOL datatypes than what is covered in this chapter. Even SQL*Loader only handles a limited subset of the possibilities. These examples of internal representations are only that—examples. For extensive information on the subject, begin with the following sources:

- The COBOL FAQ, maintained by Bill Klein. You'll find this at *http://www.cobolreport.com/faqs/cobolfaq.htm*.

- Michael Mattias' article titled "COBOL Data Conversions," and his combination graphic tutorial and article titled "Understanding COBOL Datatypes." You'll find both at *http://www.flexus.com*.

The first two bytes of this data represent the length of the character string. On Intel hardware, the least significant byte of a SHORT INT value comes first, so what you see as "0E 00" in this data really represents X'000E'. When you convert X'000E' to decimal, you get 14.

The syntax to use when declaring a VARCHAR field is:

    VARCHAR[(max_bytes)]

The default maximum size is 4 KB. If a POSITION clause with starting and ending values is used, the default maximum size is derived from that. Specifying a value for *max_bytes* overrides any default.

The main difference between VARCHAR and VARGRAPHIC is that SQL*Loader will treat VARCHAR data as character data, and will perform character set translation. Use VARCHAR when loading character columns such as VARCHAR2, CHAR, CLOB, and LONG.

VARRAW

The VARRAW type is used to load variable-length binary data. The binary data to be loaded must be preceded by a two-byte subfield that specifies the length of the data in terms of bytes. For example, on an Intel x86 system, where the least-significant byte of a binary number comes first, the following VARRAW data will result in the string "12345" (assuming ASCII) being loaded into a RAW column:

    X'05003132333435'

The syntax to use for VARRAW is:

    VARRAW[(max_bytes)]

The default maximum size is 4 KB. If a POSITION clause with starting and ending values is used, the default maximum size is derived from that. Specifying a value for *max_bytes* overrides any default. The maximum number of bytes that may be loaded with VARRAW is 65,536, or 64 KB.

LONG VARRAW

The LONG VARRAW type is used to load variable-length, binary data that is too long to be loaded using VARRAW. The difference between LONG VARRAW and VARRAW lies in the size of the length subfield. VARRAW fields use two bytes to specify the length. LONG VARRAW fields use four bytes to specify the length.

The syntax to use for LONG VARRAW is:

    LONG VARRAW[(max_bytes)]

The default maximum size is 4 KB. If a POSITION clause with starting and ending values is used, the default maximum size is derived from that. Specifying a value for *max_bytes* overrides any default. The maximum number of bytes that may be loaded with LONG VARRAW is 4 GB.

4

Loading from Fixed-Width Files

Fixed-width data is one of the two overarching classifications of data that you deal with when using SQL*Loader. Fixed-width data files consist of columnar data—each field has a specific length and position that never varies from one record to the next. The other major classification, delimited data, discussed in Chapter 5, *Loading Delimited Data*, consists of variable-length fields separated by delimiter characters. Describing the fields in a fixed-width record is mostly a matter of specifying their positions and their datatypes. Occasionally, things are actually that simple. More often, you'll encounter issues such as these:

- How do you represent null values?

- What do you do with records that are shorter than they should be?

- How do you handle trailing whitespace at the end of a record?

The issue of null values is probably the trickiest of these issues. Null refers to the absence of a value, yet in a fixed-width data file you always have *some* value for each field. Other issues occur, perhaps less frequently. At times, you may be faced with the need to concatenate multiple physical records into one long logical record. You may also find yourself faced with fixed-width fields that contain delimited data.

This chapter shows you how to define fixed-width data, and it describes the tools SQL*Loader provides that allow you to deal with the issues listed here. You'll learn how to define nulls, deal with short records and whitespace, concatenate multiple records together, and pull apart delimited, fixed-width fields.

Common Datatypes Encountered

COBOL programs almost universally generate fixed-width data, and they may in fact represent the greatest source of such data. We have certainly written enough COBOL programs over the years that transfer data between systems using flat files. If you are loading data that comes from a COBOL source, you'll most likely be working with the following SQL*Loader datatypes:

CHAR
DATE
DECIMAL
ZONED

If you need a refresher on SQL*Loader datatypes, refer back to Chapter 3, *Fields and Datatypes*.

Of course, COBOL doesn't have a lock on fixed-width data. Binary files containing data in hardware-specific numeric formats represent another source of fixed-width data. Such files could be generated by a C program, and might include the following SQL*Loader datatypes:

INTEGER
SMALLINT
FLOAT
DOUBLE
BYTEINT

Character data can appear within a binary file, and in the case of C-style strings will be delimited by X'00' characters. This can lead to some interesting complications in terms of blending fixed-width and delimited data.

Specifying Field Positions

When dealing with columnar data, each field has a starting position, an ending position, and a length. As in Chapter 3, you can specify these values for each field, or you can specify some values and allow SQL*Loader to calculate others. For each field, you can choose to specify one of the following combinations of values:

- Starting and ending position
- Starting position and length
- Field type and length

Typically it's best to be consistent and use one approach for all fields. This is especially true when you are supplying the field type and length for each field. When you do that, you're using relative positioning—the beginning position of each field depends on the ending position of the previous field, and it rarely makes sense to mix relative positioning with absolute positioning.

We are going to show some examples of each method, but before we do that, let's look at some representative columnar data:

```
MI Tie Hill Lookout Tower                    tower     Alger
MI Slowfoot Lake                             lake      Alger
MI Stella, Lake                         790  lake      Alger
MI Dam Lake                                  lake      Alger
MI Camp K Lake                               lake      Alger
MI Tie Lake                             790  lake      Alger
MI Mathias Township Park                862  park      Alger
MI Trenary Cemetery                     878  cemetery  Alger
MI Temple Lake                               lake      Alger
MI Mantila Camp                         968  locale    Alger
MI Forest Lake Lookout Tower           1036  tower     Alger
...
```

This is a list of geographic feature names for Alger County, Michigan. The columns are as follows:

- State code

- Feature name

- Elevation above sea level

- Feature type

- County name

This is typical columnar data, and the next three sections will illustrate three different techniques for specifying the location of each column in the record. The destination table, used for all the examples in this chapter, is created as follows:

```
CREATE TABLE michigan_features (
    feature_name VARCHAR2(44),
    elevation NUMBER,
    feature_type VARCHAR2(10),
    county VARCHAR2(5),
    short_feature_name VARCHAR2(10),
    latitude VARCHAR2(15),
    longitude VARCHAR2(15)
);
```

The short feature name that you see in the table doesn't correspond directly to a field in the input record. It's not used for the first example, but later you'll see how it's derived from the potentially longer feature name field.

Starting and Ending Position

Probably the most obvious method of describing columnar data is to simply specify the starting and ending position of each field in the record. That's exactly what the following LOAD statement does:

```
LOAD DATA
    INFILE 'alger_county.dat'
    REPLACE INTO TABLE michigan_features
    (
    feature_name          POSITION(4:47)   CHAR,
    elevation             POSITION(49:52)  INTEGER EXTERNAL,
    feature_type          POSITION(54:62)  CHAR,
    county                POSITION(64:68)  CHAR
    )
```

Here you see the POSITION clause used to specify the exact starting and ending location for each field. We didn't want to load the state code field, so we simply didn't list it in our INTO TABLE clause. This is one advantage of dealing with columnar data—you can simply ignore fields that you don't want to load.

Starting Position and Length

Another approach to describing columnar data is to specify the starting position and length of each record. Specify the starting position in the POSITION clause, and the length along with the datatype. For example:

```
LOAD DATA
    INFILE 'alger_county.dat'
    REPLACE INTO TABLE michigan_features
    (
    feature_name          POSITION(4)   CHAR(44),
    elevation             POSITION(49)  INTEGER EXTERNAL(4),
    feature_type          POSITION(54)  CHAR(9),
    county                POSITION(64)  CHAR(5)
    )
```

Whether you use this method or the previous method should depend on the documentation and tools available to you. If you have an editor that makes it easy to determine starting and ending column positions for each field, you might choose to use that method. On the other hand, if your documentation specifies starting position and length, go with that. Use whichever method is most convenient.

Field Type and Length

The previous two methods specify the location of each field in absolute terms—the location of one field is never dependent on another. By specifying field type and length, on the other hand, you can describe columnar data in relative terms, with the starting position of each field depending on the ending position of the previous field. For example:

```
LOAD DATA
   INFILE 'alger_county.dat'
   REPLACE INTO TABLE michigan_features
   (
   state_code      FILLER CHAR(2),
   blank_space_1   FILLER CHAR(1),
   feature_name           CHAR(44),
   blank_space_2   FILLER CHAR(1),
   elevation              INTEGER EXTERNAL(4),
   blank_space_3   FILLER CHAR(1),
   feature_type           CHAR(9),
   blank_space_4   FILLER CHAR(1),
   county                 CHAR(5)
   )
```

Two things are worth noticing about this LOAD statement:

- The starting position is never specified for any field.

- There are four fields named *blank_space_1* through *blank_space_4*.

What's going on here? First off, because each field specification contains only a datatype and a length, you know that relative positioning is being used. SQL*Loader will start with the first byte in the record, and will expect to find a two-character *state_code* field. SQL*Loader then expects to find the second field immediately following the first, and so forth. This leads to the need for several FILLER fields.

The feature name data used for this chapter has one blank between each field in the record. That blank provides visual separation of the data, but is not part of any field, and is nothing that you want to load into your database. If you were writing a COBOL record description, you would use the special name of FILLER for those blank fields. For example:

```
01 FEATURE-NAME-REC.
   05 STATE-CODE      PIC X(2).
   05 FILLER          PIC X.
   05 FEATURE-NAME    PIC X(44).
   05 FILLER          PIC X.
   05 ELEVATION       PIC 9(4).
   05 FILLER          PIC X.
   05 FEATURE-TYPE    PIC X(9).
   05 FILLER          PIC X.
   05 COUNTY          PIC X(5).
```

As mentioned earlier, SQL*Loader borrows the keyword FILLER from COBOL, but rather than have you use it as a field name, it expects you to use it as a field quali-fier. SQL*Loader does not load FILLER fields into the database. The reason we needed to specify FILLER fields in this example was because we were describing the position of the data in relative terms; the position of each field is relative to the position of the preceding field. Thus, it's necessary to account for every byte in the record—even those that we don't want to load.

 The FILLER keyword was introduced in Oracle8*i*. You can't use it with prior releases of SQL*Loader.

Relative positioning is useful if you've been handed a data file along with a COBOL record format. You can easily use the COBOL PICTURE clauses as the basis for writing a SQL*Loader field list. Chapter 3 discusses this, and also discusses some of the advantages and disadvantages of relative positioning versus absolute positioning.

Handling Anomalous Data

When you're dealing with columnar data, there are some anomalies and ambiguous situations that you need to deal with. Take a close look at the following data:

```
MI Sitka Lake                   902 lake        Alger
MI Sevenmile Lake                   lake
MI Little Beaver Creek              stream      Alger
MI Traunik                      925 ppl
```

Now, given this data, ask yourself these questions:

- Should the missing elevation values be represented in the database as zeros or as nulls?

- What should be done with records, such as those missing the county name, that are too short?

- What should be done about trailing spaces in fields? Is it "Traunik" (with no trailing spaces) or "Traunik . . ." (with 37 trailing spaces to fill out the 44-character string)?

The answers to these questions are not always as obvious as you might think. While you almost certainly want a missing elevation to be represented as a null, what if you are dealing with a missing dollar amount? Should that become a null or a zero? Application considerations sometimes trump logic. Representing missing elevations as zero may not make intuitive sense, but you may be dealing with an application that requires missing numbers to be represented as zeros. With character fields, you have the issue of trailing spaces. You would almost certainly trim trailing spaces from feature names, but what about code fields? We've seen programs that expect alphanumeric fields such as the *feature_type* field to be constant-width, even if that means including trailing spaces.

Can Fields Overlap?

Is it possible to load the same data twice by specifying the same position for two different fields? The answer is yes. Two fields can overlap, although it won't be a very common occurrence. Here's an example of a LOAD statement that loads both a short and a long version of each feature name:

```
LOAD DATA
   INFILE 'alger_county.dat'
   REPLACE INTO TABLE michigan_features
   (
   feature_name            POSITION(4) CHAR(44),
   short_feature_name      POSITION(4) CHAR(10),
   elevation               POSITION(49)
                           INTEGER EXTERNAL(4),
   feature_type            POSITION(54) CHAR(9),
   county                  POSITION(64) CHAR(5)
   )
```

The short name in this case is simply a truncated version of the full name. Such a name may be useful for indexing, or for reports where you don't have space to show the full feature name.

In this case, the overlap was from the beginning of the feature name field. However, you also can overlap the beginning of one field with the end of the previous one. It's even possible to overlap fields when you are using relative positioning, but you must be extremely careful when doing so. Here's an example:

```
LOAD DATA
   INFILE 'alger_county.dat'
   REPLACE INTO TABLE michigan_features
   (
   state_code      FILLER CHAR(2),
   blank_space_1   FILLER CHAR(1),
   short_feature_name     CHAR(10),
   feature_name    POSITION(4) CHAR(44),
   blank_space_2   FILLER CHAR(1),
   elevation               INTEGER EXTERNAL(4),
   blank_space_3   FILLER CHAR(1),
   feature_type            CHAR(9),
   blank_space_4   FILLER CHAR(1),
   county                  CHAR(5)
   )
```

Here, the POSITION clause was used with the second feature name field in order to reset SQL*Loader's position in the record back to the fourth byte. The longer of the two fields was listed last in order to allow relative positioning to take over for subsequent fields. If *short_feature_name* came after *feature_ name* instead of before it, you would also need to use a POSITION clause in the field specification for *blank_space_2* in order to point SQL*Loader at the correct starting column for that field.

SQL*Loader has default behavior with respect to each one of these issues, and that default behavior is often reasonable and sufficient. However, SQL*Loader provides you with the flexibility to override the default behavior when necessary.

Trimming Whitespace

SQL*Loader's default behavior when you are loading fixed-width, columnar data is to trim trailing whitespace from each field in the input record. *Whitespace* in this context is defined as space and tab characters. This trimming of whitespace is actually one of the first things SQL*Loader does after reading each record of data, and it's consistent with how most people intuitively look at character strings when they are arranged in a column. SQL*Loader does, however, provide you with a way to preserve trailing whitespace in your fields if you need to do that.

The PRESERVE BLANKS clause

You can use the PRESERVE BLANKS clause in your control file to prevent SQL*Loader from trimming trailing whitespace from the fields that you are loading. The PRESERVE BLANKS clause immediately precedes your first INTO TABLE clause, and it applies to all fields that you are loading.

Here is some sample data where PRESERVE BLANKS can make a difference:

```
MI Chatham                          ppl      Alger
MI Shingleton              821 ppl           Alger
MI Rumely                          ppl       Alger
MI Sundell                 1049              Alger
```

The feature names here are the names of four towns. SQL*Loader's default behavior is to trim trailing whitespace. However, the following LOAD statement uses PRESERVE BLANKS to override that default behavior:

```
LOAD DATA
   INFILE 'alger_nulltest.dat'
   REPLACE PRESERVE BLANKS INTO TABLE michigan_features
   (
   feature_name          POSITION(4) CHAR(44),
   short_feature_name    POSITION(4) CHAR(10),
   elevation             POSITION(49) INTEGER EXTERNAL(4)
                         DEFAULTIF elevation = BLANKS,
   feature_type          POSITION(54) CHAR(9),
   county                POSITION(64) CHAR(5)
   )
```

The following example is taken from SQL*Plus, and shows the results of loading these feature names using the PRESERVE BLANKS clause:

```
SQL> SELECT feature_name,LENGTH(feature_name)
  2  FROM michigan_features
```

FEATURE_NAME	LENGTH(FEATURE_NAME)
Chatham	44
Shingleton	44
Rumely	44
Sundell	44

All the names are 44 bytes in length. Most of those bytes, of course, are the trailing spaces that weren't trimmed as a result of using PRESERVE BLANKS.

 When using PRESERVE BLANKS, you'll need to use DEFAULTIF or NULLIF with any INTEGER EXTERNAL, FLOAT EXTERNAL, DECIMAL EXTERNAL, and ZONED EXTERNAL FIELDS.

Use of PRESERVE BLANKS causes an unfortunate side effect if you are loading NUMERIC EXTERNAL fields. A string of blanks cannot be translated to a number. When SQL*Loader attempts to convert a NUMERIC EXTERNAL field consisting only of blanks to a numeric value, an error will occur, and SQL*Loader will write the record to the bad file. Blank trimming normally prevents this from being an issue, but when you disable blank trimming, you suddenly have this problem to worry about. One solution is to make use of the DEFAULTIF and NULLIF clauses described later in this chapter. DEFAULTIF was used in this example to drive the numeric elevation value to zero when that field contained all spaces.

Selective trimming of whitespace

It's unfortunate that Oracle doesn't provide any mechanism to preserve blanks on a field-by-field basis. It's all or nothing. If you are loading data where you need to preserve blanks for some fields and not for others, you may be able to use built-in SQL functions to achieve the desired results. The following example shows a LOAD statement that will preserve blanks only for the *feature_type* field:

```
LOAD DATA
   INFILE 'alger_nulltest.dat'
   REPLACE PRESERVE BLANKS INTO TABLE michigan_features
   (
   feature_name        POSITION(4) CHAR(44) "RTRIM(:feature_name)",
   short_feature_name  POSITION(4) CHAR(10) "RTRIM(:short_feature_name)",
   elevation           POSITION(49) INTEGER EXTERNAL(4)
                       DEFAULTIF elevation=BLANKS,
   feature_type        POSITION(54) CHAR(9),
   county              POSITION(64) CHAR(5) "RTRIM(:county)"
   )
```

With respect to whitespace, this LOAD statement works in a three-fold manner:

1. PRESERVE BLANKS is used to inhibit the trimming of whitespace by SQL*Loader itself.

2. Oracle's built-in SQL function RTRIM is selectively used only for those fields where trailing whitespace needs to be trimmed.

3. The DEFAULTIF clause is used to cause blank elevation values to be interpreted as zeros.

The double-quoted strings at the end of each field specification represent SQL expressions that are made part of the INSERT statement that SQL*Loader uses to insert the data into the database. You'll read more about this feature in Chapter 8, *Transforming Data During a Load*. Here, RTRIM has been applied to all the fields except two. The elevation field is numeric. Whitespace doesn't matter if the field actually contains some digits—the trailing spaces won't matter when the data is converted to a number, and the DEFAULTIF clause handles the case where the field consists entirely of blanks. The *feature_type* field is a character field. Because RTRIM has not been applied to *feature_type*, each occurrence of that field will be exactly nine bytes in length.

This use of RTRIM to selectively trim fields effectively pushes the work of trimming trailing spaces from SQL*Loader into the database. It has some other ramifications as well. RTRIM will only trim trailing space characters, while SQL*Loader trims both trailing space and trailing tab characters. That subtle difference may be important to you if your data contains tab characters. The use of SQL expressions also precludes your doing a direct path load. Direct path loads are often advantageous when loading large amounts of data, and are discussed in Chapter 10, *Direct Path Loads*.

Dealing with Nulls

In a database, a null represents data that is missing or nonexistent. In a columnar data file, however, you usually have *some* value for every column. You end up with an impedance mismatch wherein you either don't allow for null values at all, or you must designate a specific field value to represent a null. If you designate a specific field value to represent a null, what then do you do when you actually need to represent that particular value in the column?

Nulls are not fun, but SQL*Loader does provide some features to help you deal with them. These features include:

The NULLIF clause
> Allows you to specify one or more conditions under which a field should be interpreted as a null.

The DEFAULTIF clause
> Allows you to specify one or more conditions under which a field should take on either a null or a zero value depending on whether the field is a character field or a numeric field.

Delimited by Whitespace?

As we were researching this entire issue of how SQL*Loader handles whitespace, it occurred to us to try mixing the use of the PRESERVE BLANKS and TERMINATED BY WHITESPACE clauses. The TERMINATED BY WHITESPACE clause applies to delimited data, and is described in Chapter 5.

Is it possible, we wondered, to use TERMINATED BY WHITESPACE on a fixed-width field in order to effectively trim the whitespace from that field? To find out, we gave it a try using a LOAD statement such as the following:

```
LOAD DATA
    INFILE 'alger_nulltest.dat'
    REPLACE PRESERVE BLANKS
    INTO TABLE michigan_features
    (
    feature_name            POSITION(4) CHAR(44)
                            TERMINATED BY WHITESPACE,
    short_feature_name  POSITION(4) CHAR(10),
    elevation               POSITION(49)
                            INTEGER EXTERNAL(4)
                            DEFAULTIF elevation=BLANKS,
    feature_type            POSITION(54) CHAR(9)
                            TERMINATED BY WHITESPACE,
    county                  POSITION(64) CHAR(5)
    )
```

This actually did work after a fashion. Trailing spaces were preserved in the *county* and *short_feature_name* fields, and they were eliminated from the *feature_name* and *feature_type* fields. We did note one odd effect, though. Not only did TERMINATED BY WHITESPACE eliminate trailing spaces, but it eliminated *leading* spaces as well. We can't think of any rational justification for that behavior. If you can live with the fact that leading whitespace is also trimmed, this appears to be a useful technique for selectively trimming whitespace on a field-by-field basis.

The NULLIF and DEFAULTIF clauses sound simple and straightforward on the surface, but Oracle's implementation of these clauses is confusing and defies logic. Many a DBA, including ourselves, has ripped his hair out trying to make DEFAULTIF work, because it just doesn't work the way you would expect after reading the Oracle manuals. Before getting into all of this, though, it's important that you understand SQL*Loader's default behavior with respect to whitespace and null values.

*SQL*Loader's default behavior*

When you are loading columnar, character-based data, SQL*Loader's default behavior is to recognize whitespace as representing a null value. Take a look at the following two rows of data:

```
MI Shingleton                                    821 ppl        Alger
MI Shingleton                                                   Alger
```

The first row contains five values. In the second row, two of those values will be interpreted as null because two fields are filled entirely with whitespace. Here is the process SQL*Loader follows by default for character-based fields:

1. SQL*Loader extracts a field from the record.

2. Trailing spaces are trimmed from the field.

3. SQL*Loader checks to see if the resulting field length is zero.

If a character field consists entirely of spaces, then after those spaces have been trimmed off, the resulting field length will be zero. SQL*Loader interprets zero-length character fields as nulls.

 As far as SQL*Loader is concerned, NUMERIC EXTERNAL fields such as INTEGER EXTERNAL and DECIMAL EXTERNAL are simply another type of character field. Trailing whitespace is trimmed, and if the resulting field length is zero, the corresponding database column is set to null.

None of what we've said here applies when you are loading binary data, or when you are using nonportable datatypes. SQL*Loader only trims whitespace on character fields. Nonportable datatypes such as INTEGER or FLOAT represent binary data—whitespace won't be trimmed, and the length will never be zero. The only way to derive null values from such fields is to use the NULLIF and DEFAULTIF clauses.

The effect of PRESERVE BLANKS

The use of PRESERVE BLANKS has some interesting, and possibly confusing, ramifications with respect to fields that consist entirely of whitespace. When you use PRESERVE BLANKS, SQL*Loader doesn't trim trailing whitespace from fields. Because trailing whitespace is not trimmed, even a completely blank field will not have a length of zero. Consequently, blank fields will no longer be treated as nulls. Instead, all those blanks will be loaded into your database. That may or may not be the behavior you are after.

Another complication with the use of PRESERVE BLANKS is the manner in which NUMERIC EXTERNAL fields are converted to numeric values. Fields with digits, even when trailing spaces are present, will still convert properly to numbers. However, NUMERIC EXTERNAL fields that are completely blank will no longer convert to nulls—they will cause errors instead. SQL*Loader will attempt to convert a string of blanks to a number, that will result in an error, and the entire record will be written to the bad file.

When you use PRESERVE BLANKS, you can work around these complications using the NULLIF and DEFAULTIF clauses.

NULLIF

The NULLIF clause allows you to specify a condition under which a field should be interpreted as a null. NULLIF is part of the field specification clause. Consider the following data:

```
MI Chatham                                       0 ppl       Alger
MI Shingleton                                  821 ppl       Alger
MI Rumely                                        0 ppl       Alger
MI Sundell                                    1049           Alger
```

The third field, the elevation field, sometimes contains a zero. You can use the NULLIF clause, as shown in the following example, to translate zero elevation value to null:

```
LOAD DATA
    INFILE 'data04.dat'
    REPLACE INTO TABLE michigan_features
    (
    feature_name            POSITION(4) CHAR(44),
    short_feature_name      POSITION(4) CHAR(10),
    elevation               POSITION(49) INTEGER EXTERNAL(4)
                            NULLIF elevation = '   0',
    feature_type            POSITION(54) CHAR(9),
    county                  POSITION(64) CHAR(5)
    )
```

Notice the three leading spaces in the constant used in the NULLIF clause. Those are present because SQL*Loader considers an INTEGER EXTERNAL value to be a character datatype. In the data file, you have a four-character long field with three leading spaces followed by a zero. That character string is what the NULLIF clause works against.

NULLIF can also be helpful if you are using PRESERVE BLANKS and you have data such as the following:

```
MI Chatham                                         ppl       Alger
MI Shingleton                                  821 ppl       Alger
MI Rumely                                          ppl       Alger
MI Sundell                                    1049           Alger
```

The elevation values for Chatham and Rumely are blank. Normally, these blank spaces are trimmed, resulting in an empty string, further resulting in a null value being stored in the destination database column. However, when you use PRE-SERVE BLANKS, SQL*Loader feeds all the spaces from the blank elevation fields into the TO_NUMBER function, which returns an error, causing the record to be rejected and written to the bad file. You can work around this by using NULLIF to specify that blank field values should be interpreted as nulls. For example:

```
LOAD DATA
    INFILE 'data04.dat'
    REPLACE INTO TABLE michigan_features
    (
    feature_name          POSITION(4) CHAR(44),
    short_feature_name    POSITION(4) CHAR(10),
    elevation             POSITION(49) INTEGER EXTERNAL(4)
                          NULLIF elevation = '    ',
    feature_type          POSITION(54) CHAR(9),
    county                POSITION(64) CHAR(5)
    )
```

The field condition used with a NULLIF clause isn't limited to only looking at the one field in question. You may reference any other field defined in the field list, so the nullability of one field may be dependent on another. In the following example, NULLIF is used to set the elevation to null whenever the feature type is "falls":

```
...
elevation          POSITION(49) INTEGER EXTERNAL(4)
                   NULLIF feature_type='falls',
feature_type POSITION(54) CHAR(9),
...
```

Include trailing spaces in your constants if you are using the PRE-SERVE BLANKS clause. For example, when PRESERVE BLANKS is being used, you would use "falls   " (four trailing spaces) rather than "falls" (no trailing spaces).

This ability to reference other fields from a NULLIF condition gives you the ability to use indicator fields. Assuming that you are in control of the data file format, you can design it such that each field that you want to load has a corresponding indicator field to indicate nullness. This is especially helpful when loading binary data. It's also helpful when you load character-based data using PRESERVE BLANKS. The following example uses an indicator field to indicate when the FIPS state code value should be null:

```
...
gfn_fips_state_code              POSITION(151) INTEGER
                                 NULLIF gfn_fips_state_code_ind=0,
gfn_fips_state_code_ind FILLER POSITION(155) INTEGER,
...
```

Such a scheme frees you from having to designate a special value in the field you are loading to represent null. With respect to this example, any integer value may be loaded into the state code field. If a null is desired, you simply need to set the indicator to zero.

With respect to character data, SQL*Loader evaluates the NULLIF clause after trimming whitespace from the field, and just prior to checking the field's length. This has ramifications for how you refer to fields in your NULLIF conditions. Refer to a character field by name, and you get the trimmed value—unless you are also using PRESERVE BLANKS. Refer to a field by position, and you get the entire value, including any trailing spaces. Here are two examples that will function identically. Both assume that you are *not* using PRESERVE BLANKS:

```
...
elevation              POSITION(49) INTEGER EXTERNAL(4)
                       ' NULLIF feature_type='falls',
feature_type POSITION(54) CHAR(9),
...


...
elevation              POSITION(49) INTEGER EXTERNAL(4)
                       NULLIF (54:62)='falls     ',
feature_type POSITION(54) CHAR(9),
...
```

In the first case, the NULLIF clause refers to the *feature_type* field by name. The result is the trimmed value, so it is compared to "falls". In the second case, the NULLIF clause refers to the *feature_type* field by specifying its position within the record. The result is the untrimmed value, which includes trailing spaces, and which will be 9 bytes long. That value must be compared to a 9-byte string, which also must contain trailing spaces. Hence, "falls   " is used in the second case.

When PRESERVE BLANKS is used, trailing whitespace is not trimmed, and you consequently get the same result whether you refer to a field by name or by position.

DEFAULTIF

The DEFAULTIF clause is primarily for use with numeric fields, and it allows you to specify a condition under which SQL*Loader will set a numeric field's value to zero. DEFAULTIF can be used with nonportable numeric datatypes such as INTEGER and FLOAT. It can also be used with any of the NUMERIC EXTERNAL types, such as INTEGER EXTERNAL and ZONED EXTERNAL.

DEFAULTIF is one of the most frustrating and unintuitive SQL*Loader features that we've ever worked with. An obvious use for it, you would think, would be to have NUMERIC EXTERNAL fields set to zero when they are all blanks. Normally those fields are set to null when they are blank. Many people, in fact try to do that by writing a clause such as the following:

```
...
elevation              POSITION(49) INTEGER EXTERNAL(4)
                       DEFAULTIF elevation=blanks,
...
```

This certainly seems logical enough. If the *elevation* field is composed of blanks, then store a zero in the corresponding database column. The problem is that this completely logical and intuitive approach simply does not work. The reason it doesn't work is that SQL*Loader determines the nullity of the field before checking the DEFAULTIF condition, and only checks the DEFAULTIF condition if the field is not null. Here's the process SQL*Loader follows:

1. SQL*Loader extracts the field from the record.

2. SQL*Loader trims any trailing blanks (unless PRESERVE BLANKS was specified).

3. SQL*Loader checks the field length, and if it is zero, sets the field to null.

4. SQL*Loader checks the NULLIF clause, if one is present.

5. SQL*Loader checks the DEFAULTIF clause, if one is present.

The problem is that SQL*Loader may stop after step 3 or 4. If the field length is zero, SQL*Loader will set the field value to null and stop after step 3. If you specify a NULLIF condition, and if that condition evaluates to TRUE, SQL*Loader stops after step 4, also setting the field value to null. The DEFAULTIF condition is checked last, and only if the field contains a non-null value. So in the case where you are most likely to need its functionality, the DEFAULTIF clause is completely useless.

Like NULLIF, the DEFAULTIF condition can reference other fields in the record. If you're using indicator fields, you could use an indicator field to determine whether or not the field you were loading should be set to zero. For example:

```
...
gfn_fips_state_code         POSITION(151) INTEGER
                            DEFAULTIF gfn_fips_state_code_ind=0,
gfn_fips_state_code_ind FILLER POSITION(155) INTEGER,
...
```

This solution is viable if you have control over the program creating the data file that you are loading. You can modify the program to generate the needed indicator values. On the other hand, if you can modify the program, you can presumably just modify it to write out zeros when necessary, and you won't have to bother using indicators at all.

Interpreting Blanks as Zeros

Is there any way to use DEFAULTIF to make SQL*Loader treat blank numeric fields as if they were zeros? There is, but it's not a good solution. You can use PRESERVE BLANKS to preserve whitespace in all your fields. Whitespace won't be trimmed, and assuming you don't use a NULLIF clause, your DEFAULTIF clause will be evaluated. For example:

```
LOAD DATA
    INFILE 'alger_nulltest.dat'
    REPLACE PRESERVE BLANKS
    INTO TABLE michigan_features
    (
    feature_name        POSITION(4) CHAR(44),
    short_feature_name  POSITION(4) CHAR(10),
    elevation           POSITION(49)
                        INTEGER EXTERNAL(4)
                        DEFAULTIF elevation=BLANKS,
    feature_type        POSITION(54) CHAR(9),
    county              POSITION(64) CHAR(5)
    )
```

The problem is that while DEFAULTIF now works as most everyone expects, you have to deal with the ramifications of using PRESERVE BLANKS discussed earlier in this chapter. There's a better approach to this problem that works as long as you are not doing a direct path load: use Oracle's built-in NVL function in an expression for the numeric field that you are loading. The following LOAD statement, for example, will translate blank elevations into zeros:

```
LOAD DATA
    INFILE 'alger_nulltest.dat'
    REPLACE INTO TABLE michigan_features
    (
    feature_name        POSITION(4) CHAR(44),
    short_feature_name  POSITION(4) CHAR(10),
    elevation           POSITION(49)
                        INTEGER EXTERNAL(4)
                        "NVL(:elevation,0)",
    feature_type        POSITION(54) CHAR (9),
    county              POSITION(64) CHAR(5)
    )
```

We personally like this method, because the NVL expression only affects the one field. The PRESERVE BLANKS solution generates side effects that change the way SQL*Loader looks at the rest of your data.

If you are doing a direct path load using a release prior to Oracle9*i*, SQL*Loader won't be able to execute SQL functions for you. In that case, you will need to use PRESERVE BLANKS and deal with the side effects, change the way your data file is generated, or load the data into a work table where you can fix up any anomalies before moving the data to its final destination.

Dealing with "Short" Records

Short records are those that contain fewer bytes than you would expect from looking at a LOAD statement. The records used for examples in this chapter have all been 68 bytes long. You can derive that value by looking at the LOAD statements and working out the math on field positions and lengths. A short record, then, with respect to this chapter, is any record containing fewer than 68 bytes.

When you are loading columnar data, there are two cases you need to be aware of with respect to short records:

* The record may end in the middle of a field.

* One or more fields may have starting positions beyond the end of the record.

If the record ends in the middle of a field, that field's value is based on whatever characters are present in the record for that field. The field's length also corresponds to whatever characters are present. This has an interesting implication when you are loading character fields and using the PRESERVE BLANKS clause. When you use PRESERVE BLANKS, trailing blanks are normally preserved, and the length of the values loaded into the database is equal to the maximum field size. Load a CHAR(5) field using PRESERVE BLANKS, and every row loaded into your database will have a 5-byte long value. The one exception is—you guessed it—when the record is truncated in the midst of such a field. SQL*Loader won't add the necessary spaces to bring the field length up to the maximum size.

The ramifications of the second case are a bit easier to describe than those of the first. If a field has a defined position and size (columnar data), and its starting position is beyond the end of the record, then SQL*Loader will set the field's value to null.

Database Column Defaults

When you create database tables, you can define default values for any or all of the columns. For example, the following CREATE TABLE statement defines a default value for the *elevation* column:

```
CREATE TABLE michigan_features (
    feature_name VARCHAR2(44),
    elevation NUMBER DEFAULT 0,
    feature_type VARCHAR2(10),
    county VARCHAR2(5),
    short_feature_name VARCHAR2(10),
    latitude VARCHAR2(15),
    longitude VARCHAR2(15)
);
```

You might think that you could take advantage of such column defaults, especially when it comes to loading empty NUMERIC EXTERNAL columns. Simply allow SQL*Loader to evaluate them as nulls, and the database default value will be used, right? Unfortunately, you can't do that. SQL*Loader always explicitly sets a value for each field that it loads, even if that value is null. In other words, SQL*Loader will do the equivalent of:

```
INSERT INTO michigan_features
    (feature_name, elevation, feature_type, county)
    VALUES ('Harbor of Refuge',NULL,'bay','Alger');
```

Because NULL is explicitly specified, in this case for the elevation, it will override any default. In short, SQL*Loader always overrides database default values for columns that you are loading. In addition, SQL*Loader's DEFAULTIF clause has nothing whatsoever to do with default values you specify at the table level.

Concatenating Records

SQL*Loader has the capability to read multiple records from a data file and concatenate those records into one longer record. When you do this, the distinction between physical and logical records becomes important. The term *physical record* is always used to refer to the records read from the input data file. The term *logical record* refers to a record that SQL*Loader loads into the database. Usually, there's a one-to-one correspondence between physical and logical records. When you concatenate records together, you are combining two or more physical records into one logical record. SQL*Loader supports two main ways of doing this:

- You can specify a fixed number of physical records to concatenate into one logical record.

- You can specify a continuation flag in the physical record that indicates whether or not a given physical record should be concatenated to another.

The distinction between physical and logical records is important when it comes to specifying the positions of fields (using the POSITION clause) in the input record. The POSITION clause always refers to byte positions in the logical record. In general, SQL*Loader always deals with the logical record. The *only* time you specify positions with respect to the physical record is when you are defining continuation fields.

CONCATENATE

Use the CONCATENATE clause if you always want to concatenate a specific number of physical records into one logical record. Consider the following data, which splits the information for each geographical feature across two physical records:

```
MI Halfmoon Lake                         798
lake      Alger
MI Cleveland Cliffs Basin                779
reservoir Alger
MI Doe Lake                              798
lake      Alger
MI Limestone                             912
ppl       Alger
MI Traunik                               925
ppl       Alger
```

In this case, you always want SQL*Loader to read two physical records, combine them into one logical record, and then load the data from that logical record. This is a job for CONCATENATE.

CONCATENATE syntax

The CONCATENATE clause immediately precedes the PRESERVE BLANKS clause. If you are not using PRESERVE BLANKS, then CONCATENATE precedes your INTO TABLE clause. The syntax is as follows:

```
CONCATENATE [(]record_count[)]
```

Replace *record_count* in the syntax with an integer indicating the number of records that you want to concatenate together. The use of parentheses is optional.

CONCATENATE example

The following LOAD statement can be used to concatenate and load the data shown earlier. Each group of two physical records will be combined into one logical record. Notice that the field positions are with respect to the logical record that results after the concatenation takes place. Also notice that this example assumes that there are no trailing spaces at the end of the first record—the *feature_type* field immediately follows the elevation:

```
LOAD DATA
   INFILE 'alger_concatenate.dat'
   REPLACE CONCATENATE 2
   INTO TABLE michigan_features
   (
   feature_name        POSITION(4:47) CHAR,
   elevation           POSITION(49:52) INTEGER EXTERNAL,
   feature_type        POSITION(53:61) CHAR,
   county              POSITION(63:67) CHAR
   )
```

CONCATENATE works well if you always have a fixed number of records to combine together. If the number of records to concatenate is variable, you should use CONTINUEIF instead.

When concatenating character data such as shown in this chapter, watch out for the issue of trailing spaces. Many text editors trim these automatically when a file is saved. If you edit your data file with a text editor, this trimming could result in non-uniform physical record lengths. That will throw off the field positions when the records are concatenated together.

CONTINUEIF

The CONTINUEIF clause allows you to specify a field in the input record to serve as an indicator when two or more physical records should be concatenated together. You specify the indicator by its position in the physical record. It can be one byte in length, or it can be multiple bytes. The indicator may be one of these two types:

Before-the-fact
   A before-the-fact indicator (our term, not Oracle's) is one that tells SQL*Loader to concatenate the next physical record to the current physical record.

After-the-fact
   An after-the-fact indicator is one that tells SQL*Loader to concatenate the current physical record with the previous one.

There's actually a third possibility—a variation on before-the-fact—that allows you to specify a continuation indicator that always occurs at the end of each physical record. This is more useful when loading variable-length and delimited data, and we discuss it in Chapter 5.

CONTINUEIF syntax

The CONTINUEIF clause appears in the same location as CONCATENATE. The syntax is as follows:

```
CONTINUEIF {THIS | NEXT} [PRESERVE] [(|start[{: | -}end][)] {= | <>}
                         {'string' | X'hex_digits'}
```

The elements in the syntax are as follows:

THIS
   Specifies that the continuation indicator is before-the-fact. Each physical record contains a flag indicating whether or not the next physical record should be concatenated to it.

NEXT

> Specifies that the continuation indicator is after-the-fact. Each physical record contains a flag indicating whether or not it should be concatenated to the previous physical record.

PRESERVE

> Causes SQL*Loader to preserve the continuation string as part of the record. This is only available in Oracle release 8.1.7 and higher.

start

> Specifies the starting byte position of the continuation indicator in the physical record.

end

> Specifies the ending byte position of the continuation indicator in the physical record.

: | -

> Separates the start value from the end value. You can use either a colon (:) or a hyphen (-).

= | <>

> The equal and not-equal operators. These are your two choices. When the condition you specify is true, concatenation occurs. When the condition is false, SQL*Loader stops concatenating physical records, and processes the logical record that it has.

string

> The text string that you want SQL*Loader to look for in the indicator field. You may enclose this value in either single or double quotes.

hex_digits

> A string of hexadecimal digits representing the value that you want SQL*Loader to look for in the indicator field.

One issue to be aware of is the manner in which SQL*Loader computes the length of the indicator field. If you specify both a starting and ending position, the length is determined from that. If you specify only a starting position, the indicator field length is based on the length of the value (*string* or *hex_digits*) that you ask SQL*Loader to look for. In either case, if the length of the indicator field does not match the length of the value that you specify, SQL*Loader pads the shorter of the two values in the following manner:

- If you specify a text string, SQL*Loader pads the shorter of the two values with spaces.

- If you specify a string of hexadecimal digits, SQL*Loader pads the shorter of the two values with X'00' characters.

Another, *very important* thing to be aware of, is that SQL*Loader removes continuation characters from each physical record that it reads. This has implications for how you specify field positions in the logical record, and it also means that you can't load the continuation data into your destination database tables. The examples in the following few sections illustrate the continuation strings being removed.

Beginning with Oracle release 8.1.7, you can use the PRESERVE keyword to retain the continuation field in the record. For example, use CONTINUEIF THIS PRESERVE or CONTINUEIF NEXT PRESERVE.

CONTINUEIF THIS

Use CONTINUEIF THIS if the continuation indicator in one physical record indicates whether the logical record continues on to the next physical record or ends at the current record. The data in the following example has the indicator in the first byte of the record. A value of "1" indicates that the record is continued. A value of "0" marks the final physical record making up a logical record:

```
1MI Halfmoon
0 Lake                          798 lake       Alger
1MI Cleveland
1 Cliffs Basin                  779
0 reservoir Alger
0MI Doe Lake                                   798 lake      Alger
1MI Limeston
0e                              912 ppl        Alger
0MI Traunik                                    925 ppl       Alger
```

You can see in this example that some logical records span multiple physical records, while others don't. The logical record for Cleveland Cliffs Basin spans three physical records. The logical records for Doe Lake and Traunik each consist of just one physical record. The remaining logical records each consist of two physical records. To load this data, you could use the following control file:

```
LOAD DATA
   INFILE 'alger_this.dat'
   REPLACE CONTINUEIF THIS (1) = '1'
   INTO TABLE michigan_features
   (
   feature_name         POSITION(4:47) CHAR,
   elevation            POSITION(49:52) INTEGER EXTERNAL,
   feature_type         POSITION(54:62) CHAR,
   county               POSITION(64:68) CHAR
   )
```

The CONTINUEIF clause in this case specifies that physical records should be concatenated together as long as the first byte contains a "1". Concatenation stops when that's no longer the case, so the "0" records in this example end up marking the end of each logical record.

SQL*Loader only looks specifically for the value that you specify. In this example, SQL*Loader looks for a "1". Any other value indicates the final record. We used a "0" uniformly for that purpose, but any value other than a "1" would serve equally well to terminate the logical record.

Remember that SQL*Loader removes the continuation characters from each physical record when assembling the logical record. Thus, the logical record for Cleveland Cliffs Basin would be assembled to appear as follows:

```
MI Cleveland Cliffs Basin                   779 reservoir Alger
```

Notice that all the "1"s and "0"s used for continuation are gone. Be sure to take this into account when computing field positions for the fields that you are loading.

CONTINUEIF NEXT

Use CONTINUEIF NEXT if your continuation indicator is in the second and subsequent records. In the following example, the first physical record for each logical record begins with four spaces. Continuation records are flagged with the text CONT:

```
        MI Halfmoon
CONT Lake                       798 lake      Alger
        MI Cleveland
CONT Cliffs Basin               779
CONT reservoir Alger
        MI Doe Lake                           798 lake      Alger
        MI Limeston
CONTe                           912 ppl       Alger
        MI Traunik                            925 ppl       Alger
```

The following control file could be used to load this data:

```
LOAD DATA
    INFILE 'alger_next.dat'
    REPLACE CONTINUEIF NEXT (1:4) = 'CONT'
    INTO TABLE michigan_features
    (
    feature_name          POSITION(4:47) CHAR,
    elevation             POSITION(49:52) INTEGER EXTERNAL,
    feature_type          POSITION(54:62) CHAR,
    county                POSITION(64:68) CHAR
    )
```

Because CONTINUEIF NEXT is used, each time SQL*Loader reads a physical record beginning with CONT, it concatenates that record to the current logical record. A physical record beginning with anything other than CONT (spaces in this example) marks the beginning of a new logical record.

The continuation indicator in this example is a string of four characters, and those are still removed when SQL*Loader builds the logical record. The logical record for Cleveland Cliffs Basin still appears as follows:

```
MI Cleveland Cliffs Basin                        779 reservoir Alger
```

Using not-equals

The use of not-equals (<>) in a CONTINUEIF expression can be somewhat confusing and unintuitive. We always need to think things through two or three times whenever we use it. Here's an example of some data where the use of not-equals is indicated:

```
aMI Halfmoon
0 Lake                           798 lake        Alger
bMI Cleveland
c Cliffs Basin                   779
0 reservoir Alger
0MI Doe Lake                                     798 lake        Alger
fMI Limeston
0e                               912 ppl         Alger
0MI Traunik                                      925 ppl         Alger
```

You'll notice here that a "0" in the first position marks the *last* physical record for each logical record, but that the first character otherwise takes on a number of different values. What you want to do here is to concatenate records so long as the indicator value is not "0". The CONTINUEIF clause in the following LOAD statement does this:

```
LOAD DATA
    INFILE 'alger_not_equal.dat'
    REPLACE CONTINUEIF THIS (1) <> '0'
    INTO TABLE michigan_features
    (
    feature_name        POSITION(4:47) CHAR,
    elevation           POSITION(49:52) INTEGER EXTERNAL,
    feature_type        POSITION(54:62) CHAR,
    county              POSITION(64:68) CHAR
    )
```

In actual practice, it's almost always possible to use the equality operator with CONTINUEIF. Only one or two times in our careers have we ever been handed data that forced us to use not-equals.

Nesting Delimited Fields

With columnar data, it's possible to take an individual field and treat it as if it were a series of delimited fields. In essence, depending on the representation used, you may be able to extract subfields. There are also some ways to deal with records that begin with fixed-width columns only to have a variable-length column thrown into the middle.

Extracting Subfields

If you've ever worked on a MUMPS system,* you are familiar with the concept of nested delimiters, and of using the $PIECE function to extract specific pieces of information from a delimited string. The following columnar data is a doctored version of the feature name data that you've seen so far in this chapter. It's not from a MUMPS system, but the records do contain one column with nested, delimited data:

```
MI Werners Creek          "46° 11' 07'' N,86° 58' 48'' W " stream Alger
MI Chapel Falls           "46° 14' 44'' N,86° 26' 40'' W " falls  Alger
MI Chapel Lake            "46° 32' N,86° 26' 40'' W      " lake   Alger
MI Birch Lakes            "46° 33' 13'' N,86° 9' 26'' W  " lake   Alger
MI Chapel Beach Campground "46° 32' 51'' N,86° 26' 29'' W " locale Alger
MI Legion Lake            "46° 31' 41'' N,186° 21' 47'' W" lake   Alger
MI Chapel Creek           "46° 32' 54'' N,86° 26' 21'' W " stream Alger
MI Nita, Lake             "46° 33' N,86° 3' 53'' W       " lake   Alger
MI West Branch Lakes      "46° 30' 47'' N,86° 6' 04'' W  " lake   Alger
MI Centerline Lake        "46° 30' 23'' N,86° 3' 50'' W  " lake   Alger
```

In this example, the latitude and longitude values for each feature are enclosed in a 30-character wide quoted string. A comma (,) serves to separate the two values, and the conventional degree, minute, and second notation is used. For example:

```
degree° minute' second''
```

The next two examples show you how to do two things. First, you'll see how to store the latitude and longitude into separate database columns. Then you'll see how to extract each degree, minute, and second value individually.

Separating the latitude and longitude

The key to separating the latitude and longitude in the data shown earlier is the comma used to delimit the two values. You can recognize the end of the latitude value by the comma. You can't, however, recognize the end of the longitude value

---

* MUMPS is a programming language sometimes used in medical and banking systems. In MUMPS, all data is character data, and fields in a record are separated by delimiters.

in the same way—there's no second comma. Instead, you can take advantage of the trailing double quote. Use the following LOAD statement:

```
LOAD DATA
   INFILE 'alger_nested.dat'
   REPLACE INTO TABLE michigan_features
   (
   feature_name   POSITION(4:26) CHAR,
   latitude       POSITION(29) CHAR TERMINATED BY ',',
   longitude      CHAR TERMINATED BY '"' "RTRIM(:longitude)",
   feature_type   POSITION(61:66) CHAR,
   county         POSITION(68:72) CHAR
   )
```

Here are some points you should note about this LOAD statement:

- The *latitude* field always begins at byte 29, but the end of the field is determined by the location of the comma.

- No POSITION clause is used for the *longitude* field, so it will begin immediately after the comma that marks the end of the previous field.

- The *longitude* field is terminated by a double quote, which leaves open the possibility that it may contain trailing spaces. Oracle's built-in RTRIM function is used to remove those.

If you're not familiar with the DELIMITED BY clause, read Chapter 5. The use of built-in functions such as RTRIM is discussed in Chapter 8.

Separating the individual latitude and longitude components

The previous example demonstrated one way to separate the latitude and longitude values into two separate, character-based database columns. Consider, for a moment, the problem of loading that same data into the following table:

```
CREATE TABLE michigan_features (
   feature_name VARCHAR2(44),
   elevation NUMBER,
   feature_type VARCHAR2(10),
   county VARCHAR2(5),
   short_feature_name VARCHAR2(10),
   lat_degrees NUMBER,
   lat_minutes NUMBER,
   lat_seconds NUMBER,
   lat_direction CHAR,
   lon_degrees NUMBER,
   lon_minutes NUMBER,
   lon_seconds NUMBER,
   lon_direction CHAR
);
```

This table requires that each individual latitude and longitude component be split out into a separate column. You can actually do this with SQL*Loader by creatively making use of the degree, minute, and second symbols as delimiters. The following, much more complex LOAD statement extracts the individual degree, minute, second, and direction components into the separate database columns:

```
LOAD DATA
   INFILE 'alger_nested.dat'
   REPLACE INTO TABLE michigan_features
   (
   feature_name  POSITION(4:26) CHAR,
   lat_degrees   POSITION(29) INTEGER EXTERNAL TERMINATED BY '°',
   lat_minutes   INTEGER EXTERNAL TERMINATED BY "'",
   lat_seconds   INTEGER EXTERNAL TERMINATED BY "''",
   blank_space_1 FILLER CHAR(1),
   lat_direction CHAR(1) TERMINATED BY ',',
   lon_degrees   INTEGER EXTERNAL TERMINATED BY '°',
   lon_minutes   INTEGER EXTERNAL TERMINATED BY "'",
   lon_seconds   INTEGER EXTERNAL TERMINATED BY "''",
   blank_space_2 FILLER CHAR(1),
   lon_direction CHAR(1),
   feature_type  POSITION(61:66) CHAR,
   county        POSITION(68:72) CHAR
   )
```

In this example the degree, minute, and second values are treated as INTEGER EXTERNAL. You would want to do that if your destination database columns for these values were numeric. Here are some other things you should note about this solution:

- POSITION(29) is used to position SQL*Loader to the *lat_degrees* field. From that point forward, SQL*Loader progresses from one delimiter to the next.

- The numeric degree, minute, and second values are delimited by the degree symbol (°), the minute symbol (′), and the second symbol (″) respectively. Since the minute and second symbols are composed of one and two apostrophes, respectively, they are enclosed within double quotes.

- The *blank_space_1* and blank_*space_2* fields are single character filler fields that absorb the space between the value for seconds and the letter indicating the compass direction.

- The *lat_direction* field is terminated by a comma (,), which causes SQL*Loader to look past the comma for the start of the next field.

- The *lon_direction* field is simply CHAR(1), with no terminating character. That's sufficient to pick up the one letter.

- The POSITION clause is used to specify the start location for the *feature_type* field that follows all the delimited latitude and longitude data.

The manner in which we've handled the two direction fields deserves some more explanation. Instead of preceding each by a "blank space" column, we could have written:

```
lat_direction CHAR(2) TERMINATED BY ',' "LTRIM(:lat_direction)",
...
lon_direction CHAR(2) "LTRIM(:lon_direction)",
```

In this way, Oracle's built-in LTRIM function would have eliminated the leading space character. The disadvantage of using LTRIM is that using any SQL function precludes you from doing a direct path load (except in Oracle9*i*). In many situations, but not all, direct path loads confer significant performance advantages.

Variable-Length Records

SQL*Loader can even deal with records that begin with fixed-width data in a columnar format, but that later include one or more variable-length fields. The following LOAD statement defines the *feature_name* field as a C-style string terminated by an X'00' character:

```
LOAD DATA
   INFILE 'alger.dat'
   REPLACE INTO TABLE michigan_features
   (
   elevation           POSITION(4) INTEGER EXTERNAL(4),
   feature_name        POSITION(8) CHAR(44) TERMINATED BY X'00',
   feature_type        CHAR(9),
   county              CHAR(5)
   )
```

The starting positions of the first two columns are fixed, so the POSITION clause is used for each. The feature name, however, is terminated by an X'00' character, and may or may not be a full 44 characters in length. Because of that, the definitions for the fields that follow all omit the POSITION clause. SQL*Loader will look for them immediately following the X'00' character used to terminate the feature name, and thus their positions will tend to change with each record that SQL*Loader processes. In this example, only the *feature_name* field is variable-length. The *feature_type* and *county* fields are still fixed in size. All the fields can be variable-length delimited fields, and the next chapter shows you how to deal with those.

5

Loading Delimited Data

Delimited data is the second of the two major classifications of data that you can load using SQL*Loader. Delimited data is usually textual in nature. Fields are separated by strings of characters referred to as delimiters. Issues you'll encounter when loading delimited data include the following:

- Some fields, notably text fields, may be enclosed by characters such as quotation marks.

- Fields may contain leading and/or trailing spaces that need to be trimmed away.

- Records may not have all the fields that the LOAD statement calls for.

This chapter shows you how to use SQL*Loader's support for delimited data. You'll learn how to define delimiters and enclosing characters, and also to deal with nested occurrences of both delimited and fixed-width fields.

Common Datatypes Encountered

Delimited data is almost always textual. Thus, the SQL*Loader datatypes that you'll most commonly use are the external types:

```
CHAR
DATE
DECIMAL EXTERNAL
ZONED
ZONED EXTERNAL
INTEGER EXTERNAL
FLOAT EXTERNAL
```

Example Data

The example data used in this chapter will be a delimited version of the same geographic feature name data that you saw in Chapter 4, *Loading from Fixed-Width Files*. The exact data format will vary with the particular aspect of SQL*Loader under discussion at any given time.

The destination table used for all examples can be created using the following statement:

```
CREATE TABLE michigan_features (
    feature_name VARCHAR2(44),
    elevation NUMBER,
    population NUMBER,
    feature_type VARCHAR2(10),
    county VARCHAR2(15),
    short_feature_name VARCHAR2(10),
    latitude VARCHAR2(15),
    longitude VARCHAR2(15),
    update_time DATE
);
```

This is very similar to what you saw in the previous chapter. The only differences are that we've added an update timestamp and a column to record the population.

Using Delimiters to Identify Fields

A *delimiter* is a character, or string of characters, used to separate two fields. One of the most common delimiters is the comma. Spreadsheet programs such as Microsoft Excel commonly generate comma-delimited files. The following is an example of comma-delimited data:

```
MI,Alger School,school,Kent,425517N,0853840W
MI,Alger Swamp,swamp,Ogemaw,442306N,0840345W
MI,Algoma Cemetery,cemetery,Kent,430923N,0853731W
MI,Algoma Church,church,Kent,430920N,0853732W
```

One issue that you run into with comma-delimited data is the occasional need to represent the delimiter character in one of the values. This is rarely an issue with numeric fields, but is almost always an issue with text fields. Look at the following example:

```
MI,Algoma, Township of,civil,Kent,430942N,0853635W
```

This line contains seven fields delimited by commas, but it was really intended to contain only six. The geographic feature name in this case is "Algoma, Township of", and the comma in the name makes that one field appear as if it were two.

There are two ways of dealing with a problem like this, at least as far as SQL*Loader is concerned:

- Use a delimiter character that never appears as part of a value.

- Enclose all string values within quotes.

Choosing a different delimiter is a simple solution. If you know that your field values might contain commas, but are certain they will never contain vertical bars (|), you might represent your data as follows:

```
MI|Algoma, Township of|civil|Kent|430942N|0853635W
```

We don't particularly like this solution, because it's too easy to get in trouble down the road. Sure, you don't use vertical bars today, but can you guarantee that you will never use one? If your input programs allow users to enter a vertical bar, you can almost count on it happening some day.

A more robust approach is to enclose each field within quotation marks. For example:

```
"MI","Algoma, Township of","civil","Kent","430942N","0853635W"
```

Comma-delimited data enclosed within quotation marks is commonly referred to as *comma-separated values* (CSV) data. Many programs, including spreadsheets such as Microsoft Excel, support the transfer of data via CSV files. The commas are only recognized as delimiters when they occur outside the quoted strings.

 When creating a CSV file, Microsoft Excel will only enclose fields within quotes when necessary. If a particular value does not include a comma or a quote, then it will not be enclosed within quotes.

The quotation mark is the enclosing character used for CSV files, but SQL*Loader allows you to define any character as an enclosing character. You can even define a string of characters to use in enclosing a field.

Specifying Termination Characters

You specify termination characters in the SQL*Loader control file using the TERMINATED BY clause. You can do it on a field-by-field basis, or you can specify one termination character for all fields. When you specify termination characters on a field-specific basis, you write the TERMINATED BY clause as part of each field description. To use one termination character for all fields, you write the TERMINATED BY clause as part of your INTO TABLE clause, but prior to your field list.

Enclosure Characters in a Value

Enclosing a field within quotes solves the problem of using delimiter characters as part of a field value, but what if you want to use a quotation mark within such a field? Aren't you right back to the same dilemma you faced when your values included commas? In a sense, you are, but fortunately there is a solution. Consider the following hypothetical geographic feature name:

```
Algoma, "Township" of
```

Since the value contains quotes, how do you enclose it within quotes? The answer is to double-up on the quotes when they appear inside a string. For example:

```
"MI","Algoma, ""Township"" of",...
```

Each occurrence of two quotes in succession is treated as one quote to be included in the field value. This is the type of data Microsoft Excel and most other desktop programs will generate if you save columns containing quote characters in a CSV file.

Syntax for TERMINATED BY

The following is a simplified syntax for the TERMINATED BY clause:

```
TERMINATED BY {WHITESPACE | X'hex_digits' | 'string'}
```

The elements in the syntax are as follows:

WHITESPACE

Any whitespace character, or string of whitespace characters, will end the field. Both space characters and tab characters count as whitespace. This is a good option to use if you have a varying number of spaces or tabs between fields. However, be sure that you either enclose your data, or that your data does not include space or tab characters.

hex_digits

Allows you to specify a termination character using hexadecimal digits. Each two hexadecimal digits represents one byte. On an ASCII system, specifying X'2C' is the same as specifying a comma (,). Use hex digits when you are dealing with binary data, or when your delimiters aren't printable characters. C strings, for example, are terminated by X'00' characters.

string

A single character, or string of characters, that marks the end of the field.

You can optionally specify enclosing characters as part of the TERMINATED BY clause. The section "Specifying Enclosing Characters," later in this chapter, shows how. In addition, if you are loading large object (LOB) columns, you can specify EOF as the field termination. The EOF option is only valid for LOBs, and is discussed in Chapter 11, *Loading Large Objects.*

Example: Field-specific delimiters

This example demonstrates how to load simple, comma-delimited data. The data to be loaded looks like this:

```
Anna River,stream,Alger,462440N,0863825W,630,08-Dec-2000 10:58 AM
Keweenaw Point,cape,Keweenaw,472406N,0874242W,610,08-Dec-2000 10:59 AM
```

The following control file can be used to load this data. It specifies the comma as the field terminator for all fields in the record:

```
LOAD DATA
    INFILE 'data01.dat'
    REPLACE INTO TABLE michigan_features
    (
    feature_name CHAR TERMINATED BY ',',
    feature_type CHAR TERMINATED BY ',',
    county CHAR TERMINATED BY ',',
    latitude CHAR TERMINATED BY ',',
    longitude CHAR TERMINATED BY ',',
    elevation INTEGER EXTERNAL TERMINATED BY ',',
    update_time DATE "DD-MON-YYYY HH:MI AM"
    )
```

No TERMINATED BY clause was used for the final field, the *update_time* field. There's no comma following *update_time*, because there's no subsequent field from which to separate it. SQL*Loader will recognize the end of the record as the end of that field. You could, however, still specify the comma as the termination character:

```
...
update_time DATE "DD-MON-YYYY HH:MI AM" TERMINATED BY ','
...
```

This won't cause a problem, even though there's really no comma following the timestamp. SQL*Loader will still end the field when it hits the end of the record.

Example: One delimiter for all fields

If your input file uses the same delimiter for all fields, you can save yourself some typing by placing the TERMINATED BY clause just before the field list. For example, the following LOAD statement will load the same comma-delimited data shown in the previous example:

```
LOAD DATA
    INFILE 'data01.dat'
    REPLACE INTO TABLE michigan_features
```

```
FIELDS TERMINATED BY ','
(
feature_name CHAR,
feature_type CHAR,
county CHAR,
latitude CHAR,
longitude CHAR,
elevation INTEGER EXTERNAL,
update_time DATE "DD-MON-YYYY HH:MI AM"
)
```

Note the FIELDS keyword that precedes the TERMINATED BY clause. That needs to be there when you specify the termination character globally, for all fields.

You can actually mix the two methods. You can specify one delimiter globally, and then override it for specific fields. Consider the following data:

```
Anna River,stream,Alger,462440N|0863825W,630,08-Dec-2000 10:58 AM
Keweenaw Point,cape,Keweenaw,472406N|0874242W,610,08-Dec-2000 10:59 AM
```

Here all the fields are delimited by commas (,), except for the latitude and longitude fields. Between latitude and longitude, you see a vertical bar (|). The following LOAD statement will load this data:

```
LOAD DATA
    INFILE 'data02.dat'
    REPLACE INTO TABLE michigan_features
    FIELDS TERMINATED BY ','
    (
feature_name CHAR,
feature_type CHAR,
county CHAR,
latitude CHAR TERMINATED BY '|',
longitude CHAR,
elevation INTEGER EXTERNAL,
update_time DATE "DD-MON-YYYY HH:MI AM"
    )
```

Notice here that TERMINATED BY ',' has been specified in front of the field list. That terminator applies to all fields but latitude. The TERMINATED BY '|' clause for the latitude field overrides the global setting for that one field.

Example: Multi-character delimiters

Previous examples have all illustrated single-character delimiters, but SQL*Loader also allows you to specify delimiters of any arbitrary length. The following data uses two characters—a double asterisk (**)—between each field:

```
Anna River**stream**Alger**462440N**0863825W**630**12/8/2000 10:58 AM
Keweenaw Point**cape**Keweenaw**472406N**0874242W**610**12/8/2000 10:59 AM
```

The fact that the delimiter is two characters does not present a problem for SQL*Loader. You could use the following LOAD statement to load this data:

```
LOAD DATA
   INFILE 'data03.dat'
   REPLACE INTO TABLE michigan_features
   FIELDS TERMINATED BY '**'
   (
   feature_name CHAR,
   feature_type CHAR,
   county CHAR,
   latitude CHAR,
   longitude CHAR,
   elevation INTEGER EXTERNAL,
   update_time DATE "MM/DD/YYYY HH:MI AM"
   )
```

The FIELDS TERMINATED BY '**' clause in this LOAD statement specifies the field delimiter as a double asterisk.

While SQL*Loader does support multiple-character termination strings, you'll get your best performance using a single-character terminator.

Specifying Enclosing Characters

As we mentioned earlier, there's always a risk that text fields might contain the very character that you are using as a delimiter. Consequently, such fields are often enclosed within quotation marks. SQL*Loader allows you to specify any character as the enclosing character for a field. To do this, you use the ENCLOSED BY clause. As with termination characters, your enclosure may be a string of characters rather than just one. You can specify that enclosing characters are optional, and you can specify different characters for the beginning and end of a field.

Syntax for ENCLOSED BY

The ENCLOSED BY clause allows you to specify enclosure characters for a field. The clause may immediately follow the TERMINATED BY clause, or it may replace that clause altogether. Following is the syntax:

```
[OPTIONALLY] ENCLOSED [BY] {'string' | X'hex_digits'}
            [AND {'string' | X'hex_digits'}]
```

The syntax elements are as follows:

OPTIONALLY

Indicates that the enclosing characters are optional. SQL*Loader won't require them to be present, but will recognize them if they are. This keyword may only be used following the TERMINATED BY clause.

string

> A single character, or string of characters, that encloses the field.

hex_digits

> Allows you to specify an enclosure string using hexadecimal digits. Each two hexadecimal digits represents one byte. On an ASCII system, specifying X'22' is the same as specifying a double quote ("). Use hex digits when you are dealing with non-printable characters.

AND

> Allows you to specify a second enclosing string. If you do this, the first string that you specify marks the beginning of the field value, while the second string marks the end of the field value.

Example: Loading CSV files

Comma-separated values (CSV) data provides a good example of when you would need to specify enclosing characters. Here's some typical CSV data you might get from Microsoft Excel:

```
"Baraga, Township of",civil,Baraga,464419N,0883419W,0,200012081404
"Ontonagon, Township of",civil,Ontonagon,464904N,0891640W,0,200012081405
Anna River,stream,Alger,462440N,0863825W,630,200012081058
Keweenaw Point,cape,Keweenaw,472406N,0874242W,610,200012081059
```

Notice that only the feature name fields are enclosed in quotes, because only they contain delimiters embedded within their values. This is exactly how Microsoft Excel writes data when you save a spreadsheet as a CSV file. Fields are only enclosed when they need to be. Since you don't know when, or even if, a field might be enclosed within quotes, you must make the quotes optional. The following LOAD statement will do that for all fields:

```
LOAD DATA
   INFILE 'data05.dat'
   REPLACE INTO TABLE michigan_features
   FIELDS TERMINATED BY ',' OPTIONALLY ENCLOSED BY '"'
   (
   feature_name CHAR,
   feature_type CHAR,
   county CHAR,
   latitude CHAR,
   longitude CHAR,
   elevation INTEGER EXTERNAL,
   update_time DATE "YYYYMMDDHH24MI"
   )
```

This is the best approach to take if you are generating a CSV file using an off-the-shelf program, because it allows for any field to be enclosed by quotes. You don't have to specify ahead of time precisely which fields may or may not be enclosed.

If you knew for certain that the feature name field was the only one ever enclosed within quotes, and you didn't want to specify the delimiter globally, you could do the following:

```
LOAD DATA
    INFILE 'data05.dat'
    REPLACE INTO TABLE michigan_features
    (
    feature_name CHAR TERMINATED BY ',' OPTIONALLY ENCLOSED BY '"',
    feature_type CHAR TERMINATED BY ',' ,
    county CHAR TERMINATED BY ',' ,
    latitude CHAR TERMINATED BY ',' ,
    longitude CHAR TERMINATED BY ',' ,
    elevation INTEGER EXTERNAL TERMINATED BY ',' ,
    update_time DATE "YYYYMMDDHH24MI"
    )
```

Here, delimiters have been defined at the individual field level, and the definition for the feature name field specifies an optional enclosing character.

Here's one final variation on the theme of loading CSV data:

```
LOAD DATA
    INFILE 'data05.dat'
    REPLACE INTO TABLE michigan_features
    FIELDS TERMINATED BY ','
    (
    feature_name CHAR OPTIONALLY ENCLOSED BY '"',
    feature_type CHAR,
    county CHAR,
    latitude CHAR,
    longitude CHAR,
    elevation INTEGER EXTERNAL,
    update_time DATE "YYYYMMDDHH24MI"
    )
```

In this example, the field termination character, the comma, is specified globally. But enclosing characters have been specified for only the feature name field.

Example: Whitespace as a delimiter

Whitespace may be used as a delimiter, and it's particularly helpful when you have fields separated by varying amounts of space and/or tab characters. For example:

```
"Baraga, Township of" civil     Baraga 464419N 0883419W 0     200012081404
"Ontonagon, Township of" civil   Ontonagon 464904N 0891640W 0 200012081405
```

Use the keyword WHITESPACE to specify that you want to use any amount of whitespace between fields as a delimiter. For example:

```
LOAD DATA
    INFILE 'data06.dat'
    REPLACE INTO TABLE michigan_features
```

```
FIELDS TERMINATED BY WHITESPACE OPTIONALLY ENCLOSED BY '"'
(
feature_name CHAR,
feature_type CHAR,
county CHAR,
latitude CHAR,
longitude CHAR,
elevation INTEGER EXTERNAL,
update_time DATE "YYYYMMDDHH24MI"
)
```

When WHITESPACE is used as the delimiter between fields, SQL*Loader will recognize any combination of space and tab characters as the delimiter. While often helpful, there are two issues that arise out of this behavior:

- Leading and trailing spaces are trimmed from any field that is terminated by whitespace.

- You can't use two delimiters together to represent a null field.

The exception to these rules is that they really don't apply when you use enclosing characters such as quotation marks. Consider the following example:

```
"Big Powderhorn Mountain" " summit " "Gogebic"
"Lake Gogebic" "" "Ontonagon"
```

The data within the enclosing characters, quotation marks in this case, is protected. Thus, " summit " will retain its leading and trailing spaces. The feature type for Lake Gogebic will be interpreted as a null. The enclosing characters break up the string of whitespace, allowing SQL*Loader to recognize the field.

 The keyword WHITESPACE cannot be used to specify an enclosing character.

Example: Enclosing characters with no delimiters

It's actually possible to specify enclosing characters for a field without specifying any termination characters, although it usually doesn't make sense to do so. The following data provides one possible case where it might make sense to use ENCLOSED BY without first using TERMINATED BY:

```
"Big Powderhorn Mountain"(summit),Gogebic,
"Lake Gogebic"(reservoir),Ontonagon,
```

Each field in this record is enclosed, and in each case the enclosing characters are different. You can load this data using the following LOAD statement:

```
LOAD DATA
    INFILE 'data07.dat'
```

```
REPLACE INTO TABLE michigan_features
(
feature_name CHAR ENCLOSED BY '"',
feature_type CHAR ENCLOSED BY '(' AND ')',
county CHAR ENCLOSED BY ','
)
```

Now you might think that you could simplify things, and use the same enclosing characters for each field. For example:

```
"Big Powderhorn Mountain""summit""Gogebic"
"Lake Gogebic""reservoir""Ontonagon"
```

Unfortunately, you can't easily load this data because SQL*Loader interprets each back-to-back occurrence of the quotation mark character as a single quotation mark to be included as part of the first field's value. If you specified just ENCLOSED BY '"' for this data, then SQL*Loader would see each record as containing only one field. In order to load the data as three separate fields, you need to delimit it.

Example: Different beginning and ending enclosing characters

When you specify enclosing characters for a field, there's no reason you have to specify the same characters for the end of the field as for the beginning. Use the AND keyword, and you can specify both separately. Consider the following data:

```
(Big Powderhorn Mountain)(summit)(Gogebic)
(Lake Gogebic)(reservoir)(Ontonagon)
```

Each field is enclosed within parentheses, and of course the opening and closing parentheses are not the same character. You can load this data using the following LOAD statement:

```
LOAD DATA
   INFILE 'data10.dat'
   REPLACE INTO TABLE michigan_features
   FIELDS ENCLOSED BY '(' AND ')'
   (
   feature_name CHAR,
   feature_type CHAR,
   county CHAR
   )
```

The fact that there are no spaces or other delimiters between fields in this example doesn't matter, because the beginning and ending enclosing characters are not the same. There's no ambiguity about whether a field should end.

Common Issues with Delimited Data

As we mentioned at the beginning of the chapter, there are a number of common issues that arise when dealing with delimited data. These include:

- Dealing with nulls
- Dealing with short records
- Skipping fields you don't want to load

The next few sections talk about these issues and demonstrate some of the solutions available with SQL*Loader.

Dealing with Nulls

Null values are usually less of an issue with delimited data than they are with columnar data. When you load columnar data, the only time you don't have a value for each field is when the record is short. The problem then is to decide which value should represent the lack of a value—in other words, a null. With delimited data, null values are easily represented by placing two delimiters in succession. For example, in the following data, the record for Escanaba Light contains six fields, with fields four and five being the latitude and longitude (the record for Vulcan Lookout Tower, on the other hand, is missing those two values):

```
"Escanaba Light","locale","Delta","454448N","0870213W","582"
"Vulcan Lookout Tower","tower","Dickinson",,,0
```

This data can easily be loaded using the following LOAD statement, and the two missing values will be represented as null values in the destination database table. In the case of delimited data, it's not necessary to use the NULLIF clause:

```
LOAD DATA
   INFILE 'data11.dat'
   REPLACE INTO TABLE michigan_features
   FIELDS TERMINATED BY ',' OPTIONALLY ENCLOSED BY '"'
   (
   feature_name CHAR,
   feature_type CHAR,
   county CHAR,
   latitude CHAR,
   longitude CHAR,
   elevation INTEGER EXTERNAL
   )
```

It all seems too easy, doesn't it? But unfortunately, there are still some quirks and gotchas to be aware of.

Enclosures must be optional

When you're loading delimited data that may possibly include missing, or null, values, you can run into problems with enclosing characters. Consider the following record:

```
"Vulcan Lookout Tower","tower","Dickinson",,,0
```

This record is missing values for two fields. If you try to load this data using the following FIELDS clause, you'll get an error:

```
FIELDS TERMINATED BY ',' ENCLOSED BY '"'
```

The reason you'll get an error is that the data does not include enclosing characters for the two missing values. If enclosing characters are required, they must be present. In this case, either you need to use the OPTIONAL keyword in front of the ENCLOSED BY clause, or you need to generate a data file that includes enclosing quotes even for null fields. Here's an example:

```
"Vulcan Lookout Tower","tower","Dickinson","","","0"
```

This time, because the enclosing quotes surround all fields, including those that are empty, you can get away without making those quotes optional.

The presence of enclosing characters affects the treatment of spaces

The presence or absence of enclosing characters such as quotation marks affects the manner in which SQL*Loader treats leading and trailing spaces in delimited data. The following records provide some examples. Focus on the feature type value, which is the second field in the record:

```
"Menominee, City of","  civil   ","Menominee","450716N","0873725W","0"
Blind Sucker River,   stream   ,Luce,464047N,0854040W,0
Tahquamenon Falls State Park,    ,Chippewa,463547N,0851230W,0
"Brevoort Lake","     ","Mackinac","460000N","0845600W","625"
```

The feature type values in this set of records will be treated as follows:

- When you use enclosing characters, both leading and trailing spaces are preserved. As a result, the City of Menominee's feature type will still continue to be " civil ", and the type for Brevoort Lake will contain all spaces.

- When no enclosing characters are used, SQL*Loader trims both *leading* and *trailing* spaces. The feature type for Blind Sucker River, therefore, will be "stream", and not " stream ".

- A string of all spaces will be interpreted as a NULL, but only when no enclosing characters are used. So Tahquamenon Falls State Park gets a feature type of null, while Brevoort Lake gets a feature type of " ".

If this seems like too much complexity, try to remember the simple rule that leading and trailing spaces are always trimmed when enclosing characters are not used. Everything else flows logically from that rule.

Errors result if the final field is missing

SQL*Loader will usually recognize two delimiters in a row as a missing value, but if the missing value is at the end of the record, SQL*Loader treats that record as a short record. A *short record* is one that does not contain the required number of delimited values, and SQL*Loader sees it as a possible error. Following are two example records:

```
Driggs River,stream,Schoolcraft,461134N,0855916W,""
Seney National Wildlife Refuge,park,Schoolcraft,461600N,0860600W,
```

Both of these records end with a null value, but one is enclosed within quotes, while the other is not. SQL*Loader will see six fields in the Driggs River record. However, SQL*Loader will see only five fields in the record for Seney National Wildlife Refuge. If your LOAD statement calls for six fields, the Driggs River record will be loaded, while the Seney National Wildlife Refuge record will be rejected because it is short.

Dealing with Short Records

As we just mentioned, a short record is a delimited record that does not contain as many fields as you have specified in your LOAD statement. SQL*Loader's default behavior is to reject such records and write them to the bad file. When this happens, you'll see errors such as the following in your log file:

```
Record 6: Rejected - Error on table MICHIGAN_FEATURES, column ELEVATION.
Column not found before end of logical record (use TRAILING NULLCOLS)
```

You can change SQL*Loader's default behavior by using the TRAILING NULLCOLS clause. This clause causes SQL*Loader to treat missing fields as null values.

TRAILING NULLCOLS syntax

The TRAILING NULLCOLS clause appears within the INTO TABLE clause. The following syntax highlights its proper location with respect to other, optional, clauses:

```
INTO TABLE table_name
    [({PARTITION | SUBPARTITION} partition_name)]
    {INSERT | REPLACE | TRUNCATE | APPEND}
    [SORTED [INDEXES] (index_list)] [SINGLEROW]
    [{INSERT | REPLACE | TRUNCATE | APPEND}]
    [OPTIONS (FILE=database_filename)]
    [REENABLE [DISABLED_CONSTRAINTS][EXCEPTIONS exception_table_name]]
    [WHEN field_conditions]
    [{OID(fieldname) | SID(fieldname)}]
```

```
[FIELDS [delimiter_clause]]
[TRAILING [NULLCOLS]
[SKIP skip_count]
(field_list)
```

The NULLCOLS keyword is optional. You can save typing, but be less clear, by using just TRAILING.

Example: TRAILING NULLCOLS

The following comma-delimited records typify a case where you might want to use TRAILING NULLCOLS. The first record contains six fields, but the remaining records vary from two to four fields:

```
"Keweenaw Waterway","canal","Houghton","471258N","0883712W","601"
"Ishpeming, City of","civil","Marquette"
"Marquette State Prison","locale","Marquette","463043N",
"Tilden Mine","mine",
```

The following LOAD statement—note the TRAILING NULLCOLS clause—will load this data:

```
LOAD DATA
    INFILE 'data13.dat'
    REPLACE INTO TABLE michigan_features
    FIELDS TERMINATED BY ',' ENCLOSED BY '"'
    TRAILING NULLCOLS
    (
    feature_name CHAR,
    feature_type CHAR,
    county CHAR,
    latitude CHAR,
    longitude CHAR,
    elevation INTEGER EXTERNAL
    )
```

Because TRAILING NULLCOLS has been used, any trailing fields not represented in the record are represented as null values in the destination database table.

Skipping Fields You Don't Want to Load

The problem of how to skip columns that you don't want to load used to be one of the most vexing problems encountered when loading delimited data. The problem is so common, and the solution so obvious, that it amazes us that Oracle didn't provide a solution until Oracle8*i* was released.

The following records each contain four fields: state code, feature name, feature type, and county name:

```
"MI","Maxton Plains","flat","Chippewa"
"MI","Marble Head","summit","Chippewa"
"MI","Potagannissing River","stream","Chippewa"
```

What would you do if you wanted to load all but the state code field? What if you also wanted to skip the feature type field? If you're using Oracle8*i* or higher, you can use the FILLER clause to skip fields. Prior to Oracle8*i*, there was no easy solution to the problem of skipping a field.

Using the FILLER clause

The obvious solution to the problem of skipping a field in the input record is to simply have some way to define a field and specify that it not be loaded into the database. You can do that now using the FILLER keyword. The following LOAD statement makes use of FILLER to load only the feature and county names from the data shown previously:

```
LOAD DATA
    INFILE 'data14.dat'
    REPLACE INTO TABLE michigan_features
    FIELDS TERMINATED BY ',' ENCLOSED BY '"'
    TRAILING
    (
    state_code FILLER CHAR,
    feature_name CHAR,
    feature_type FILLER CHAR,
    county CHAR
    )
```

Fields marked as FILLER fields are parsed out of the input record by SQL*Loader, but are not loaded into the database.

Skipping a fixed portion of the record

Prior to Oracle8*i*, the FILLER keyword was not available. If you were lucky, the fields you wanted to skip would be in a fixed-length portion of the input record. The state field in the data shown previously is always two characters in length, always enclosed within quotes, and always delimited by a comma. The data that you want to load, therefore, always begins in the sixth column. You can take advantage of that fact to skip the state field by specifying POSITION(6) for the first field in your LOAD statement. For example:

```
LOAD DATA
    INFILE 'data14.dat'
    REPLACE INTO TABLE michigan_features
    FIELDS TERMINATED BY ',' ENCLOSED BY '"'
    TRAILING
    (
    feature_name POSITION(6) CHAR,
    feature_type CHAR,
    county CHAR
    )
```

Unfortunately, this is a very limited solution. You can only use it if the data that you want to skip occurs at the beginning of the record and is fixed in length.

Skipping columns before Oracle8i

Prior to the release of Oracle8*i*, there was no mechanism that you could use from within SQL*Loader to skip a delimited field in your input file. If you're using a pre-Oracle8*i* release of SQL*Loader, you have the following options for skipping fields:

- Load all fields into a work table, and then use SQL or PL/SQL to move whichever columns you desire into your production table.

- Remove the unwanted column from your data prior to loading it.

If you are on a Unix or Linux system, you can use the *cut* utility to extract only the columns you desire to load from your data file. The following example demonstrates the action of the *cut* utility. First, the *cat* command is used to show the contents of a data file. The *cut* command is then used to eliminate one column. Finally, the *cat* command is used again to show new version of the data:

```
[oracle@localhost oracle]$ cat data14.dat
"MI","Maxton Plains","flat","Chippewa"
"MI","Marble Head","summit","Chippewa"
"MI","Potagannissing River","stream","Chippewa"
[oracle@localhost oracle]$ cut -f2,4 -d"," data14.dat > data14cut.dat
[oracle@localhost oracle]$ cat data14cut.dat
"Maxton Plains","Chippewa"
"Marble Head","Chippewa"
"Potagannissing River","Chippewa"
```

The elements of the *cut* command used in this example are as follows:

cut
> Invokes the *cut* utility.

–f2,4
> Extracts fields 2 and 4 from each input record.

–d","
> Specifies the delimiter as the comma. The default delimiter is the tab character. It's not always necessary to enclose the delimiter within quotes (*–d,* works just as well as *–d","*), but spaces and other special characters must be quoted.

data14.dat
> The input file.

> data14cut.dat
> Redirects output to create a new file named *data14cut.dat*.

Other solutions besides the one shown here are possible. Perl and awk, for example, can both be applied to solving this same problem.

Concatenating Records

Physical records containing delimited data may be concatenated together into one logical record, but the solutions presented in Chapter 4 for fixed-width data often don't apply to delimited data. The issue is that with delimited data, the location of any continuation character is unlikely to remain fixed.

If you have a continuation flag in your input record, and the position of that flag happens to remain fixed from one record to the next, you should investigate one of the concatenation solutions described in Chapter 4. Otherwise, you should look at the CONTINUEIF LAST clause. This lets you designate a continuation character that always occurs at the end of each physical record. For example, the following two lines represent one logical record that has been written as two physical records:

```
"Grace Harbor","bay","Keweenaw","475215N",
"0891330W","610"
```

A trailing comma in this example marks the end of the first physical record. If you had an entire file of such data, with the comma consistently at the end of each continued record, you could use the CONTINUEIF LAST clause to cause SQL*Loader to look to that last character as a continuation flag.

Syntax for CONTINUEIF LAST

Following is the syntax for the CONTINUEIF LAST clause:

```
CONTINUEIF LAST [(]operator {'char' | X'hex_digits'}[)]
```

The elements in the syntax are as follows:

CONTINUEIF LAST

Causes SQL*Loader to look at the final character, or string of characters, in each physical record to determine whether or not it is continued.

operator

Specifies the condition under which a physical record is continued. The following operators are valid:

=

Continues the record if the specified string matches the corresponding characters at the end of the record.

<>

Continues the record if the characters at the end of the record do not match the specified string.

char

> The text character that you want SQL*Loader to look for as a continuation value.

hex_digits

> A two-digit string of hexadecimal digits representing the character that you want SQL*Loader to look for as a continuation value.

Unlike the case with the other CONTINUEIF options, when LAST is used, the continuation character is preserved in the logical record.

CONTINUEIF LAST Examples

The following two examples show possible approaches to using CONTINUEIF LAST. The first example is straightforward, and looks for a trailing comma as a continuation indicator. The second example looks for an asterisk character to mark the end of each logical record.

Example: A trailing comma as a continuation character

The following data uses a trailing comma as a continuation character. Whenever a logical record has been broken over two or more physical lines, it's been done immediately after the occurrence of a comma.

```
"Grace Harbor","bay","Keweenaw","475215N",
"0891330W","601"
"Minong Ridge","ridge","Keweenaw","480115N","0885348W","800"
"Siskiwit Lake",
"lake",
"Keweenaw",
"480002N",
"0884745W",
"659"
```

The following LOAD statement can be used to load this data. Note especially the CONTINUEIF LAST clause in the third line:

```
LOAD DATA
   INFILE 'data15.dat'
   REPLACE CONTINUEIF LAST = ','
   INTO TABLE michigan_features
   (
   feature_name CHAR TERMINATED BY ',' ENCLOSED BY '"',
   feature_type CHAR TERMINATED BY ',' ENCLOSED BY '"',
   county CHAR TERMINATED BY ',' ENCLOSED BY '"',
   latitude CHAR TERMINATED BY ',' ENCLOSED BY '"',
   longitude CHAR TERMINATED BY ',' ENCLOSED BY '"',
   elevation INTEGER EXTERNAL TERMINATED BY ',' ENCLOSED BY '"'
   )
```

It's important to understand that the continuation indicator, a trailing comma in this case, is preserved in the logical record. After reassembly, the logical records in this example would appear as follows:

```
"Grace Harbor","bay","Keweenaw","475215N","0891330W","601"
"Minong Ridge","ridge","Keweenaw","480115N","0885348W","800"
"Siskiwit Lake","lake","Keweenaw","480002N","0884745W","659"
```

It is this logical record that you must keep in mind when writing the field descriptions in your LOAD statement. The logical record is what SQL*Loader looks at when parsing out the fields that you've described.

Unfortunately, SQL*Loader makes no provision for any arbitrary delimited field to be treated as a continuation indicator. You can't, for example, look at the third field or the fourth field. You must always look at a fixed character position, (as discussed in Chapter 4) or at the end of the record.

Example: Marking the end of each logical record

Another twist on the use of CONTINUEIF LAST is to mark not the end of each continued physical record, but rather the end of each logical record. The following data, for example, contains an asterisk at the end of each logical record:

```
"Grace Harbor","bay","Keweenaw","475215N",
"0891330W","601",*
"Minong Ridge","ridge","Keweenaw","480115N","0885348W","800",*
"Siskiwit Lake",
"lake",
"Keweenaw",
"480002N",
"0884745W",
"659",*
```

The challenge now is to concatenate each physical record until you get to one that ends with an asterisk. The CONTINUEIF LAST <> '*' clause in the following LOAD statement does this:

```
LOAD DATA
    INFILE 'data15.dat'
    REPLACE CONTINUEIF LAST <> '*'
    INTO TABLE michigan_features
    FIELDS TERMINATED BY ',' ENCLOSED BY '"'
    (
    feature_name CHAR,
    feature_type CHAR,
    county CHAR,
```

```
    latitude CHAR,
    longitude CHAR,
    elevation INTEGER EXTERNAL
    )
```

The trailing asterisk in this example will be preserved in each logical record, but that doesn't present any problem since it's set off by a comma as a separate field that isn't loaded by this LOAD statement.

Handling Nested Fields

Sometimes you have a field of delimited data that's made up of two or three values that you'd like to extract separately. These values may themselves be delimited, or they may be fixed-width.

Nested Delimited Fields

MUMPS programmers are familiar with the concept of nested delimited fields. For example, you might have a string of values delimited by commas, and one of those values is further delimited by some other character. For example, the individual pieces of the latitude and longitude values in the following comma-delimited data are themselves delimited by vertical bars:

```
Muskrat Point,cape,Alger,46|27|36|N,086|38|34|W
```

SQL*Loader doesn't really recognize the concept of a nested field, but you can still extract these individual subfields. Just specify the appropriate delimiter. For example:

```
LOAD DATA
    INFILE 'data16.dat'
    REPLACE
    INTO TABLE michigan_features
    (
    feature_name CHAR TERMINATED BY ',',
    feature_type CHAR TERMINATED BY ',',
    county CHAR TERMINATED BY ',',
    lat_degrees INTEGER EXTERNAL TERMINATED BY '|',
    lat_minutes INTEGER EXTERNAL TERMINATED BY '|',
    lat_seconds INTEGER EXTERNAL TERMINATED BY '|',
    lat_direction CHAR TERMINATED BY ',',
    long_degrees INTEGER EXTERNAL TERMINATED BY '|',
    long_minutes INTEGER EXTERNAL TERMINATED BY '|',
    long_seconds INTEGER EXTERNAL TERMINATED BY '|',
    long_direction CHAR TERMINATED BY '"'
    )
```

Notice that the termination character specified for the first three fields was a comma. Beginning with the *lat_degree* field, the termination character is changed to a vertical bar (|). The vertical bar is used up until the *lat_direction* field, which ends with a comma. The same pattern is repeated for the longitude values.

What if the data is enclosed? For example:

```
'Muskrat Point","cape","Alger","46|27|36|N","086|38|34|W"
```

This gets tougher, because the entire collection of degree values is enclosed within quotes, but each individual value is not. However, as long as the enclosing quotes are not optional, you can work around this by cleverly adjusting your termination strings. For example:

```
LOAD DATA
    INFILE 'data16.dat'
    REPLACE
    INTO TABLE michigan_features
    (
    feature_name CHAR TERMINATED BY ',',
    feature_type CHAR TERMINATED BY ',',
    county CHAR TERMINATED BY ',"',
    lat_degrees INTEGER EXTERNAL TERMINATED BY '|',
    lat_minutes INTEGER EXTERNAL TERMINATED BY '|',
    lat_seconds INTEGER EXTERNAL TERMINATED BY '|',
    lat_direction CHAR TERMINATED BY '","',
    long_degrees INTEGER EXTERNAL TERMINATED BY '|',
    long_minutes INTEGER EXTERNAL TERMINATED BY '|',
    long_seconds INTEGER EXTERNAL TERMINATED BY '|',
    long_direction CHAR TERMINATED BY '"'
    )
```

The *county* field is terminated by ',"'. That clears out both the comma and the quote that begins the latitude value. The *lat_direction* field is terminated by '","', which serves to clear out the delimiting and enclosing characters between it and the *long_degrees* value. As long as you don't have any extra space characters surrounding your delimiters, and your enclosing characters are always present, this approach will work.

Nested Fixed-Width Fields

It's also possible to extract fixed-width data from a delimited field. The latitude value in the following example has the degrees, minutes, and seconds all expressed in fixed, two-digit fields. The direction adds yet another character. The longitude value is similar, except that three digits are used for the degrees:

```
"Wagner Falls","falls","Alger","462316N","0863846W"
"Tannery Falls","falls","Alger","462456N","0863737W"
```

The exact character position of the latitude and longitude fields is not consistent from one record to the next, but the length of those fields is. You can take advantage of that fact to pull apart the individual latitude and longitude elements. The trick is to specify each element's length as part of the SQL*Loader datatype. For example:

```
LOAD DATA
    INFILE 'data17.dat'
    REPLACE INTO TABLE michigan_features
    (
    feature_name CHAR TERMINATED BY ',',
    feature_type CHAR TERMINATED BY ',',
    county CHAR TERMINATED BY ',"',
    lat_degrees INTEGER EXTERNAL(2),
    lat_minutes INTEGER EXTERNAL(2),
    lat_seconds INTEGER EXTERNAL(2),
    lat_direction CHAR TERMINATED BY '","',
    long_degrees INTEGER EXTERNAL(3),
    long_minutes INTEGER EXTERNAL(2),
    long_seconds INTEGER EXTERNAL(2),
    long_direction CHAR TERMINATED BY '"'
    )
```

Delimiters are specified for each field until the latitude is reached. At that point, the *lat_degrees* field is described as INTEGER EXTERNAL(2). This causes SQL*Loader to pick up the first two digits of the latitude value to use for *lat_ degrees*. The *lat_minutes* field will immediately follow that, and will also consist of two digits. The *lat_seconds* value is handled in the same manner. The *lat_direction* field is again delimited in order to absorb the '","' characters that separate it from the longitude values. The entire pattern is then repeated for the four longitude values.

6

Recovering from Failure

What do you do when you are loading data with SQL*Loader, and something goes wrong, and the load fails? That's an important question, because sooner or later you'll find yourself in just that situation. In some cases, you may be able to restart the load from the beginning. Otherwise, you'll need to determine how many records were successfully processed and loaded, so that you can restart the load from that point forward.

It's important to think through your plans for restarting a load before you actually begin a load operation. In some cases, it can be very difficult to determine the precise point from which to restart.

There are many reasons why a load might fail. Problems you might encounter include the following:

- A table or index may reach its maximum allowed number of extents.

- You may run out of space in a tablespace.

- You may suffer an instance crash during a load.

Whichever problem occurs, you obviously need to fix it before you restart the load. If you run out of space in a tablespace, for example, you'll need to add a datafile to the tablespace, or increase the size of an existing datafile, before you try the load again.

An easy solution, when a load fails, is to simply start over and redo the entire load. However, if a lot of data is involved, starting over is not very efficient. SQL*Loader provides a mechanism to restart a load and pick up from the point where the previous attempt failed. By using this mechanism, you avoid the need to reprocess data that has already been successfully loaded.

The issues involved with using SQL*Loader's restart mechanism differ depending on whether you are doing a conventional path load or a direct path load. The conventional path load, where SQL*Loader uses standard SQL INSERT statements to load data, represents the simplest case. When doing a direct path load, SQL*Loader writes data directly into the database datafiles. Because of the way in which direct path loads work, there are some circumstances in which such loads cannot reliably be restarted.

Deleting and Starting Over

Restarting a load from the beginning is often the easiest approach. You should consider it in cases where no data was actually saved to the database, or in cases where you can reliably delete any data that was saved prior to the failure. Note that I said "consider." If you are loading a large amount of data, you may not want to spend the time loading the same data twice. Instead, you'll want to continue processing from the point at which the failure occurred.

When You're Loading an Empty Table

Regardless of the load type, if you were loading into a table that was empty to begin with, and you are sure that no other processes have modified that table, then you can delete the partially loaded data from the table and run the load again. For this exact reason, it's not uncommon to load data from an external file into a work table using a LOAD statement such as one of the following:

```
LOAD DATA ...
TRUNCATE INTO TABLE ...

LOAD DATA ...
REPLACE INTO TABLE ...
```

The TRUNCATE keyword causes SQL*Loader to truncate the table prior to loading it, while the REPLACE keyword causes SQL*Loader to delete all rows from the table prior to loading it. Either way, any existing data in the table is deleted. If the load fails, you simply need to correct the problem and run the load again. You can repeat that cycle any number of times, until the load completes successfully.

When You're Appending to a Table with Existing Data

If you are using the APPEND keyword to load data into a table along with whatever existing data might be there, starting over from the beginning becomes more difficult. If you can reliably identify the rows that were loaded, you can delete just those rows, and then rerun the load. For example, if you were loading geographic names for the State of Michigan, and you knew that there was no preexisting data for Michigan, you could delete all the Michigan data and then rerun the load. This approach is especially attractive if you are loading a specific partition of a large table because you can simply truncate that partition before restarting the load.

Restarting a Conventional Path Load

To restart a conventional path load, you need to determine the number of input records that were successfully processed, and then you need to restart the load, telling SQL*Loader to skip those previously processed records.

Determining the Number of Records to Skip

During a conventional path load, SQL*Loader reads and processes input records one at a time. If data is being loaded into one table, then each input record will result in one INSERT statement being executed. If you are loading data into multiple tables, then each input record may result in several INSERT statements being executed. SQL*Loader will periodically execute COMMIT statements during the load process. Each COMMIT corresponds to an input record number. When one input record generates multiple INSERT statements, SQL*Loader ensures that they are all part of the same transaction, so an input record is either entirely loaded or not loaded at all.

Each COMMIT executed by SQL*Loader represents one *commit point*. A log of the commit points reached during a SQL*Loader session is displayed in your command prompt window as the load progresses. The following example shows the commit points for a conventional path load that failed because a table reached its maximum number of extents:

```
$ sqlldr gnis/gnis@herman control=gnis_load_multi.ctl
        log=gnis_load_multi.log rows=100 direct=n

SQL*Loader: Release 8.1.5.0.0 - Production on Tue Jun 6 13:48:14 2000

(c) Copyright 1999 Oracle Corporation.  All rights reserved.

Commit point reached - logical record count 107
Commit point reached - logical record count 229
Commit point reached - logical record count 295
Commit point reached - logical record count 447
Commit point reached - logical record count 491
Commit point reached - logical record count 613
Commit point reached - logical record count 785
Commit point reached - logical record count 921
Commit point reached - logical record count 983
```

```
SQL*Loader-605: Non-data dependent ORACLE error occurred -- load discontinued.
```

```
Commit point reached - logical record count 1015
```

The most recent successful commit point corresponds to logical record #983. The final commit point is the one that caused the error to occur. It does seem rather odd that the error message precedes the commit point message, but that's the way it is. To find the number of records to skip when continuing a conventional path load, look for the most recent commit point prior to any error message. In this case, you would want to skip the first 983 records, and continue the load starting with record 984.

> Once you've determined the number of records to skip, you should verify that by checking to see if the last record that you think was loaded successfully really was. Do that by querying your database table to see if the record exists. Conversely, you should find the next record in your file that should have been loaded, and verify that it hasn't been. With respect to the example in this chapter, you should query the table to verify that record 983 was loaded, and that 984 was not.

You might think that the number of records to be skipped could also be derived from the SQL*Loader log file. Unfortunately, that often cannot be done. Here's the summary portion of the log file from the same load used to generate the previous example:

```
Table CHU_CHURCH:
    163 Rows successfully loaded.
    0 Rows not loaded due to data errors.
    831 Rows not loaded because all WHEN clauses were failed.
    0 Rows not loaded because all fields were null.
```

The number of rows loaded is incremented after each successful commit, and corresponds to the most recent successful commit point. However, because some rows were discarded, the number of rows loaded in this example does not correspond to the number of input records that were successfully processed. Nor does the sum of the rows loaded plus the rows not loaded give you that information. The count of rows not loaded is incremented independently of the commit point. Adding 163 to 831 gives you 994, which is well beyond the most recent successful commit point of 983.

The only case where you can reliably use the summary information in the log file to continue a conventional path load is when all the "Rows not loaded" values are zero. If that's the case, then you can continue the load by skipping the number of rows that were successfully loaded.

Using the SKIP Command-Line Parameter

Once you know how many records to skip, you can use the SKIP command-line parameter to have SQL*Loader skip over those records and continue the load from where it left off previously. Before you do that, check your SQL*Loader control file. When continuing a load, you need to use the APPEND keyword in your LOAD DATA statement. For example:

```
LOAD DATA
   INFILE 'al_deci.'
   BADFILE 'al_deci.bad'
   DISCARDFILE 'al_deci.dis'
   APPEND INTO TABLE air_airport
   ...
```

If you use TRUNCATE or REPLACE instead of APPEND, then your new load will wipe out the data that was previously loaded successfully. If you use the INSERT keyword, or no keyword at all, your second load attempt might fail because of existing records in your destination table. If you are loading multiple tables, you should use APPEND with each of your INTO TABLE clauses.

 Be sure to use APPEND INTO TABLE when continuing a load. Check all your INTO TABLE clauses.

Once you've modified your control file to append new data to the data loaded previously, you can restart the load using the SKIP command-line parameter. For example:

```
sqlldr gnis/gnis@herman control=gnis_load_multi.ctl
       log=gnis_load_multi.log rows=100 direct=n SKIP=983
```

This command specifies SKIP=983, so SQL*Loader will begin loading with record 984. The number used with SKIP is in terms of logical records. If you are combining multiple physical records together into one logical record, then the number used with SKIP won't correspond to a physical record number in your input file. That's OK, and everything will still work out, because the record numbers reported with the commit point messages are also logical records.

Continuing a Continued Load

What if you continue a load, and the continuation fails? The short answer is that you fix the problem and continue the load again. A longer answer would include an explanation of how SQL*Loader computes logical record numbers. In any load, logical record 1 is the first record that is actually processed. Skipped records are

Saving the Commit Point Log

Why SQL*Loader writes the commit point log only to the display, and not also to the SQL*Loader log file, is a mystery to us. It doesn't really make sense, but that's the way SQL*Loader works.

Regardless of how SQL*Loader is designed, the commit point log provides important information that you will need if you want to continue a conventional path load. Fortunately, the record of commit points is written through the standard output device. On Windows NT, Linux, and Unix operating systems, you can redirect that output to a file by appending > *filename* to the end of your SQL*Loader command. For example:

```
sqlldr gnis/gnis@herman control=gnis_load_multi.ctl log=gnis_load_multi.log
        rows=100 direct=n SKIP=983 > gnis_load_multi.commit_log
```

If you are on a Unix system, there's even a way that you can watch the commit point log while it's being redirected to a log file. Simply run your load in the background, and use the *tail –f* command to display the log file as it is being written. For example:

```
sqlldr gnis/gnis@herman control=gnis_load_multi.ctl log=gnis_load_multi.log
        rows=100 direct=n SKIP=983 > gnis_load_multi.commit_log &
tail -f gnis_load_multi.commit_log
```

The ampersand (&) at the end of the *sqlldr* command causes it to run in the background. This frees your terminal session so that you can enter another command while the load is running. Enter the *tail –f* command as shown in the example, and you can monitor the log file as it is being written.

excluded. Thus, if you start a load using SKIP=983, record 1 corresponds to the record you would normally think of as 984.

When continuing a load that was started using the SKIP command-line parameter, you need to take into account not only the logical record number reported by the most recent successful commit point, but also the number of skipped records. Take a look at the following example:

```
$ sqlldr gnis/gnis@herman control=gnis_load_multi.ctl log=gnis_load_multi.log
        rows=100 direct=n SKIP=983

SQL*Loader: Release 8.1.5.0.0 - Production on Tue Jun 6 13:48:14 2000

(c) Copyright 1999 Oracle Corporation.  All rights reserved.

Commit point reached - logical record count 107
Commit point reached - logical record count 229
SQL*Loader-605: Non-data dependent ORACLE error occurred -- load discontinued.

Commit point reached - logical record count 295
```

This continued load failed after the commit point for logical record 229. To continue the load again, you need to skip 983 + 229, or 1212 records.

Restarting a Direct Path Load

Restarting a direct path load is often more difficult than restarting a conventional path load. The biggest problem is that when the direct path is used, there's no easy way to determine the exact record number at which the load should continue after a failure occurs. To make matters even worse, if you are loading multiple tables using a direct path load, the number of records that you need to skip is very likely to be different for each table.

Determining the Number of Records to Skip

The default behavior for a direct path load results in no data being saved until the entire load is complete. Essentially, SQL*Loader does the following:

1. Loads all the data into blocks above the table's current high-water mark.

2. Adjusts the high-water mark so that the newly loaded data is now included in the table.

3. Rebuilds any indexes on the table.

If a direct path load fails while the data is being loaded, steps two and three might or might not take place, depending on the reason for the failure. If the Oracle instance is still running when a direct path load fails, SQL*Loader will perform steps two and three as part of its cleanup process. If the load fails because the instance fails, then obviously no cleanup can occur. Thus, if a table fails to extend, you might see output from SQL*Loader that looks like this:

```
SQL*Loader: Release 8.1.5.0.0 - Production on Tue Jun 6 17:17:51 2000

(c) Copyright 1999 Oracle Corporation.  All rights reserved.

Save data point reached - logical record count 101.
ORA-02356: The database is out of space.  The load cannot continue
ORA-01631: max # extents (1) reached in table GNIS.GFN_GNIS_FEATURE_NAMES

Load completed - logical record count 510.
```

This example was taken from a single-table, direct path load. The problem in this case is that none of the logical record numbers shown are useful. In this particular load, a WHEN clause was used in the control file to restrict the load to records meeting a certain criteria. Here is the corresponding log file summary:

```
Table GFN_GNIS_FEATURE_NAMES:
  101 Rows successfully loaded.
  0 Rows not loaded due to data errors.
```

```
324 Rows not loaded because all WHEN clauses were failed.
  0 Rows not loaded because all fields were null.
```

Looking at the log file summary, you can see that 101 rows were loaded, and that 324 were skipped. Those 101 rows do not necessarily correspond to the first 101 logical records in the input file. The "Load completed" message in the earlier example indicates that SQL*Loader read 510 records. Those 510 records generated 101 inserts into table *gfn_gnis_feature_names*. 324 of those records were discarded because they didn't match the WHEN criteria. The remaining 85 records probably represent records that would have been saved had the table not failed to extend. There's nothing to tell you how many rows to skip when you try to continue the load. As Figure 6-1 illustrates, none of these record counts necessarily represents a contiguous block of records.

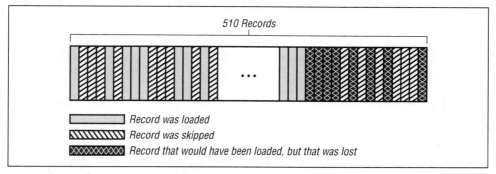

*Figure 6-1. Different record counts reported by SQL*Loader don't represent contiguous records*

Because the records are interspersed as shown in Figure 6-1, none of the counts are really useful for the purpose of determining the point from which to continue a load. The situation gets even worse when you perform a direct path load involving several tables. Here is the output from a failed direct path load involving three tables:

```
SQL*Loader: Release 8.1.5.0.0 - Production on Tue Jun 6 17:44:16 2000

(c) Copyright 1999 Oracle Corporation.  All rights reserved.

Save data point reached - logical record count 1.
Save data point reached - logical record count 1.
Save data point reached - logical record count 1.
Save data point reached - logical record count 1.
Save data point reached - logical record count 2.
Save data point reached - logical record count 2.
Save data point reached - logical record count 2.
Save data point reached - logical record count 3.
Save data point reached - logical record count 4.
ORA-02356: The database is out of space.  The load cannot continue
ORA-01631: max # extents (1) reached in table GNIS.CHU_CHURCH
```

```
Save data point reached - logical record count 4.
ORA-02356: The database is out of space.  The load cannot continue
ORA-01631: max # extents (1) reached in table GNIS.CHU_CHURCH

Save data point reached - logical record count 4.
ORA-02356: The database is out of space.  The load cannot continue
ORA-01631: max # extents (1) reached in table GNIS.CHU_CHURCH

Save data point reached - logical record count 5.
ORA-02356: The database is out of space.  The load cannot continue
ORA-01631: max # extents (1) reached in table GNIS.CHU_CHURCH

Save data point reached - logical record count 5.
ORA-02356: The database is out of space.  The load cannot continue
ORA-01631: max # extents (1) reached in table GNIS.CHU_CHURCH

Save data point reached - logical record count 6.

Load completed - logical record count 1484.
```

The log summary from the same load looks like this:

```
Table AIR_AIRPORT:
  1484 Rows successfully read.
  6 Rows successfully loaded.
  0 Rows not loaded due to data errors.
  1478 Rows not loaded because all WHEN clauses were failed.
  0 Rows not loaded because all fields were null.

Table CHU_CHURCH:
  1299 Rows successfully read.
  181 Rows successfully loaded.
  0 Rows not loaded due to data errors.
  1118 Rows not loaded because all WHEN clauses were failed.
  0 Rows not loaded because all fields were null.

Table HOS_HOSPITAL:
  1471 Rows successfully read.
  4 Rows successfully loaded.
  0 Rows not loaded due to data errors.
  1467 Rows not loaded because all WHEN clauses were failed.
  0 Rows not loaded because all fields were null.
```

The number of rows successfully read can't be used as a basis for continuing a load, because not all those rows are necessarily saved to the database. In this case, the load failed because the *chu_church* table failed to extend. You know that SQL*Loader tried to insert the *chu_church* rows corresponding to 1299 logical records, and you know that 181 rows were successfully loaded, but you don't know which logical record corresponds to the most recently loaded row. With the data that we used to generate this example, record 1012 was the last logical record to be loaded into the *chu_church* table. Record 1013 was also a church, so the load would need to be continued by skipping the first 1012 records. SQL*Loader does not give you the information that you need to determine that. You have to manually go in and look at the data, and that's not always an easy thing to do. If you're dealing with a large amount of data, it may be virtually impossible to manually look at the data and determine what was loaded and what was not.

The only case in which the log file summary from a direct path load can reliably be used to determine the number of records to skip is when the three "Rows not loaded" values are all zero. In that case, and only in that case, you can use the number of rows successfully loaded as your skip value.

Using the SKIP Command-Line Parameter

If your direct path load only involves one table, you can continue it in the same manner as a conventional path load. Change the LOAD DATA statement in your control file to use the APPEND keyword, and then use the SKIP parameter on the command line to tell SQL*Loader how many logical records to skip before starting to load data again.

The SKIP command-line parameter applies to all tables being loaded. If your load involves multiple tables, you'll probably find that the number of records to skip is different for each table. In that case, you need to specify the number of records to skip on a table-by-table basis in your control file. The next section shows you how to do that. Only if the skip value is the same for all tables can you continue a multi-table direct path load using SKIP on the command line.

Using SKIP in the Control File

When a multiple-table direct path load fails, you'll often find that the number of records to skip varies from one table to the next. This comes about because the normal transaction mechanisms do not apply when a direct path load is done. SQL*Loader doesn't process all the INSERTs for one record, and then issue a COMMIT. In a direct path load, SQL*Loader fills database blocks and writes them to the database when they are full. Different tables will have different row sizes, so the blocks will fill at different rates. When you need to continue such a load, you'll need to specify a different skip value for each table.

To specify skip values on a table-by-table basis, you need to do two things. First, you need to change your LOAD DATA statement to a CONTINUE_LOAD DATA statement. Next, you need to add a SKIP clause to each of your INTO TABLE clauses. For example:

```
CONTINUE_LOAD DATA
    INFILE 'al_deci.' BADFILE 'al_deci.bad' DISCARDFILE 'al_deci.dis'
    INFILE 'mn_deci.' BADFILE 'mn_deci.bad' DISCARDFILE 'mn_deci.dis'
    INFILE 'ia_deci.' BADFILE 'ia_deci.bad' DISCARDFILE 'ia_deci.dis'
```

```
INFILE 'ak_deci.' BADFILE 'ak_deci.bad' DISCARDFILE 'ak_deci.dis'
INFILE 'mi_deci.' BADFILE 'mi_deci.bad' DISCARDFILE 'mi_deci.dis'
INFILE 'oh_deci.' BADFILE 'oh_deci.bad' DISCARDFILE 'oh_deci.dis'
APPEND
INTO TABLE air_airport
WHEN gfn_feature_type = 'airport'
SKIP 1482
(
air_airport_state POSITION (1) CHAR TERMINATED BY "," ENCLOSED BY '"',
air_airport_name CHAR TERMINATED BY "," ENCLOSED BY '"',
gfn_feature_type FILLER CHAR TERMINATED BY "," ENCLOSED BY '"',
air_airport_county CHAR TERMINATED BY "," ENCLOSED BY '"'
)
INTO TABLE chu_church
WHEN gfn_feature_type = 'church'
SKIP 1012
(
chu_church_state POSITION (1) CHAR TERMINATED BY "," ENCLOSED BY '"',
chu_church_name CHAR TERMINATED BY "," ENCLOSED BY '"',
gfn_feature_type FILLER CHAR TERMINATED BY "," ENCLOSED BY '"',
chu_church_county CHAR TERMINATED BY "," ENCLOSED BY '"'
)
INTO TABLE hos_hospital
WHEN gfn_feature_type = 'hospital'
SKIP 804
(
hos_hospital_state POSITION (1) CHAR TERMINATED BY "," ENCLOSED BY '"',
hos_hospital_name CHAR TERMINATED BY "," ENCLOSED BY '"',
gfn_feature_type FILLER CHAR TERMINATED BY "," ENCLOSED BY '"',
hos_hospital_county CHAR TERMINATED BY "," ENCLOSED BY '"'
)
```

This control file continues a load that reads data from six input files, and distributes that data among three tables. Notice that there is a SKIP clause associated with each table, and that the number of rows to skip is table-specific. CONTINUE_LOAD has been used at the beginning of the control file instead of LOAD. CONTINUE_LOAD enables the SKIP clause to be used at the table level. Without CONTINUE_LOAD, the table-level SKIP clauses would cause errors. As with any other continued load, the APPEND keyword is used in the LOAD command so that SQL*Loader will preserve the rows that are already in the table.

Index-Related Issues

Indexes on tables loaded using the direct path are usually rebuilt after the data has been loaded. If a load aborts because a table reaches its maximum number of extents, SQL*Loader will rebuild the indexes using whatever data was successfully loaded. If a failure occurs that prevents SQL*Loader from rebuilding the indexes, they will be left in an unusable state, and you'll need to either drop them or rebuild them yourself. An index running out of extents is an example of the type of failure that results in an index being left in an unusable state.

7

Validating and Selectively Loading Data

SQL*Loader can create two types of output data files during a load: the bad file and the discard file. The *bad file* is where SQL*Loader writes input records that cause errors. The *discard file* is where SQL*Loader writes records that do not match conditions that you specify in your LOAD statement. We first mentioned these files in Chapter 1, *Introduction to SQL*Loader*. In this chapter, we'll delve more deeply into the use of the bad and discard files.

Handling Rejected Records

While loading data from an input data file into an Oracle database, SQL*Loader may encounter records that cause errors, and that consequently cannot be loaded. There are many reasons why a given record might cause an error. Some of the more common reasons include the following:

- The fields in the record may not match the field descriptions in the LOAD statement.

- The record may cause a database integrity constraint to be violated.

- An Oracle server error might occur due to lack of free space or some other problem.

- An insert trigger may fire on the table being loaded, and that trigger may raise an application error, causing the record to be rejected.

Regardless of the underlying cause, SQL*Loader cannot load a record that causes an error. When a record causes an error, SQL*Loader does two things. It records the error in the log file, and it writes a copy of the record causing the error to the bad file. It will then continue with the load process.

Naming the Bad File

By default, SQL*Loader implements an automatic method for naming the bad file. The bad file name is derived by taking the name of the input data file and replacing its extension with *.bad*. So if your input file is named *feature_names.dat*, your bad file will be named *feature_names.bad*. If you are loading from multiple input files, you'll get a separate bad file for each input file.

If you don't want to use the default name for your bad file, you can specify any name you like using the BADFILE clause in your LOAD statement. Here's an example:

```
LOAD DATA
    INFILE 'michigan_feature_names.dat'
       BADFILE 'michigan.bad'
    INFILE 'wisconsin_feature_names.dat'
       BADFILE 'wisconsin.bad'
    APPEND INTO TABLE features
    (
    state CHAR TERMINATED BY ',' ENCLOSED BY '"',
    feature_name CHAR TERMINATED BY ',' ENCLOSED BY '"',
    feature_type CHAR TERMINATED BY ',' ENCLOSED BY '"',
    county CHAR TERMINATED BY ',' ENCLOSED BY '"'
    )
```

As you can see, the BADFILE clause is subordinate to the INFILE clause. Each input file is associated with its own bad file. Be careful not to specify the same bad file name for two input file names. Bad files are created in order, as each input file is processed. If you specify the same bad file name for two input files, or allow SQL*Loader to derive the same bad file name for two input files, SQL*Loader will overwrite the first occurrence of the file with the second. Thus, if you have two input files of the same name, but in different directories, you should use the BADFILE clause to specify a unique bad file name for each of them.

Specifying a bad file name in your control file doesn't necessarily mean that the bad file will always be created. A bad file will be created only if at least one record is rejected from the corresponding input file. If no records are rejected, then no bad file will be created. This can cause some confusion if you are running the same load over and over in order to get the kinks worked out. Consider the following sequence of events:

1. You run the load and get a bad file because some records cause errors.

2. You make corrections to your data, or changes to your database, in order to eliminate the root cause of the errors.

3. You run the load again, and no errors occur.

4. You still have a bad file, but it's the one left over from Step 1.

The issue here is that SQL*Loader won't attempt to open or write to a bad file unless it encounters a record that causes an error. SQL*Loader also won't delete bad files left over from previous loads. It's convenient sometimes to look for the presence of a bad file in order to determine whether any errors occurred. However, that can be misleading if a bad file happens to be left over from a previous run. You can avoid being misled by checking the log file for errors. You may also find it helpful to delete any existing bad files before rerunning a load.

Bad Records in the Log File

Any time a record is rejected and written to the bad file because of an error, SQL*Loader writes an entry to the log file. That log file entry gives the logical record number of the bad record, and also explains the reason for the rejection. If the rejection is associated with an Oracle error, such as a constraint violation, you'll see the corresponding Oracle error number in the log file as well. The following example shows some typical log file entries for bad records:

```
Record 5: Rejected - Error on table GNIS.FEATURES, column FEATURE_NUM.
ORA-01722: invalid number

Record 7: Rejected - Error on table GNIS.FEATURES.
ORA-00001: unique constraint (GNIS.FEATURES_PK) violated

Record 10: Rejected - Error on table GNIS.FEATURES.
ORA-02291: integrity constraint (GNIS.FEATURE_STATE_FK) violated -
           parent key not found
```

The log file also indicates the total number of records read and the number of records rejected. SQL*Loader writes that information when the load is complete, and you'll find it at the bottom of the log file. For example:

```
Table GNIS.FEATURES:
  7 Rows successfully loaded.
  3 Rows not loaded due to data errors.
  0 Rows not loaded because all WHEN clauses were failed.
  0 Rows not loaded because all fields were null.
  ...
Total logical records skipped:          0
Total logical records read:            10
Total logical records rejected:         3
Total logical records discarded:        0
```

If errors occur during a load, you can look at the log file to find out why they occurred. Then it's up to you to decide what corrective action to take.

Fixing Bad Records

When you run a load and records are rejected because of errors, there are at least three things that you can do about those errors:

- You can ignore them, leaving the bad data out of the database.
- You can fix the root cause of the errors and rerun the load.
- You can fix and reload just the bad records.

Sometimes, you may need to do a combination of all three. Leaving the bad data out of your database is easy—just don't load it. The other two approaches each require a bit of thought.

Rerunning the load is also a fairly easy concept to grasp. However, you need to think about the records that were successfully loaded the first time. If you are using REPLACE or TRUNCATE to completely replace existing data in the table you are loading, then you don't need to worry about those records. If you used the INSERT keyword on your first load in order to ensure that the table was empty to begin with, you'll need to use REPLACE or TRUNCATE when you rerun the load. In both cases, you also need to give thought to the possibility that online users have already updated some of the records that you have loaded, or that they have inserted new records.

Having a primary key defined for your target table can really help when it comes to rerunning a load. The primary key constraint will prevent any records loaded on the first pass from being inserted as duplicates. Of course, this will be at the expense of a very large number of errors and, consequently, a whole new set of records being written to your bad file. Also, this technique only works for conventional path loads.

Rerunning the load using just the records that were rejected the first time around represents the most surgical approach. Records written to the bad file are exact copies of those read from the input file. The data format is the same, and the same control file can be used to attempt to load them again. So the sequence of events can look like this:

1. Run a load the first time. Bad records are written to a bad file.
2. Edit the bad file. Fix the data in the bad records.
3. Change the control file so that the input file is now the bad file.
4. Change the bad file name so that it does not match the current input file.
5. Run the load again.

The following LOAD statement, for example, will pull data from the bad files created from the LOAD statement shown earlier in this chapter. Pay careful attention to how the file names have been changed:

```
LOAD DATA
    INFILE 'michigan.bad'
        BADFILE 'michigan_very.bad'
    INFILE 'wisconsin.bad'
        BADFILE 'wisconsin_very.bad'
    APPEND INTO TABLE features
    (
    state CHAR TERMINATED BY ',' ENCLOSED BY '"',
    feature_name CHAR TERMINATED BY ',' ENCLOSED BY '"',
    feature_type CHAR TERMINATED BY ',' ENCLOSED BY '"',
    county CHAR TERMINATED BY ',' ENCLOSED BY '"'
    )
```

If necessary, you can repeat this process multiple times until you get a clean run that doesn't generate any more bad records. At that point, you will have successfully loaded all your data.

Limiting the Number of Errors

Sometimes you'll find yourself loading very bad data that causes an inordinate number of errors, or you'll have some database problem that causes all or most records to be rejected. Perhaps you're trying to load a child table without first having populated the parent table, and all the child records are being rejected because of foreign key constraint violations. Whatever the cause, if things go bad in a big way, you don't want to waste resources by attempting to load each record only to have it rejected. For this reason, SQL*Loader provides you with a mechanism to abort a load when the number of errors crosses a threshold that you specify.

You place a limit on the number of errors to allow for a load using the ERRORS command-line option. For example, the following command will initiate a load that is limited to a maximum of 50 errors:

```
sqlldr system/manager control=features.ctl errors=50
```

In this case, if the error count exceeds 50, SQL*Loader will abort the load. This actually can save you a lot of time. You don't want to run a large load for hours only to discover that nothing got loaded because you flubbed a POSITION clause in your control file.

The value of 50 shown here happens to be SQL*Loader's default limit on the number of errors that will be allowed to occur for a load. That limit applies even if you don't specify a value for ERRORS on the command line. There's no way to disable the error limit completely. If you want to allow an unlimited number of errors, the best you can do is to specify a very high number.

Selectively Loading Data

When you load data using SQL*Loader, it is not necessary for you to load all the records contained in your input data file into the target database table. SQL*Loader can selectively load data based on conditions that you specify. Using this feature, you can choose to load certain records and not others. The conditions that determine whether or not a record is loaded are referred to as *field conditions*, and you specify them using the WHEN clause inside the INTO TABLE clause in your LOAD statement.

Writing Field Conditions

Field conditions are written as part of a WHEN clause. The WHEN clause is part of your INTO TABLE clause and is table-specific. If you are loading multiple tables, you can specify different WHEN clauses for each table.

The syntax for the WHEN clause is as follows:

```
WHEN [(]condition[)] [AND [(]condition[)]]...]

condition := {field_name|position} {= | <> | !=} {'string'
                                                 | X'hex_digits'
                                                 | BLANKS}
position := POSITION({start[{: | -}end])
```

The elements in the syntax are as follows:

condition
> A WHEN clause can have any number of conditions ANDed together. Conditions may optionally be enclosed within parentheses.

field_name
> The name of a field in your LOAD statement's field list.

position
> A POSITION clause using syntax similar to that used for the POSITION clause in a field description.

=
> The equality operator.

<> and !=
> Two operators that you can use to test for inequality.

string
> A character string.

hex_digits
> A string of hexadecimal digits.

BLANKS

> A keyword that allows you to test the input data to see if it is composed entirely of space characters. This is helpful for variable-length fields that might contain differing numbers of space characters in each record. It's also helpful with character sets that have more than one space character.

start

> The starting position of the field in the input record. The first byte is position 1, the second byte is position 2, and so forth.

end

> The position of the last blyte of data in the field. This is optional. If you omit the ending position, SQL*Loader will determine it based on information that you supply in your datatype specification.

When you write a field condition, you can specify the data that you want SQL*Loader to look at either by field name or by position. It's usually most convenient to reference fields by name.

The following LOAD statement provides an example of a WHEN clause. It loads feature names, but only for waterfalls located in Alger County:

```
LOAD DATA
   INFILE 'michigan_feature_names.dat'
      BADFILE 'michigan.bad'
   APPEND INTO TABLE features
   WHEN (feature_type='falls') AND (county='Alger')
   (
   state CHAR TERMINATED BY ',' ENCLOSED BY '"',
   feature_name CHAR TERMINATED BY ',' ENCLOSED BY '"',
   feature_type CHAR TERMINATED BY ',' ENCLOSED BY '"',
   county CHAR TERMINATED BY ',' ENCLOSED BY '"'
   )
```

It's an unfortunate fact of life that you can only link field conditions together using the AND keyword. You can't OR two conditions, nor can you use operators other than the ones used to test for equality and inequality.

When you run a load like this that has a WHEN clause attached, SQL*Loader will load only the records that contain data conforming to the conditions you specify. Other records will not be loaded. Instead, they will be discarded.

Naming the Discard File

When using the WHEN clause to selectively load records, you have the option of writing any discarded record to SQL*Loader's discard file. The discard file is similar in concept to the bad file. The difference is that the discard file contains records that fail the WHEN clause conditions, while the bad file contains records that cause errors.

Unlike the case with the bad file, SQL*Loader will not create a discard file by default. If you want one created, you should specify a name using the DISCARD-FILE clause. For example:

```
LOAD DATA
  INFILE 'michigan_feature_names.dat'
    BADFILE 'michigan.bad'
    DISCARDFILE 'michigan_not_falls.dsc'
  APPEND INTO TABLE features
  WHEN (feature_type='falls') AND (county='Alger')
(
  state CHAR TERMINATED BY ',' ENCLOSED BY '"',
  feature_name CHAR TERMINATED BY ',' ENCLOSED BY '"',
  feature_type CHAR TERMINATED BY ',' ENCLOSED BY '"',
  county CHAR TERMINATED BY ',' ENCLOSED BY '"'
  )
```

There is one other way to have SQL*Loader create a discard file, and that is to specify the DISCARDMAX option on your SQL*Loader command line. If you specify DISCARDMAX without explicitly using DISCARDFILE to specify a file name, SQL*Loader will create a discard file using a default name. The name is derived in the same manner as the bad file name, except that the extension is set to *.dsc*. You can read more about DISCARDMAX in the section "Limiting the Number of Discards," later in this chapter. If you think there are too many caveats with respect to discard files, we agree. We think Oracle should have made these rules much simpler than they are.

> As is the case with bad files, the format of discard file records matches the format of the data records in the original input file.

Discarded Records in the Log File

When SQL*Loader discards a record, it writes a record of that operation into the log file. SQL*Loader also keeps track of the cumulative number of discards, and reports that number at the end of the load. The following log file excerpt shows an example of a log file entry for a discarded record, and also shows how the cumulative number of discards is reported at the end of a load:

```
  ...
Record 6: Discarded - failed all WHEN clauses.
  ...
Table GNIS.FEATURES:
  9 Rows successfully loaded.
  0 Rows not loaded due to data errors.
  1 Row not loaded because all WHEN clauses were failed.
```

```
   0 Rows not loaded because all fields were null.
   ...
Total logical records skipped:        0
Total logical records read:          10
Total logical records rejected:       0
Total logical records discarded:      1
   ...
```

In this instance, a total of 10 records was read from the input file. Only one record, logical record number 6, was discarded. The other 9 were successfully loaded.

Limiting the Number of Discards

SQL*Loader allows you to place an upper limit on the number of records that may be discarded during a load. If that limit is exceeded, SQL*Loader stops and aborts the load. The DISCARDMAX command-line option is used for this purpose. In the following example, it's used to limit the number of discards to 1000:

```
sqlldr system/manager control=features.ctl errors=50 discardmax=1000
```

This is the same concept as using the ERRORS option to limit the number of records written to the bad file. There is, however, one key difference. By default, SQL*Loader allows an unlimited number of discards. While there is no explicit way to specify an unlimited number of discards, that's the behavior you get if you omit the option. In the example shown here, DISCARDMAX=1000 was used to limit the number of discarded records to 1000.

A rather subtle effect of using the DISCARDMAX option is that it causes SQL*Loader to generate a discard file. Typically, you won't get a discard file unless you use the DISCARDFILE clause in your control file to specify a discard file name. However, even if you don't explicitly specify a discard file name, the DISCARD-MAX option causes SQL*Loader to generate a discard file using a default name. See the section "Naming the Discard File," earlier in this chapter, for more details.

 If no records are actually discarded, then a discard file will not be created regardless of your DISCARDMAX and DISCARDFILE values.

Loading Multiple Tables

One very useful application of the WHEN clause is to load multiple tables from the same input file. The WHEN clause allows you to filter out, for each table, just those records that you want inserted into that table. For example, consider the

problem of loading geographic feature name data such that all the airport names
go into one table and all the school names go into another. One solution, if you
don't want to use the WHEN clause, would be to load all the data into a work
table. If you give your work table the name *all_names*, you could then issue
INSERT . . . SELECT FROM statements such as the following:

```
INSERT INTO AIRPORT
SELECT *
FROM all_names
WHERE FEATURE_TYPE='airport';

INSERT INTO SCHOOL
SELECT *
FROM all_names
WHERE FEATURE_TYPE='school';
```

This solution is time-consuming, consists of multiple steps, and requires you to
make room for all of the data in your database whether you need it or not. Using
the WHEN clause, you can have SQL*Loader do all the work in one pass. The following LOAD statement will load airport names into a table named *airport*, and
school names into a table named *school*. Notice the use of POSITION(1) in the
second field list. This resets SQL*Loader back to the beginning of the record so
that it can pick up the same fields again for the second table:

```
LOAD DATA
    INFILE 'michigan_feature_names.dat'
        BADFILE 'michigan.bad'
        DISCARDFILE 'michigan.dsc'
    INFILE 'wisconsin_feature_names.dat'
        BADFILE 'wisconsin.bad'
        DISCARDFILE 'wisconsin.dsc'
    APPEND INTO TABLE school
        WHEN (feature_type='school')
    (
    state CHAR TERMINATED BY ',' ENCLOSED BY '"',
    feature_name CHAR TERMINATED BY ',' ENCLOSED BY '"',
    feature_type CHAR TERMINATED BY ',' ENCLOSED BY '"',
    county CHAR TERMINATED BY ',' ENCLOSED BY '"'
    )
    INTO TABLE airport
        WHEN (feature_type='airport')
    (
    state POSITION(1) CHAR TERMINATED BY ',' ENCLOSED BY '"',
    feature_name CHAR TERMINATED BY ',' ENCLOSED BY '"',
    feature_type CHAR TERMINATED BY ',' ENCLOSED BY '"',
    county CHAR TERMINATED BY ',' ENCLOSED BY '"'
    )
```

Not only does this method have the advantage of being less work for you, but it is
also less work for your database server. Rows other than those for airports and

schools won't be loaded at all. You don't need to expend CPU time loading unneeded rows into your database, nor do you need to allocate space for those rows. Finally, the airport and school names are inserted into the proper tables by SQL*Loader. All the work is done in one pass.

One important thing to be aware of when loading multiple tables is that any record that causes an error is not loaded at all. If, for example, you are trying to load the same record into two tables, and an error results because of a constraint violation on one table, the record will not be loaded into either table.

8

Transforming Data During a Load

It sure would be nice if all the data to be loaded was in exactly the right format to be dumped directly into our databases. Unfortunately, in the real world, that's often not the case. For example, you may need latitude and longitude expressed as decimal numbers, but instead you might get separate degree, minute, and second values. If you control the source of the data, you probably can format and organize it in a way that makes it easy to load using SQL*Loader. But if you're working with data from an external source, you may have to take it the way you get it. That's when it's nice to have some options for manipulating data as you load it.

One of the most convenient mechanisms for manipulating data during a load is to take advantage of the ability to define SQL expressions for the fields that you are loading. These SQL expressions operate on the data in one or more fields in order to return a result that is then loaded into the destination database column. When writing SQL expressions, you can draw from Oracle's rich palette of built-in functions, or you can write your own functions. Another approach to modifying data is to load it into a temporary work table from which you can further read and process the data. A creative variation on the work table approach is to use triggers to automatically kick off processing of the new rows being loaded.

Using Oracle's Built-in SQL Functions

One of the most powerful capabilities at your disposal when using SQL*Loader is the ability to define a SQL expression that operates on a field being loaded. Instead of loading the contents of the field, SQL*Loader loads the results of the expression.

Consider the following book price data that was shown back in Chapter 3, *Fields and Datatypes*:

```
Oracle Essentials                3495
SQL*Plus: The Definitive Guide   3995
```

```
Oracle PL/SQL Programming          4495
Oracle8 Design Tips                1495
```

This price data contains an assumed decimal point. The cost of *Oracle Essentials* is not $3,495.00, it's $34.95. If you load this data as is into a numeric database column, all the prices will end up being off by a factor of 100. However, by passing the values through a SQL expression, you can cause the correct prices to be stored in the database.

Syntax for SQL Expressions

Before getting into specific examples, let's review the syntax to use for defining a SQL expression. Recall from Chapter 3 that the following syntax is used to describe a scalar field to SQL*Loader:

```
column_name [POSITION({start | *[+offset]}[{: | -}end])]
            [datatype] [PIECED]
            [NULLIF condition [AND condition...]]
            [DEFAULTIF condition [AND condition...]]
            ["sql_expression"]
```

The *sql_expression* piece of this syntax is what we are concerned with now. It may be any expression that is valid in a SQL INSERT statement. You can use all the standard arithmetic operators supported by SQL, and you can use Oracle's comprehensive library of built-in SQL functions. You can also use user-defined functions, which you'll read more about later in this chapter.

SQL expressions can refer to any SQL*Loader field, not just the one on which the expression has been defined. However, this does not include FILLER fields. To refer to a SQL*Loader field in a SQL expression, use the field name preceded by a colon. For example, the following field description could be used for the book price field:

```
price POSITION(37:40) "TO_NUMBER(:book_price)/100"
```

The are several things to notice about this field description:

- The SQL expression is enclosed within double quotes. You must use double quotes for this purpose. You'll get an error if you try to enclose an expression within single quotes.

- The SQL expression uses *:book_price* to refer to the *book_price* field.

- No datatype is given for the field.

The reason we didn't specify a datatype in this example is that we were already using TO_NUMBER in our expression to convert the price to a number before dividing it by 100. There's no need to specify the conversion redundantly. However, specifying CHAR in this case would not lead to any extra work on SQL*Loader's part. The underlying INSERT statement that SQL*Loader constructs is the same either way—it uses the specified SQL expression to derive the column value.

The use of a leading colon in the expression syntax is no doubt familiar to anyone who has used a precompiler such as SQLJ or Pro*C. In the context of a SQL expression, a colon marks a bind variable. SQL*Loader makes all fields into bind variables. So any expression can reference any, all, or none of the field values.

> FILLER fields cannot be used in SQL expressions, because FILLER fields are not loaded into the bind array, and thus are not available to be evaluated by the Oracle SQL engine in the server. Oracle9*i*, however, introduces a BOUND FILLER field type that is loaded into the bind array and that can be used in SQL expressions.

The results of the expression are what SQL*Loader actually loads into the database. With respect to the example just shown, SQL*Loader would generate an INSERT statement resembling this one:

```
INSERT INTO book_prices (price) VALUES (TO_NUMBER(:price)/100)
```

It's most common for expressions to operate on just the one field for which they have been defined, but it's important to understand any expression you write may refer to any scalar field you are loading. You may also write expressions that don't refer to any field at all. For example, you could use the expression SYSDATE to load the current date into a DATE column.

Example: Loading Book Price Data

This example focuses on loading book price data into a table named *book*. The primary key for the table is derived from an Oracle sequence named *book_seq*. You can create the table and the sequence using the following statements:

```
CREATE TABLE book (
    book_id NUMBER,
    book_title VARCHAR2(35),
    book_price NUMBER,
    book_pages NUMBER,
    CONSTRAINT book_pk
        PRIMARY KEY (book_id)
    );

CREATE SEQUENCE book_seq
    START WITH 1
    INCREMENT BY 1
    NOMAXVALUE
    NOCYCLE;
```

Null Values in Expressions

Whenever you write SQL expressions, you need to be aware of the possible effects of null values. The general rule is that null values propagate, so if one value in an expression is null, the result of the expression will also be null. The exceptions to this rule involve functions such as NVL and DECODE that are specifically designed to deal with nulls. The following expression will return a null if the value for the price is null:

```
TO_NUMBER(:price)/100
```

You can use Oracle's built-in NVL function to ensure that you always get a numeric value. In the following example, the NVL function is applied to the *price* field. If the price is not null, then NVL simply returns the value of that field. If the price is null, then NVL returns the alternate value, which in this case is a zero:

```
TO_NUMBER(NVL(:price,0))/100
```

Remember that SQL expressions are evaluated inside the database server. The values they are dealing with are the ones passed in by SQL*Loader to be loaded. All SQL*Loader processing occurs first, which means that any NULLIF or DEFAULTIF clauses will already have been applied.

The data to be loaded resides in an operating system data file, and consists of the book title, price, and page count arranged in the following columnar format:

```
Oracle Essentials                3495 355
SQL*Plus: The Definitive Guide   3995 502
Oracle PL/SQL Programming        4495 987
Oracle8 Design Tips              1495 115
```

The price in this data has an assumed decimal point, which we'll deal with using a SQL expression. To further complicate matters, we'll make up a rule that sets the minimum price for a book at 10 cents per page. The SQL expression for the price field will also enforce that rule. Finally, we'll generate the *book_id* primary key field entirely from an expression. The resulting LOAD statement looks like this:

```
LOAD DATA
   INFILE 'book_prices.dat'
   REPLACE INTO TABLE book
   (
   book_title POSITION(1) CHAR(35),
   book_price POSITION(37)
            "GREATEST(TO_NUMBER(:book_price)/100,
             TO_NUMBER(:book_pages*0.10))",
   book_pages POSITION(42) INTEGER EXTERNAL(3),
   book_id "book_seq.nextval"
   )
```

Notice that the expression for the *book_id* field doesn't refer to any of the fields being loaded. Instead, the value for that field is derived from the Oracle sequence using the *book_seq.nextval* expression. The SQL expression used for the *book_price* field refers not only to the *book_price* field, but also to the *book_pages* field. It's worth pointing out that SQL*Loader allows newline characters within SQL expressions, so the fact that the *book_price* expression takes up two lines is not a problem.

SQL Expressions and Direct Path Loads

SQL expressions represent a powerful feature of SQL*Loader, but up until the Oracle9*i* release, you could only use them in conventional path loads. Direct path loads, which we'll cover in detail in Chapter 10, *Direct Path Loads*, are in many cases more efficient, but prior to Oracle9*i* they did not support the use of SQL expressions. In the past, this has caused a great deal of consternation among programmers and DBAs who wanted to take advantage of both features—SQL expressions and direct path loads—at the same time.

The good news is that Oracle has listened to these frustrations, and if you're running Oracle9*i*, you can perform a direct path load that makes use of SQL expressions. But what do you do if you haven't upgraded to Oracle9*i* yet? If you have to manipulate the data, then the processing to do that manipulation has to take place. Period. End of story. Your only choice is where and when that happens. At a very basic level, you have the following choices:

- Manipulate the data prior to the load.
- Manipulate the data during the load (using SQL expressions).
- Manipulate the data after the load.

You can use SQL expressions in Oracle8 or Oracle8*i*, but that forces you to do a conventional path load, so you'll have to consider the performance hit that you'll take from that. Weigh that against the performance hit that you'll take from pursuing the other two options. Then consider your own capabilities. Sure, it may be more efficient to write a program to reformat your data, but what if you are not a programmer? Or, perhaps you have a PL/SQL programmer in-house who can modify the data, but only after it hits the database. You have to weigh all these options and make some intelligent decision based on your performance needs and your capabilities.

Writing Your Own Functions

You can gain even more flexibility by writing your own functions for use in SQL expressions that you write in SQL*Loader control files. Consider the problem we looked at earlier in this chapter—determining a minimum price for a book based on the page count. The solution shown previously for that problem set the minimum price at 10 cents per page, and is rather simplistic. A more realistic solution would be to define minimum prices that apply as specific page count thresholds are reached. In the following example, the PPT_PAGES column defines a page count at which the corresponding minimum price begins to apply:

```
SQL> SELECT * FROM price_page_threshold;

PPT_PAGES PPT_MIN_PRICE
---------- -------------
        0          9.95
      100         12.95
      200         14.95
      300         29.95
      400         34.95
      500         39.95
      600         43.95
      700         45.95
      800         47.95
      900         49.95
     1000         59.95
```

To get the minimum price for a given page count, you need to find the row with the highest page count that is less than or equal to the number of pages in the book. For example, any page count from 400 to 499 carries a minimum price of $34.95. At 500 pages, the minimum price jumps to $39.95. The following stored PL/SQL function takes current price and page counts as parameters, queries the *price_page_threshold* table, and returns the greater of the current price or the minimum price:

```
CREATE OR REPLACE FUNCTION price_check
                     (price_in NUMBER, pages_in NUMBER)
RETURN NUMBER IS
   min_price NUMBER;
BEGIN
   /* Retrieve the mininum price for the number of pages in question. */
   SELECT ppt_min_price INTO min_price
   FROM price_page_threshold
   WHERE pages_in >= ppt_pages
   AND ppt_pages = (
      SELECT MAX(ppt_pages)
      FROM price_page_threshold
      WHERE pages_in >= ppt_pages);

   /* Return the greater of the minimum or the book price. */
   RETURN GREATEST(min_price,price_in);
END;
/
```

With this function in place, the following LOAD statement can be used to load the book price data shown earlier. Notice that the *price_check* function is invoked in the SQL expression defined for the *book_price* field:

```
LOAD DATA
    INFILE 'book_prices.dat'
    REPLACE INTO TABLE book
    (
    book_title POSITION(1) CHAR(35),
    book_price POSITION(37)
            "price_check(:book_price,:book_pages)",
    book_pages POSITION(42) INTEGER EXTERNAL(3),
    book_id "book_seq.nextval"
    )
```

Remember that any functions you use in a LOAD statement end up being called as part of a SQL INSERT statement. Consequently, the following restrictions apply:

- All your function parameters must be IN parameters. Your function must not attempt to change any of the values that you pass to it.

- Parameter datatypes are limited to database datatypes. These include VARCHAR2, DATE, NUMBER, and CHAR. You cannot use PL/SQL-specific datatypes such as BOOLEAN or PLS_INTEGER.

- Your function must not alter transaction state by issuing a COMMIT, ROLL-BACK, SAVEPOINT, or SET TRANSACTION statement.

- Your function must not issue any ALTER SYSTEM or ALTER SESSION commands.

- Your function should not query any of the tables into which SQL*Loader is inserting data. If you query a table that you are also modifying, you'll get a mutating table error. A *mutating table* is a table that is currently being modified.

- The datatype of your function's return value must be a database datatype such as VARCHAR2, DATE, NUMBER, or CHAR. It cannot be a PL/SQL-specific type.

These restrictions aren't as bad as they may seem. Just stick to database datatypes and SELECT statements, let SQL*Loader handle the transaction logic, and you'll be fine.

Passing Data Through Work Tables

A very general solution to the problem of manipulating data during the load process is to pass the data through a work table. Your load process then becomes something like the following:

1. Load data into the work table.

2. Run programs to manipulate, validate, and modify the data in the work table.

3. Move the data from the work table to your production table.

You have an almost infinite amount of flexibility with this technique. You are essentially writing procedural code to do the actual loading, and using SQL*Loader only for the task of placing the data where your procedural code can easily access it. If the scope of what you need to do can't easily be accommodated using any of the other techniques described in this chapter, you should use this approach.

The disadvantages to using work tables are that you must create and maintain those work tables, and that you must write code—usually PL/SQL code—to manipulate the data that you load into them. You must also move the data twice: once to get it into the work table, and once to move it from the work table to the ultimate destination. Under the right circumstances, some of the other solutions discussed in this chapter allow you to load and modify data in one pass.

Using Triggers

Triggers can sometimes be used to good advantage during a load. If you're loading data into a work table, you can define an INSERT trigger that processes each row as it is loaded. In fact, triggers can be used to preprocess rows that go into any table. This saves you the trouble of invoking a separate program to do that work.

 INSERT triggers are disabled during direct path loads. If you want to use INSERT triggers to manipulate data that you are loading, you need to perform a conventional path load.

One approach to using triggers is to load data into a work table, and create an INSERT trigger on that table to process each row as it is loaded. The INSERT trigger takes care of moving the data to the final destination table. The following statement creates a work table for use when loading the book data shown earlier:

```
CREATE TABLE book_work (
    book_title VARCHAR2(35),
    book_price NUMBER,
    book_pages NUMBER,
    load_flag CHAR(1)
    );
```

With the *book_work* table as the target table for your load, you can then write an INSERT trigger with code to do the following:

1. Compensate for the assumed decimal point in the price.

2. Verify that the price exceeds the minimum for each book's page count.

3. Set the primary key for each book record.

4. Insert the modified record into the *book* table.

5. Set the *load_flag* field in the *book_work* table to indicate whether or not a record has been loaded into the *book* table.

The following trigger, defined as an INSERT trigger on the *book_work* table, will do all these things. Records for books with prices that meet the minimums will be inserted into the *book* table, and the corresponding *book_work* record will have the *load_flag* column set to a 'Y'. When a book price does not meet the minimum, the record will not be inserted into the *book* table, and the *load_flag* value in the *book_work* table will be set to 'N':

```
CREATE OR REPLACE TRIGGER book_work_ins
BEFORE INSERT ON book_work
FOR EACH ROW
DECLARE
    next_book_id NUMBER;
    min_price NUMBER;
BEGIN
    /* Divide price by 100 to compensate for assumed decimal place. */
    :new.book_price:=:new.book_price/100;

    /* Retrieve the minimum price for the number of pages in question. */
    SELECT ppt_min_price INTO min_price
    FROM price_page_threshold
    WHERE :new.book_pages >= ppt_pages
    AND ppt_pages = (
        SELECT MAX(ppt_pages)
        FROM price_page_threshold
        WHERE :new.book_pages >= ppt_pages);

    /* Only load the row if the book price equals or exceeds the minimum. */
    IF :new.book_price >= min_price THEN
        /* Set the BOOK_ID column from the Oracle sequence */
        SELECT book_seq.nextval INTO next_book_id
        FROM dual;

        /* Insert the modified values into the book table. */
        INSERT INTO book
        (book_id, book_title, book_price, book_pages)
        VALUES (next_book_id, :new.book_title, :new.book_price,
                :new.book_pages);

        /* Set the flag to indicate that this record has been processed. */
        :new.load_flag:='Y';
    ELSE
        :new.load_flag:='N';
    END IF;
END;
/
```

With this trigger in place, the LOAD statement for the book price data becomes very simple. No SQL expressions are needed. All you want SQL*Loader to do now is to load the data as is, straight into the *book_work* table. Every row that SQL*Loader inserts will fire the INSERT trigger. The INSERT trigger then computes the book price and inserts the resulting row into the *book* table. The following LOAD statement could be used:

```
LOAD DATA
    INFILE 'book_prices.dat'
    REPLACE INTO TABLE book_work
    (
    book_title POSITION(1) CHAR(35),
    book_price POSITION(37) INTEGER EXTERNAL(4),
    book_pages POSITION(42) INTEGER EXTERNAL(3)
    )
```

Once the load is complete, you can query the *book_work* table to find out which records did not load. For example, you could use a query such as this:

```
SELECT *
FROM book_work
WHERE load_flag='N';
```

You can also issue a DELETE statement to remove records from the work table that have been successfully loaded. Alternatively, you can just leave all the records in the work table, and ensure that you use REPLACE or TRUNCATE the next time you load data. That way, the work table will be cleared out at the beginning of each load.

One issue to be aware of when using triggers as described here is that the REPLACE, TRUNCATE, and APPEND clauses of the LOAD statement will apply to the table being loaded, and that will be the work table, not the ultimate destination table.

Performing Character Set Conversion

Character set conversion is another of SQL*Loader's many capabilities. The term *character set* refers to the specific numeric encoding used to represent characters in a data file. ASCII encoding, or some variation of it, is probably the most common encoding encountered today. However, a very large number of different encodings exist. EBCDIC is an example of another, somewhat less common, encoding. If you've ever worked on an IBM mainframe, or loaded data originating from such a legacy system, you're no doubt familiar with EBCDIC. In addition, if you work with languages other than English, you may be familiar with one of the many language-specific encoding schemes that allow for characters other than the 26 letters used in the English alphabet.

INSTEAD OF Triggers

Can you leverage the power of INSTEAD OF triggers using SQL*Loader? As you may know, INSTEAD OF triggers allow you to define PL/SQL code that is executed instead of an INSERT, UPDATE, or DELETE statement. Is it possible, then, to create an INSTEAD OF trigger for a work table to intercept INSERT statements executed by SQL*Loader? Such a trigger, if it could be created, would result in an empty work table when the load was finished.

Unfortunately, you can't make use of INSTEAD OF triggers in the same manner that the examples in this chapter make use of regular triggers. First, INSTEAD OF triggers may only be defined against views, not tables. Second, SQL*Loader always checks to be sure you are loading a table by executing a SQL statement such as the following:

```
SELECT 'X'
FROM all_objects
WHERE object_name = :1
   AND owner = :2
   AND object_type = 'TABLE'
```

You can easily verify this by enabling Oracle's built-in SQL Trace facility and running a SQL*Loader session. If you could specify a view as the target of a load, you could take advantage of INSTEAD OF triggers. But you can't specify a view. You can only load into a table, so you can only utilize the standard DML triggers.

*SQL*Loader and Character Sets*

With respect to SQL*Loader and character sets, you need to think in terms of the following:

- The character set used in the SQL*Loader control file. This is referred to as the *session character set.*

- The character set used in the data file that you are loading. You can specify this using the CHARACTERSET clause in your SQL*Loader control file.

- The character set used in the destination database. This is referred to as the *database character set.* If you are loading an NCHAR, NVARCHAR2, or NCLOB column, this ends up being the *national character set* that you have specified for such columns.

It's entirely possible that all three character sets are one and the same, but that doesn't need to be the case. If the character set used in your data file differs from that used in the database itself, SQL*Loader may be able to convert between the two. How that's done depends in part on whether you are doing a direct path load or a conventional path load. Figure 8-1 illustrates the difference between the two paths when it comes to character set conversion.

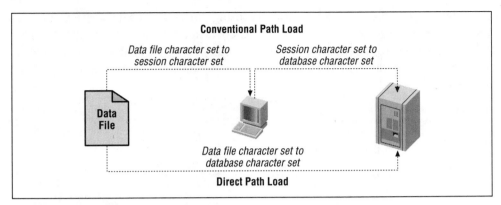

Figure 8-1. Character set conversion

In a conventional path load, data is read from the data file, and inserted into the database using standard INSERT statements. The database server expects the incoming data to match the session character set being used by SQL*Loader. The session character set refers to the character set used by the operating system session from which the SQL*Loader executable is running, and is controlled by the NLS_LANG environment variable setting. If NLS_LANG is not set, the character set defaults to a platform-specific value. For example, on Windows systems, the default session character set is WE8ISO8859P1. The key point, though, is that in a conventional path load, SQL*Loader converts data from the data file character set to the session character set. The Oracle server then converts from the session character set to the database character set.

Things are very different when a direct path load is done. In a direct path load, SQL*Loader formats database blocks and passes them directly to the server where they are written to disk. The server never processes any INSERT statements; hence, the server never does any character set conversion of its own. In this case, SQL*Loader must convert directly from the data file character set to the database character set.

Data in the SQL*Loader control file

SQL*Loader always expects the control file to be in the session character set. This is true not only for the LOAD statement, but also for any data that happens to be in the control file. You cannot perform character set conversion on control file data. If you specify terminating or enclosing characters as strings in the control file, SQL*Loader is supposed to convert those from the session character set used in the control file to the data file character set used for the data. In Oracle release 8.1.6

this didn't work correctly. The workaround—if you are using release 8.1.6—is to specify terminating and enclosing characters in hexadecimal.

Consider the problem of a control file using an ASCII character set such as US7ASCII, and a data file using an EBCDIC character set such as WE8EBCDIC37C. A comma in ASCII is represented by the value X'2C' (decimal 44). A comma in EBCDIC is X'6B' (decimal 107). You could try writing a LOAD statement such as the following:

```
LOAD DATA
   CHARACTERSET 'WE8EBCDIC37C'
   INFILE 'ebcdic.dat'
   REPLACE INTO TABLE book_work
   (
   book_title CHAR TERMINATED BY ','
   ...
   )
```

The problem is that SQL*Loader would read the control file and see that comma as X'2C', but that value would never be found in the data file. Because the data file is in EBCDIC, the comma delimiter would be represented there as X'6B'. The only way around this is to use hexadecimal notation in your control file to specify the delimiter. For example:

```
LOAD DATA
   CHARACTERSET 'WE8EBCDIC37C'
   INFILE 'ebcdic.dat'
   REPLACE INTO TABLE book_work
   (
   book_title CHAR TERMINATED BY X'6B'
   ...
   )
```

Now SQL*Loader will see the termination character as X'6B', and that will match the "comma" used in the EBCDIC data file.

Datatypes affected

Character set conversion does not apply to all datatypes supported by SQL*Loader. It's only applicable to character datatypes. The following SQL*Loader datatypes are character datatypes for which character set conversion takes place:

CHAR
DATE
VARCHARC
VARCHAR
INTEGER EXTERNAL
DECIMAL EXTERNAL
ZONED EXTERNAL

FLOAT EXTERNAL
DOUBLE EXTERNAL

The many machine-specific binary types are not subject to character set conversion. If you need a refresher on the use of these datatypes, refer back to Chapter 3.

Characters that can't be converted

Sometimes when data is converted between two character sets, you run into situations where a character in the source character set has no analog in the destination character set. This is definitely a situation you want to avoid, because you'll lose data. When SQL*Loader, or the Oracle server for that matter, is unable to convert a character to the destination character set, that character will be replaced with a default character. A default character is simply one that has been designated for use in representing a character that couldn't be converted. In some ASCII-based character sets, this default character is a question mark (?). When you convert data from one character set to another, you need to make sure that at least one of the following conditions is true:

- The destination character set must be a superset of the first. In other words, it must contain all the characters in the source character set.

- Your data must not use any characters in the source character set that are not represented in the destination character set.

Failure to meet at least one of these conditions will result in data loss due to characters that cannot be converted.

Syntax for Specifying the Character Set

You specify the character set of your input data using the CHARACTERSET clause of the LOAD statement. By default, SQL*Loader expects the data file to use the session character set. Use the CHARACTERSET clause when that's not the case. The following syntax highlights the location of this clause, which appears just prior to your INFILE clauses:

```
[UNRECOVERABLE | RECOVERABLE] {LOAD | CONTINUE_LOAD} [DATA]
    [CHARACTERSET character_set]
    [INFILE clause [INFILE clause...]]
```

Oracle supports a huge variety of character sets, and it's not possible to describe, or even list, them all here. If you need detailed information on the character sets that Oracle supports, see the *Oracle8i National Language Support Guide*.

Character Set Example

The following LOAD statement provides an example of how to specify a character
set. In this case, the character set is an EBCDIC character set named
WE8EBCDIC37C. Look for the CHARACTERSET clause in the second line of the
LOAD command:

```
LOAD DATA
    CHARACTERSET 'WE8EBCDIC37C'
    INFILE 'book_prices.dat'
    REPLACE INTO TABLE book
    (
    book_title POSITION(1) CHAR(35),
    book_price POSITION(37)
            "GREATEST(TO_NUMBER(:book_price)/100,
             TO_NUMBER(:book_pages*0.10))",
    book_pages POSITION(42) INTEGER EXTERNAL(3),
    book_id "book_seq.nextval"
    )
```

In a conventional path load, SQL*Loader will convert input data from EBCDIC to
the session character set, and the database server will convert from the session
character set to the database character set. If a direct path load is done,
SQL*Loader will convert directly from EBCDIC to the database character set.

Transaction Size and Performance Issues

Performance plays a very important role in the success of any system—hardware, software, utility—anything you can think of. SQL*Loader provides many ways to control or improve its performance. Previous chapters occasionally discussed performance issues, or mentioned parameters, clauses, or keywords that relate to the performance of SQL*Loader. In this chapter, we consolidate the discussion of SQL*Loader's performance, explore issues involved with it, and show you ways to control and improve it.

The discussion in this chapter mainly focuses on performance when doing a conventional path load. Direct path loads, because they are performed so differently from conventional path loads, lead to an almost completely different set of performance issues. You'll find a detailed discussion of direct path loads, including performance issues, in Chapter 10, *Direct Path Loads*.

Transaction Processing in SQL*Loader

When you load data using SQL*Loader, it prepares SQL INSERT statements for the input data, and passes those statements to the Oracle server. The Oracle server then processes those statements as it loads the data. From the standpoint of the Oracle server, this insertion of data into Oracle tables is nothing but a series of regular transactions. The Oracle server handles these transactions just as it does any other transactions. For each transaction, the Oracle server does the following:

1. Obtains a lock on the table being loaded.

2. Records undo information in the rollback segments.

3. Inserts the input data in the appropriate data blocks in the database buffer cache.

4. Records the changes in the redo log files.

5. Updates any indexes that are affected by the new rows. Steps two through four are applied to each index being updated.

As you can see, there's quite a bit of overhead involved in this transaction logic. But there's more work yet to come. A transaction completes with a commit, and at every commit, the Oracle server does the following:

1. Records a commit entry into the database redo log.

2. Releases the rollback segment space for reuse.

3. Releases the lock on the table.

4. Releases any index locks.

SQL*Loader provides ways to control the size and frequency of these transactions during a data load process. You can divide a data load into several transactions, or you can perform it as one, very large transaction. As you no doubt surmise by now, this is a game of tradeoffs. The larger the size of your transactions, the more rollback segment space you'll need. On the other hand, smaller transaction sizes lead to more frequent commits and all the overhead that goes with them. It follows that controlling your commit frequency, and thus the size of your transactions, is the most important key to the performance of a conventional path load.

Commit Frequency and Load Performance

SQL*Loader prepares an area in memory where it stores the data for the rows to be loaded. This area is called the *bind array*. SQL*Loader reads multiple records from your input data files, parses out the fields in those records according to your field specifications, and places the resulting data into the bind array. When the bind array becomes full, all the data in it is inserted into the database in one transaction. In essence, the size of the bind array determines the maximum number of rows that will be inserted in one transaction, and thus plays a very important role in the performance of SQL*Loader.

You can use the following three command-line parameters to control the size of the bind array:

READSIZE
BINDSIZE
ROWS

You can specify these parameters on the command line as shown in the following example:

```
sqlldr CONTROL=places.ctl READSIZE=20971520 BINDSIZE=20971520 ROWS=20000
```

As discussed in Chapter 2, *The Mysterious Control File*, you can also specify these parameters in the control file using the OPTIONS statement. For example:

```
OPTIONS (READSIZE=20971520, BINDSIZE=20971520, ROWS=20000)
LOAD DATA
...
```

Options specified on the command line always override those specified in the control file. So if you specify the same option in both places, the command-line value will be the one that is used. The following sections describe the three bind array parameters.

READSIZE

The READSIZE parameter specifies the size of the buffer used by SQL*Loader when reading data from the input data file. The default size of this buffer is 64K, or 65,536 bytes. You can specify a different buffer size using the READSIZE parameter. The value that you specify for READSIZE must be in terms of bytes, and it is subject to a platform-specific limit. For Windows NT and most Unix platforms, the maximum value possible for the READSIZE parameter is 20,971,520 bytes, which works out to 20 MB. If you specify a value larger than the upper limit supported by your platform, SQL*Loader will generate an error as shown in the following example:

```
D:\testdb>sqlldr user/pass@db control=seller.ctl readsize=40000000

SQL*Loader: Release 8.1.6.0.0 - Production on Tue Jan 2 12:52:32 2001

(c) Copyright 1999 Oracle Corporation.  All rights reserved.

SQL*Loader-500: Unable to open file (seller2.dat)
SQL*Loader-555: unrecognized processing option
```

The error messages shown here are a bit misleading. The first error—"Unable to open file"—may lead to you to believe that the input file is nonexistent or corrupt. That's not the case. The second error—"unrecognized processing option"—makes the source of the problem a bit clearer, but we wonder why Oracle couldn't just program in an error message stating that the user had specified too large a value for READSIZE.

The value you specify for READSIZE affects the minimum value for the BINDSIZE setting. If you specify both a BINDSIZE and a READSIZE, and your BINDSIZE is smaller than your READSIZE, SQL*Loader will automatically increase BINDSIZE to match the larger READSIZE value. It's important to realize, though, that the bind array size might actually end up being less than the BINDSIZE value. This interplay between BINDSIZE, READSIZE, and ROWS can sometimes be rather difficult to follow.

BINDSIZE

The BINDSIZE parameter specifies the maximum size of the bind array. The default value for the BINDSIZE parameter is 65,536, or 64 KB (256 KB in Oracle9*i*). The BINDSIZE value is specified in bytes and, like READSIZE, is subject to a platform-specific limit. For Windows NT and most Unix platforms, the BINDSIZE limit is the same as the READSIZE limit of 20,971,520 bytes (20 MB). If you specify a value larger than the upper limit supported by your platform, SQL*Loader will generate errors similar to those you get when you specify too large a value for the READSIZE parameter. In the following command, the BINDSIZE parameter is used to specify a bind array size of 500,000 bytes:

```
sqlldr user/pass@db control=gnis.ctl bindsize=500000
```

At a minimum, the bind array must be able to hold one row of data. If you specify a value for BINDSIZE such that the resulting bind array can't hold a single row of data to be inserted into the database, then SQL*Loader will abort with an error, as shown in the following example:

```
D:\testdb>sqlldr user/pass@db control=gnis.ctl readsize=20 bindsize=20

SQL*Loader: Release 8.1.6.0.0 - Production on Thu Jan 11 16:22:01 2001

(c) Copyright 1999 Oracle Corporation.  All rights reserved.

SQL*Loader-510: Physical record in data file (gnis.dat) is longer than the
maximum(20)
```

Another important point regarding the bind array is that the entire memory allocated for it need not be contiguous. However, the memory allocated for each field within the bind array must be contiguous. In extreme situations, where your memory is highly fragmented, you might also receive an error if SQL*Loader can't find a contiguous block of memory large enough for each field that you are loading.

There's a strange interplay between BINDSIZE and READSIZE. You read in the previous section that READSIZE imposes a lower limit on the size of the bind array. The converse is also true. The BINDSIZE value places a lower limit on the size of the input buffer. If you specify different values for these two parameters, SQL*Loader will adjust them in such a way that the higher of the two values will be used for both parameters. When SQL*Loader adjusts the READSIZE, you'll get a message such as the one shown in the following example:

```
D:\testdb>sqlldr tstusr/tstusr@testdb control=seller.ctl readsize=200000
              bindsize=400000

SQL*Loader: Release 8.1.6.0.0 - Production on Tue Jan 2 21:04:54 2001

(c) Copyright 1999 Oracle Corporation.  All rights reserved.

specified value for readsize(200000) less than bindsize(400000)
...
```

The message is only informational. Processing will continue without any problem. Oddly enough, when you specify a BINDSIZE that is lower than the READSIZE value, SQL*Loader will silently adjust BINDSIZE to the READSIZE value, and no messages will be displayed.

ROWS

The ROWS parameter specifies the number of rows in the bind array. This represents the number of rows that SQL*Loader loads with each INSERT statement and, therefore, represents the commit frequency. The default value for the ROWS parameter is 64.

The relationship between ROWS and BINDSIZE is complex and a bit confusing. It's best to think of BINDSIZE as specifying the maximum amount of memory to allocate for the bind array. The amount of memory actually allocated will be the amount required to accommodate the number of rows of data specified by the ROWS parameter. If you specify too large a value for ROWS, BINDSIZE will not be increased to accommodate that value. Instead, ROWS will be decreased to a value that can be accommodated by the BINDSIZE. In addition to all of this, SQL*Loader will only allocate as much memory as is required to hold the number of rows that you specify. If you specify a BINDSIZE value far larger than that required for the number of rows specified by ROWS, SQL*Loader will not waste memory. The bind array size will be limited to that necessary to accommodate the number of rows you requested.

The SQL*Loader log file indicates the value of the BINDSIZE parameter. You'll see a log entry like this:

```
Bind array:     20000 rows, maximum of 20971520 bytes
```

This indicates that a bind array will be allocated to hold 20,000 rows, limited to a maximum size of 20,971,520 bytes. The log file also indicates the actual size of the bind array allocated. Look for a line such as the following:

```
Space allocated for bind array:              20640000 bytes(20000 rows)
```

This indicates that 20,000 rows were accommodated in 20,640,000 bytes, which is less than the maximum number of 20,971,520, as specified by the BINDSIZE parameter. We used a row size of 1032 bytes to generate this example. If the rows were larger, say 2048 bytes each, then the bind array would have been the maximum size of 20,971,520 bytes, and the number of rows would have been adjusted downwards to the 10,240 that would fit in that space.

Large Versus Small Bind Arrays

You now know how to control the size of SQL*Loader's bind array, and thus its commit frequency. This naturally leads to the question of how to make the right choices. There's no easy answer to the question of what size bind array to use. Sizing the bind array involves a set of tradeoffs, which are highlighted in Table 9-1.

Table 9-1. Sizing the Bind Array

	Small Bind Array	Large Bind Array
Advantages	Requires less memory. More frequent commits mean less data lost in the event of a failure. Rollback segments can be smaller.	Fewer commits result in less transaction-related overhead.
Disadvantages	More frequent commits result in more transaction-related overhead.	Requires more memory. Fewer commits mean more data lost in the event of a failure. Rollback segments must be correspondingly large.

Generally speaking, the larger your bind array, the better will be your performance. The tradeoff is that you need enough memory to support the bind array, and the rollback segments in your database need to be large enough to accommodate the resulting transactions.

It is also true that a larger transaction size means that more data is lost in the event that SQL*Loader aborts because of an error. When SQL*Loader aborts, none of the records processed since the most recent commit will be saved in the database. If you restart the load, you'll need to read those records again. The number of rows that you need to reread is limited to the number of rows in your bind array, so the larger your bind array, the more data file records you will potentially need to reprocess. In our experience, this is usually a secondary issue. The time required to recover from a failure is not the primary driver behind the size of the bind array. It's just something to be aware of.

Let's look at an example that shows the impact of the size of the bind array on load performance. The following control file loads 120,001 records into a table:

```
OPTIONS (READSIZE=20971520, BINDSIZE=20971520)
LOAD DATA
INFILE waterfalls.dat
INSERT INTO TABLE gnis.waterfalls
FIELDS TERMINATED BY '^'
(falls_name, falls_county, falls_state TERMINATED BY WHITESPACE)
```

Notice that we have not specified any value for the ROWS parameter. Therefore, SQL*Loader will use the default value of 64. A section of the resulting log file follows; it indicates the size of the bind array allocated and the time taken for the load:

```
...
Bind array:     64 rows, maximum of 20971520 bytes
...
Space allocated for bind array:                   66048 bytes(64 rows)
Space allocated for memory besides bind array:       0 bytes

Total logical records skipped:         0
Total logical records read:       120001
Total logical records rejected:        0
Total logical records discarded:       0

Run began on Tue Jan 02 12:22:30 2001
Run ended on Tue Jan 02 12:23:41 2001

Elapsed time was:     00:01:10.48
CPU time was:         00:00:05.37
```

Even though a value of 20,971,520 was specified for BINDSIZE, SQL*Loader allocated only 66,048 bytes for the bind array. That's because 66,048 bytes was all that it took to hold 64 rows. The elapsed time for the load was 1 minute and 10.48 seconds. Now, let's try the same load again, but after increasing the bind array so that it holds 5000 rows. The following control file does this:

```
OPTIONS (READSIZE=20971520, BINDSIZE=20971520, ROWS=5000)
LOAD DATA
INFILE waterfalls.dat
INSERT INTO TABLE gnis.waterfalls
FIELDS TERMINATED BY '^'
(falls_name, falls_county, falls_state TERMINATED BY WHITESPACE)
```

Following is the same section of the log file as before, but for this new load. Notice the difference in the bind array size, and in the elapsed time for the load:

```
...
Bind array:     5000 rows, maximum of 20971520 bytes
...
Space allocated for bind array:                 5160000 bytes(5000 rows)
Space allocated for memory besides bind array:       0 bytes
```

```
Total logical records skipped:        0
Total logical records read:      120001
Total logical records rejected:       0
Total logical records discarded:      0

Run began on Tue Jan 02 12:25:15 2001
Run ended on Tue Jan 02 12:26:00 2001

Elapsed time was:       00:00:45.32
CPU time was:           00:00:03.93
```

With ROWS specified as 5000, SQL*Loader allocated 5,160,000 bytes for the bind array. That was the size required to store 5000 records. The increase in bind array size led to an increase in performance. The load time decreased from 1 minute, 10.48 seconds to 45.32 seconds.

Setting READSIZE, BINDSIZE, and ROWS

You can see after reading the material in the past few sections that the relationships between the values for READSIZE, BINDSIZE, and ROWS can be complex and a bit confusing. In the following list, we provide a few practical tips for setting these values:

- Default values are usually adequate for loads involving small amounts of data.

- For loads involving large amounts of data, you should override the defaults and specify larger values to get better performance.

- It is general practice to set READSIZE and BINDSIZE to the same value. There is no point in setting these to different values, because SQL*Loader changes the settings to use the higher of the two values for both the parameters. Some people set only BINDSIZE and allow SQL*Loader to automatically adjust the READSIZE value to match.

- There is a hard limit on the maximum permissible value of READSIZE and BINDSIZE. On Windows NT and on most Unix platforms, that limit is 20 MB.

- There is no limit on the value of ROWS per se, but the actual number of rows is limited by the maximum limit on the BINDSIZE value.

- You should try to accommodate from 1000 to 5000 rows in the bind array. We have seen, on most machines, that a bind array with 1000 to 5000 rows gives reasonably good performance. Experiment to find the best values for your own environment.

Commit Frequency and Rollback Segments

So far in this chapter, you've learned how you can influence SQL*Loader's performance by controlling the commit frequency. You've seen that you can improve load performance by increasing the size of the bind array. However, a larger bind array equates to a longer time between commits, which, in turn, means that more undo information needs to be maintained. In other words, the larger your bind array, the larger your rollback segments need to be.

Rollback Segment Errors

If you specify a large bind array, and your rollback segments are not large enough to record all the undo information for the resulting transaction size, you'll receive an error when you run your load. You'll actually receive an error for each record that fails to load up to the limit you specify using the ERRORS option. With respect to rollback segments and transaction size, there are two potential problems you need to be aware of:

- Your rollback segments may not be able to extend because they hit the MAXEXTENTS limit.

- Your rollback segments may not be able to extend due to a lack of free space in the rollback segment tablespace.

If you're running a load with large transactions, and your rollback segments cannot extend enough to accommodate those transactions, you will see errors such as the following in your SQL*Loader log file:

```
Record 3286: Rejected - Error on table GNIS.WATERFALLS.
ORA-01562: failed to extend rollback segment number 5
ORA-01628: max # extents (6) reached for rollback segment RB4
```

This particular error indicates that the rollback segment reached its maximum extent (MAXEXTENTS) limit. To solve this problem, you need to increase the maximum number of extents allowed for the rollback segment. You can do that from SQL*Plus using an ALTER ROLLBACK SEGMENT statement such as the following:

```
ALTER ROLLBACK SEGMENT rb4
    STORAGE (MAXEXTENTS 200);
```

The other type of error you may encounter is that of insufficient free space in the rollback segment tablespace. For example:

```
Record 2306: Rejected - Error on table GNIS.WATERFALLS.
ORA-01562: failed to extend rollback segment number 1
ORA-01650: unable to extend rollback segment RB1 by 13 in tablespace RBS
```

The rollback segment in this example wasn't limited by MAXEXTENTS. It should have been able to extend, but it couldn't because there wasn't enough free space remaining in the rollback segment tablespace to accommodate the new extent. To solve this problem, you need to increase the size of your tablespace. One way to do that is by adding a new datafile to it. For example, the following statement adds a 20-megabyte datafile to the tablespace named RBS:

```
ALTER TABLESPACE RBS
    ADD DATAFILE '/u01/oradata/rbs_02.dat' SIZE 20M;
```

As an alternative to adding a new datafile, resize one of the existing datafiles.

Estimating Rollback Segment Requirements

Because you don't want to run a load only to have it fail, it follows that you should make sure you have sufficiently large rollback segments before you begin. To estimate the rollback segment size requirement for a load, we recommend that you start with the size of the bind array, and increase that by 30% to account for overhead. You can use the following procedure to do this:

1. Determine the size of a single row.

2. Determine the size of the bind array.

3. Estimate the size of the rollback segment required.

The following sections describe each step in detail.

Step 1: Determine the size of a single row

Your first step is to determine the size of a single row for the table you are load-ing. You can do this by running a fictitious load prior to running the actual load. By "fictitious load," we mean one that doesn't really load any data. Consider the following control file:

```
OPTIONS(ROWS=1)
LOAD DATA
    INFILE *
    INSERT INTO TABLE tstusr.seller
    FIELDS TERMINATED BY '^'
    (falls_name, falls_county, falls_state TERMINATED BY WHITESPACE)
BEGINDATA
```

As you can see, there's no actual data in this control file. The INFILE * clause causes SQL*Loader to read data from the control file. It will expect that data to fol-low the BEGINDATA keyword. Since there is no data, nothing will be loaded. That's OK, though, because you are really interested only in getting the row size from the log file. The ROWS=1 option was used to allocate a bind array for just one row. The result is that the bind array size will match the row size. You can get the bind array size, and hence the row size, from the log file. Look for a message in the log file such as the following:

```
Space allocated for bind array:                    1028 bytes(1 rows)
```

This particular message indicates that SQL*Loader allocated a bind array of 1028 bytes for one row. Therefore, the row size is 1028 bytes.

Step 2: Determine the size of the bind array

Now that you know the size of a single row, you can determine the size of the bind array for your actual load. Get the values of ROWS and BINDSIZE for your actual load, and compute the size of the required bind array using the following formula:

```
memory = ROWS * rowsize
bindArraySize = min(BINDSIZE,memory)
```

Getting back to our example with a 1028-byte row size, the following calculations show the ultimate size of the bind array that would result from specifying ROWS=1000 BINDSIZE=10000000:

```
1028000 = 1000 * 1028
bindArraySize = min (10000000,1028000)
bindArraySize = 1028000
```

As you can see, a 10,000,000-byte bind array is far larger than is necessary to accommodate 1000 rows of 1028 bytes each. SQL*Loader won't waste the space. It will allocate only the amount of memory necessary for the number of rows that you specify. When you specify a value for ROWS, the BINDSIZE value serves as an upper limit on the bind array size.

Step 3: Estimate the size of the rollback segment required

When estimating the needed rollback segment size, our recommendation is to add 30% for overhead to the bind array size. The following continues our example, and illustrates how this is done:

```
rollbackSegmentSize = 1.3 * bindArraySize
rollbackSegmentSize = 1.3 * 1028000
rollbackSegmentSize = 1336400
```

Once you get an idea of the total size required, you can create one or more rollback segments for the load by specifying suitable values for their INITIAL, NEXT, and MAXEXTENTS storage parameters. The following example shows one approach that will work for our example:

```
CREATE ROLLBACK SEGMENT RBS10
    STORAGE (INITIAL 256K NEXT 256K MAXEXTENTS 8)
    TABLESPACE RBS;
```

The INITIAL and NEXT values specify extent sizes of 256K. We recommend that you always use the same value for both INITIAL and NEXT. The MAXEXTENTS value limits this rollback segment to a maximum of eight such extents. The maximum size for the rollback segment as a whole can then be computed as follows:

```
8 * 256K = 2MB
```

Two megabytes (2,097,152 bytes) is actually substantially more than our estimated requirement of 1,336,400 bytes.

Don't forget that rollback segment size can be limited not only by MAXEXTENTS, but also by the amount of free space in your rollback segment tablespace. Make sure you have enough free space for your rollback segments to grow to their maximum size.

Using the Right Rollback Segments

A database generally has a pool of rollback segments. Transactions, including those started by SQL*Loader, select a rollback segment randomly from this pool. Therefore, you never know which rollback segment, or segments, will be picked up for your SQL*Loader transactions. If you're writing your own code, you can use the SET TRANSACTION USE ROLLBACK SEGMENT statement to specify the rollback segment to use for a given transaction. Unfortunately, SQL*Loader doesn't provide you with any mechanism for doing that. If you have a mix of rollback segments of varying sizes in your database, how then do you get SQL*Loader to use the ones that are right for your load? There are two options that we can suggest:

- Make all rollback segments large enough for your load.

- Take all rollback segments offline except for those large enough to handle your load.

If you make all rollback segments large enough to handle your load, you don't need to worry about which one randomly gets picked. It won't matter, because each is as good as the others. This approach is usually feasible only when you're loading a small amount of data, because in such cases the required rollback segment size will be reasonably small. This approach is also useful if you need to perform your load during normal business hours when other users are using the database.

The second option is to create one rollback segment large enough to handle your load, and then take all other rollback segments offline right before you begin the load. That way, the only rollback segment online and available will be the one that you want SQL*Loader to use. The drawback here, of course, is that this interferes with the normal use of the database. It's a good solution for loads done during off hours, but it won't work if your users need to have access to the database while you are loading your data.

Performance Improvement Guidelines

The bind array size is just one factor to look at when considering SQL*Loader performance. In our own personal experience, we've found that there are a number of other things that you can consider doing in order to improve load performance. These are described in the following list:

Drop indexes before loading

> If you are loading a substantial amount of data, we recommend dropping the indexes on the table before loading. After the load is complete, you can recreate the indexes. At some point, when you load enough data, it becomes less costly to rebuild the indexes from scratch than to maintain them during the load. However, indexes associated with primary key and unique key constraints should never be dropped. To do so sacrifices data integrity.

Use TRUNCATE instead of REPLACE

> If you want to delete existing data from a table before loading it, we recommend using the TRUNCATE keyword instead of REPLACE in your INTO TABLE clause. The TRUNCATE keyword results in a TRUNCATE statement being executed to remove existing data, and that will execute much, much faster than the DELETE statement used as a result of the REPLACE keyword. See Chapter 2 for more details on this issue.

Use a larger bind array

> We've already discussed this issue earlier in the chapter. Generally, the bigger the bind array, the better your performance. Oracle recommends that you use a bind array that's at least large enough to accommodate 100 rows. Our own experience has been that bind arrays large enough to accommodate 1000 to 5000 rows yield the best performance.

Use larger redo log files

> Redo log files record all transactions against a database. Every time a redo log file gets filled, a checkpoint occurs, and the Oracle server must write all modified data blocks from the buffer cache to the disk. Frequent checkpoints are a common performance bottleneck. If you are loading a large amount of data, you will generate a large amount of redo. Creating larger redo log files is one way to minimize the resulting checkpoint activity.

Adjusting redo log file sizes is usually considered an instance-level tuning activity. There's more at stake than just the performance of SQL*Loader. Your DBA may not want to make such adjustments to improve the performance of a single load job.

Disable archiving while loading

Database archiving is necessary if you want to recover lost data in the event of a drive or other media failure. However, if you are loading an extremely large amount of data, the redo log files will fill up frequently, and consequently they will frequently need to be copied to the archive log destination. This may reduce load performance. If circumstances allow, and the amount of data is extremely large, your DBA may be able to disable archiving for the duration of your load, thus eliminating this potential overhead. Bear in mind that there are many reasons why this may not be feasible.

Avoid use of CONTINUEIF and CONCATENATE

If at all possible, prepare your input data in such a way that you have a one-to-one correspondence between physical and logical records. The use of CONTINUEIF and CONCATENATE to join multiple logical records into one physical record involves some amount of overhead. If you can avoid that overhead, so much the better.

Load fixed-width data instead of delimited data if at all possible

If you have the option of loading from either fixed-width or delimited data files, choose the fixed-width data. You'll save the rather significant overhead of scanning each record for delimiters. In one experiment we conducted it took 1 minute, 50.25 seconds to load 120,000 records from a delimited file. It only took 1 minute, 3.42 seconds to load that same data from a file that had the data arranged in fixed-width columns.

Avoid character set conversion

SQL*Loader supports character set conversion between the character set used in the input data file and the character set used by the database server. However, character set conversion takes time and requires CPU resources. If you can keep all character sets the same, you avoid that overhead and speed up your load.

Avoid unnecessary NULLIF and DEFAULTIF clauses

Any NULLIF or DEFAULTIF clauses that you specify in your control file need to be evaluated for each row in your input file. This poses a considerable amount of processing overhead. Avoid any NULLIF and DEFAULT clauses that you can, and your load will run that much faster.

Perform direct path loads

A direct path load is one in which SQL*Loader writes directly to your database's datafiles. This results in a significant performance improvement—often by one or two orders of magnitude. Direct path loads can't be used in all circumstances, but when they can be used, the performance benefits are significant. Read more about direct path loads in Chapter 10.

Please bear in mind that this is just a list of suggestions that you may be able to take advantage of in order to improve the performance of a load. It's unlikely that you will be able to follow all these suggestions, or even that you will need to follow them all. You have to consider the particular requirements associated with the data being loaded. For example, the format of your incoming data may require that you use CONTINUEIF to concatenate records. You also must consider the resources at your disposal. There are a variety of reasons why you may not be in a position to drop and recreate indexes. You may not be a DBA. You may not have the time. Your users may need access to the tables while data is being loaded, and thus require that the indexes remain. If you can take advantage of some of these suggestions, by all means do so, but don't look at them as hard-and-fast rules that you must follow at any cost.

Direct Path Loads

All the SQL*Loader examples that we've discussed in previous chapters have been conventional path loads. These use the standard SQL interface to load data into an Oracle database—in other words, conventional INSERT statements are used. Conventional path loads involve all the overhead of standard SQL statement processing. Consequently, severe bottlenecks may occur while loading large amounts of data. To help you avoid these bottlenecks, Oracle provides another load mechanism—the direct path load—that bypasses standard SQL processing. Under the right circumstances, direct path loads can be orders of magnitudes faster than conventional path loads. However, like any other performance-enhancing feature, direct path loads come with a set of tradeoffs.

What is the Direct Path?

You really have to understand direct path loads in terms of what they are *not*. Let's look at how a conventional path load works. When you invoke SQL*Loader to load data from a file into an Oracle database, SQL*Loader goes through the process shown in Figure 10-1.

A direct path load works differently. Rather than load data using a series of INSERT statements, a direct path load results in data being written directly into the database datafiles. SQL*Loader reads the input data, formats it into database blocks that match the Oracle data block format, and writes those blocks directly into new extents above the high-water mark (HWM) of the table being loaded. Figure 10-2 illustrates this.

As you can see from Figure 10-2, much of the overhead involved with executing INSERT statements has been eliminated. No SQL statements need to be parsed and executed. Blocks in the database buffer cache are not accessed. No attempt is made

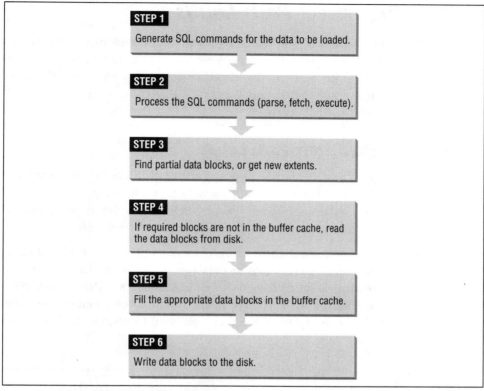

Figure 10-1. A conventional path load

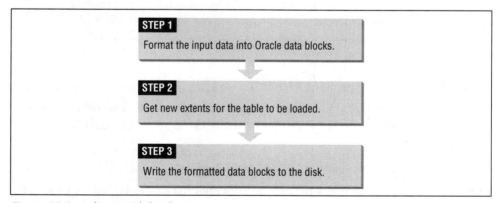

Figure 10-2. A direct path load

to search out free space in existing blocks, and no rollback information is written to the rollback segments. The need to write rollback information is avoided by writing the new data blocks above the high-water mark. If the load succeeds, SQL*Loader adjusts the HWM to include the new data in the table. If the load fails, SQL*Loader does not adjust the HWM, and it will be as if the load was never performed.

Performing Direct Path Loads

Now that you know that direct path loads improve load performance significantly, you probably would like to know how to actually perform a direct path load. We discuss this in detail in this section. We also discuss various keywords that you need to know and use while performing direct path loads, and various issues and restrictions associated with such loads.

Preparing to Use Direct Path Loads

Several data dictionary views exist to support direct path loads. These views are created by a SQL*Plus script named *catldr.sql*, which resides in your *$ORACLE_HOME/rdbms/admin* directory. They are used by SQL*Loader when performing a direct path load, so you can't perform such a load unless the views exist.

The *catldr.sql* script is one of the scripts invoked by *catalog.sql*, and it should have been executed when you first created your database. If, for some reason, you do not have the SQL*Loader direct path views (e.g., LOADER_TAB_INFO, LOADER_PART_INFO) in your database, or if you are in any doubt about whether you have them, you can invoke *catldr.sql* to create them. Be sure to connect as SYS or as INTERNAL before doing so.

You should never need to run *catldr.sql* separately. You should always run *catalog.sql* when creating a new database, and *catalog.sql* always runs *catldr.sql*. If you need to run *catldr.sql* separately, it's a sign that the proper database creation process was not followed.

Invoking a Direct Path Load

You invoke a direct path load as you would any other load. The only additional thing that you need to do is to specify DIRECT=TRUE as a command-line option. For example:

```
sqlldr USER=smishra@testdb DIRECT=TRUE CONTROL=waterfalls.ctl
```

The DIRECT option controls whether the conventional or direct path is used. The default value for DIRECT is FALSE, which is why you get a conventional path any time you don't specifically ask for the direct path to be used. The DIRECT option is one of the options that you can also specify using the OPTIONS clause in the control file. For example:

```
OPTIONS (DIRECT=TRUE)
LOAD DATA
```

```
INFILE 'waterfalls.dat'
INSERT INTO TABLE waterfalls
...
```

Any DIRECT option that you specify on the command line will override any value that you specify in the control file. With respect to this example, specifying DIRECT=FALSE on the command line would cause a conventional path load to be performed even though the control file specified DIRECT=TRUE.

That's all there is to it. Invoking a direct path load couldn't be simpler. If you have a conventional path load that works, you can try it as a direct path load simply by adding DIRECT=TRUE to your command line. As with any performance-enhancing feature, though, there are some restrictions and issues that you need to take into account. Not every load can be a direct path load.

Restrictions on Direct Path Loads

A direct path load provides improved performance while loading large volumes of data, but this performance does come with a price. Certain types of data cannot be loaded with the direct path, and certain SQL*Loader features cannot be used with the direct path. The following list enumerates column and table types that are not supported for direct path loads. Oracle9*i* is expected to remove some of these restrictions, and we've noted that fact in parentheses where appropriate:

* Clustered tables

* Object columns (Oracle9*i* can handle these)

* LOB columns (Oracle9*i* can handle these)

* VARRAY columns

* Nested tables (Oracle9*i* can handle these when they are loaded separately)

* REF columns (Oracle9*i* can handle these)

* BFILE columns

If you are working on a load that involves anything on this list, you'll need to use the conventional path. In addition to not being able to use the direct path to load any of the items on this list, when you perform a direct path load you give up the ability to invoke SQL functions to manipulate the data that you are loading. At least, that was true prior to Oracle9*i*. Beginning in Oracle9*i*, you can use SQL expressions that return simple scalar data such as character strings, numbers, and dates.

When you perform a direct path load into a partition of a table using the PARTITION clause in the INTO TABLE statement, you must disable all constraints and triggers, and you must drop all global indexes.

Storage Issues with Direct Path Load

As discussed earlier in this chapter, a direct path load prepares data blocks from the input data and writes those data blocks directly into the database datafiles, bypassing the SQL statement processing layer and the database buffer cache. When doing this, SQL*Loader writes the new blocks above the current high-water mark of the table (or tables) being loaded. By adding data blocks above the HWM, SQL*Loader eliminates the processing needed to scan the table and find partially filled blocks. The HWM is adjusted to a new value after the load.

Since a direct path load adds data blocks above the high-water mark, it can't use any existing space under the HWM. Therefore, you need to consider two important space management issues when performing direct path loads:

- The initial extent of a table can never be used.
- Free space below the high-water mark will not be used.

Direct path loads insert data into new extents, and do not use any existing extents. Therefore, the initial extent of a table can never be used by a direct path load. Sometimes, especially in data warehouse environments, you may have tables that are populated solely through direct path loads. If you have such a table, you should consider creating it with a very small INITIAL extent size, and a larger NEXT extent size. The INITIAL extent will never be used, so you want to keep it small in order to save space. Your NEXT extent size controls the size of the extents to be created by direct path loads, so you'll probably want it to be reasonably large with respect to the ultimate size of the table.

This idea of wasting space by wasting extents may seem a bit untidy, but the performance increase from performing a direct path load far outweighs the loss of a single extent. And remember, the space is only lost if direct path loads are the only data source. Any data inserted using conventional methods will make use of that first extent. If you feel that you absolutely must use the space in the initial extent of a table for which SQL*Loader represents the only source of data, then you need to use the conventional path.

The second space management issue is that of free space below the high-water mark. Direct path loads do not use any space below the HWM. If you have significant unused space below the HWM prior to a load, and you want to use that space, you must rebuild the table in order to reset the HWM before you start the load. By "rebuild the table," we mean that you must export (or copy) the data, drop the table, recreate it, and reload the data. With large tables, this is not a trivial exercise, and you should carefully think through the costs and benefits before you undertake it.

If you always remove all the data from a table before loading it with new data, you should truncate the table in order to remove existing data. You can truncate the table externally to SQL*Loader by issuing a TRUNCATE TABLE statement from SQL*Plus, or you can use the TRUNCATE keyword in the INTO TABLE clause in your control file. The reason it's better to truncate a table is that doing so resets the high-water mark of the table to the INITIAL extent. A direct path load can then begin using the extents beyond that INITIAL extent. A DELETE statement, on the other hand, doesn't reset the HWM. A direct path load following a DELETE will allocate new extents following all the existing, empty ones, thus wasting a lot of space.

Index Maintenance with Direct Path Loads

During a conventional path load, any indexes on the table being loaded are updated as each row is inserted. This index maintenance adds to the processing load, and of course has a negative impact on the performance of the load. For direct path loads, a different approach is taken to index maintenance in order to minimize the performance impact. Indexes are essentially rebuilt at the end of the load.

During a direct path load, new index keys for the new rows are written to a temporary segment. SQL*Loader will create one temporary segment for each index on the table being loaded. At the end of the load, each temporary segment is sorted, and then merged with the corresponding old index in order to create a new index. After the new indexes are created, the old indexes and the temporary segments are removed. Merging all the new index entries at once like this usually requires less processing overhead than would be required to insert each new index entry one at a time. The exception to this is when you load a very small number of rows into a large table. In such a case, it might be more advantageous to update the indexes in the traditional manner rather than rebuild them. You can use SQL*Loader's SINGLEROW option—described later in this chapter—to do that.

Storage requirements for index maintenance

The manner in which a direct path load manages indexes has a significant effect on the amount of disk storage needed for a load. You need space not only for the data being loaded, but also for the temporary segments and the new copy of the index. At the end of the load, when the indexes are being rebuilt, and the new index entries are being merged in, you need enough disk space for all of the following:

- Each of the old indexes

- The temporary segments containing the new index entries

- Each of the new indexes

If you don't have this much space available, you can do a conventional path load, or you can use the SINGLEROW option.

Unusable index state

During a direct path load, any indexes on the table being loaded are not usable by user applications. When a direct path load starts saving data into the destination table, it marks the indexes on that table as unusable to indicate that the index data is out of date with respect to the data in the table. During such a load, you can see this characteristic indicated in the *status* column of the *user_indexes* (also *all_ indexes* or *dba_indexes*) data dictionary view. For example:

```
SQL> SELECT index_name, status FROM user_indexes;

INDEX_NAME                     STATUS
------------------------------ --------
WATERFALLS_PK                  UNUSABLE
```

If a SQL statement attempts to access an unusable index, an error is returned, as shown in the following example:

```
SQL> SELECT /*+ INDEX(waterfalls waterfalls_pk) */ COUNT(*)
  2  FROMwaterfalls;
select /*+ index(waterfalls waterfalls_pk) */ count(*)
*
ERROR at line 1:
ORA-01502: index 'GNIS.WATERFALLS_PK' or partition of such index is in unusable
state
```

After the direct path load completes loading of the data into the destination table, it creates new indexes and attempts to bring those indexes online in a valid state. If everything works correctly, the index *status* column will show a status of VALID after the load is complete. For example:

```
SQL> SELECT index_name, status FROM user_indexes;

INDEX_NAME                     STATUS
------------------------------ --------
WATERFALLS_PK                  VALID
```

Unfortunately, there are some situations that prevent SQL*Loader from bringing an index back to a valid state. Any of the following situations will cause an index to remain unusable:

- The SQL*Loader process fails or is killed while the index is being rebuilt.

- An instance failure occurs while the index is being rebuilt.

- SQL*Loader runs out of space while rebuilding the index.

- The index is a unique index, and some of the data that was loaded violates that constraint.

- The data being loaded is not in the order specified by the SORTED INDEXES clause.

If any of the above situations occur for an index, SQL*Loader will put a message into the log file to indicate the index and the specific reason for leaving it in an unusable state. For example:

```
The following index(es) on table GNIS.WATERFALLS were processed:
index GNIS.WATERFALLS_PK was made unusable due to:
ORA-01452: cannot CREATE UNIQUE INDEX; duplicate keys found
```

In this particular example, one of the rows loaded into the table violates the table's primary key. To fix the problem, you would need to find that row and delete it. Then you could rebuild the primary key index.

SINGLEROW index option

SQL*Loader's default behavior during a direct path load is to update all indexes at the end of the load. You can change that behavior through the use of the SINGLE-ROW keyword. This keyword causes SQL*Loader to update any indexes as each new row is inserted, rather than deferring index maintenance to the end of the load. The SINGLEROW keyword is an optional part of the INTO TABLE clause discussed in Chapter 2, *The Mysterious Control File*. For example:

```
OPTIONS (DIRECT=TRUE)
LOAD DATA
    INFILE seller.dat
    APPEND INTO TABLE seller
    SINGLEROW
    FIELDS TERMINATED BY ','
    (falls_name, falls_county, falls_state)
```

The advantage of using the SINGLEROW option is that less storage is required. No temporary segments are required to hold new index keys, because index maintenance is done on a per-row basis. You also avoid the need to temporarily have two copies of each index, because indexes are not rebuilt at the end of the load.

The disadvantages of using the SINGLEROW option are performance-related, and include the following:

- Oracle calls are made to insert keys into a table's indexes for each new row that is loaded.

- Oracle maintains undo information for each index insert.

- The index is not resorted and rebuilt at the end of the load, and thus may not be as optimal as it could be.

From a practical standpoint, the SINGLEROW option is useful when a small number of rows is being loaded into a large table. This is the one case where the processing required to update the index for each row may be less than that required to rebuild the index at the end of the load. Oracle recommends using the SINGLE-ROW option if the ratio of new rows to existing rows is 1:20 or less.

You should not use the SINGLEROW option if you are loading data into an empty table, or if you are using the DELETE or TRUNCATE keywords to remove existing data prior to the load. If there is no data in the table to begin with, you'll always get better performance from the default behavior.

Presorting your input data

The performance of a direct path load can be significantly enhanced by presorting your input data to match at least one of the indexes on your destination table. This eliminates the space and time requirements for sorting the new index entries. When your input data is presorted, you indicate this to SQL*Loader by using the SORTED INDEXES clause in your control file. The SORTED INDEXES clause is part of the INTO TABLE clause, and occurs following the table name. Here is an example:

```
OPTIONS (DIRECT=TRUE)
LOAD DATA
   INFILE waterfalls.dat
   INSERT INTO TABLE waterfalls
   SORTED INDEXES (waterfalls_pk)
   FIELDS TERMINATED BY ','
   (falls_name, falls_county, falls_state)
```

In this case, the SORTED INDEXES clause tells SQL*Loader that the input data provided in the *waterfalls.dat* file is sorted on the column(s) of the index named *waterfalls_pk*. SQL*Loader can then take advantage of that fact by not resorting the data when it comes time to rebuild that index at the end of the load.

You may not always have control over the input data that you receive; many applications extract data from legacy systems and load it into Oracle tables. In these situations, it may be more efficient to introduce a sorting operation (e.g., an ORDER BY clause) in the extract programs than to let Oracle sort the data when you load it.

While it's unusual to do so, you can specify more than one index in the SORTED INDEXES clause. Just separate the index names using commas. However, specifying two indexes is an unusual case, because data that is sorted for one index is not usually also sorted for another index. You would have to have multiple indexes with the same set of leading columns.

If you have specified the SORTED INDEXES clause, then it is up to you to ensure that your input data is sorted in a way that corresponds to the index that you specified. Otherwise, SQL*Loader won't be able to rebuild that index, and it will remain in an unusable state after the load completes. Then you'll need to manually rebuild the index by issuing an ALTER INDEX . . . REBUILD statement.

If a table has multiple indexes, and you have the option to choose the sort order of your input data, try to sort your data to match the index with the greatest width. By "width" in this instance, we mean the number of bytes in each index entry. You can get a rough estimate of that number by summing the number of bytes in each column that makes up the index. If you can eliminate only one sort, you want it to be the one that consumes the greatest amount of disk space and memory.

Direct Path Loads and Integrity Constraints

During a conventional path load, any integrity constraints on the table being loaded are verified for each row as it is inserted. If any row violates any of the constraints, it gets rejected. This is simple and intuitive. Direct path loads deal with integrity constraints in a very different way. A direct path load disables some constraints at the beginning of the load, while some others remain enabled throughout. In addition, much of the work of validating new rows against these constraints is deferred until the end of the load.

The fact that SQL*Loader alters constraints when a direct path load is performed has an impact on the privileges that you need in order to load a table. When performing a direct path load, you must have the necessary privileges to enable and disable constraints on the table(s) being loaded. If you are not the table's owner, this means you need the ALTER TABLE privilege on the corresponding table(s). If you attempt a direct path load without having the privileges needed to enable and disable constraints on the target tables, you will get an error similar to the following:

```
SQL*Loader-965: Error 1031 disabling constraint WATERFALLS_CK on table
                GNIS.WATERFALLS
```

The following constraint types remain enabled throughout a direct path load:

NOT NULL constraints
> These constraints remain enabled and enforced during a direct path load. Rows violating NOT NULL constraints will be rejected, and will be written to the bad file.

UNIQUE KEY and PRIMARY KEY constraints
> These constraints remain enabled during a direct path load, but new rows are only verified against these constraints at the end of the load process when the underlying indexes are rebuilt. If a row violates a UNIQUE KEY or PRIMARY KEY constraint, then it is not rejected; it still gets loaded. However, the corresponding index will remain in the UNUSABLE state after the load completes. You need to locate the duplicate row(s), resolve the problem, and then rebuild the index manually.

> If the underlying index for a UNIQUE KEY or PRIMARY KEY constraint is in an unusable state, that doesn't, in and of itself, disable the constraint.

The following constraint types are disabled during a direct path load. Their validation status will be set to NOT VALIDATED to indicate that Oracle doesn't know whether they are met by all the rows currently in the table or tables being loaded:

CHECK constraints
> You need to ensure that the data you are loading meets any CHECK constraints that you have defined; otherwise, you won't be able to reenable those CHECK constraints at the end of the load.

FOREIGN KEY constraints
> SQL*Loader disables FOREIGN KEY constraints during a load, probably to avoid the overhead of querying related tables in order to check each row that is loaded. Be sure that you load valid data into your FOREIGN KEY columns.

Beginning with Oracle9*i*, CHECK constraints are enforced during a
direct path load.

When disabling these constraints, SQL*Loader will write a message such as the following into the log file:

```
Constraint GNIS.WATERFALLS.WATERFALLS_CK was disabled and novalidated before the
load.
Constraint GNIS.WATERFALLS.WATERFALL_COUNTY_FK was disabled and novalidated before
the load.
```

You can verify the status of constraints on a table by querying the *user_constraints* (also *all_constraints* or *dba_constraints*) data dictionary view. The query in the following example retrieves the status of the constraints on the table named *waterfalls*:

```
SQL> SELECT constraint_name, status, validated
  2  FROM user_constraints
  3  WHERE table_name = 'WATERFALLS';

CONSTRAINT_NAME                   STATUS    VALIDATED
------------------------------    --------  -------------
WATERFALLS_PK                     ENABLED   VALIDATED
WATERFALLS_CK                     DISABLED  NOT VALIDATED
WATERFALLS_COUNTY_FK              DISABLED  NOT VALIDATED
```

By default, at the end of a direct path load, any constraints that SQL*Loader disabled are left in that disabled state. You'll need to reenable and revalidate the constraints yourself. Recognizing that few users want to do that manually, Oracle provides a way for you to have SQL*Loader reenable the constraints automatically. You do that through the use of the REENABLE DISABLED_CONSTRAINTS clause, which is part of the INTO TABLE clause. The following LOAD statement specifies this clause:

```
OPTIONS (DIRECT=TRUE)
LOAD DATA
   INFILE waterfalls.dat
   INSERT INTO TABLE waterfalls
      SORTED INDEXES (waterfalls_pk)
      REENABLE DISABLED_CONSTRAINTS
   FIELDS TERMINATED BY ','
   (falls_name, falls_county, falls_state)
```

The DISABLED_CONSTRAINTS keyword is an optional noise word that makes the meaning of the clause clear to people who aren't familiar with it. If you don't like to type, you can just specify REENABLE.

While SQL*Loader is reenabling previously disabled constraints at the end of a direct path load, it may encounter one or more rows that violate a constraint. If this happens, the violated constraint is enabled, but not validated. SQL*Loader will also write an error message to the log file mentioning the constraint and the reason it couldn't be validated. The log file also mentions the constraints that were enabled and validated successfully. The following example shows both types of messages:

```
GNIS.WATERFALLS.WATERFALLS_CK was re-enabled.
GNIS.WATERFALLS.WATERFALLS_COUNTY_FK was re-enabled.

Constraint GNIS.WATERFALLS.WATERFALLS_CK was validated
GNIS.WATERFALLS.WATERFALLS_COUNTY_FK was not re-validated due to ORACLE error
2298.
```

This example indicates that SQL*Loader re-enabled both the *waterfalls_ck* and *waterfalls_county_fk* constraints. However, it could validate only *waterfalls_ck*. The constraint *waterfalls_county_fk* could not be validated because of Oracle error 2298, which is a shortened form of ORA-02298. If you look that error up in the *Oracle8i Error Messages* manual, you'll find that it's a "parent key not found" error. This means at least one row of the data just loaded contains a county name that is not found in the parent table to which the FOREIGN KEY constraint refers. If you query the *user_constraints* view now, you'll find that the *validated* column for the constraint contains a value of NOT_VALIDATED:

```
SQL> SELECT constraint_name, status, validated
  2  FROM user_constraints
  3  WHERE table_name = 'WATERFALLS';

CONSTRAINT_NAME                      STATUS    VALIDATED
------------------------------------ --------- -------------
WATERFALLS_PK                        ENABLED   VALIDATED
WATERFALLS_CK                        ENABLED   VALIDATED
WATERFALLS_COUNTY_FK                 ENABLED   NOT VALIDATED
```

Because the constraint has not been validated, the Oracle database engine can no longer count on it to represent the true state of the data within the table.

Because of the danger that some constraints may not get revalidated after a direct path load, even though you have specified the REEN-ABLE clause, you must explicitly check the log file, or use the query shown here, to verify the validation status of all constraints on the table(s) that you loaded. You must manually deal with any constraints not automatically revalidated by SQL*Loader.

As you've seen, SQL*Loader writes an error message to the log file if it can't validate a constraint. However, to solve the problem, you really need to know more than just that the problem occurred. You need to know the error that prevented the constraint from being validated, and you also need to know which rows of data led to the error occurring. Using the optional EXCEPTIONS keyword in the REENABLE clause, you can cause the ROWIDs of all problem rows to be inserted into an exceptions table. In the following example, the exceptions table is named *waterfalls_exc*:

```
REENABLE DISABLED_CONSTRAINTS EXCEPTIONS waterfalls.exc
```

Using the EXCEPTIONS clause in the control file in this way causes SQL*Loader to use the EXCEPTIONS INTO clause of the ALTER TABLE statement when it goes to reenable constraints at the end of a direct path load. Oracle then inserts the ROWID and constraint name into the exceptions table for every constraint violation that it finds. The exceptions table must be in a specific format. You can use the *$ORACLE_HOME/rdbms/utlexcpt1.sql* script to create an exceptions table, which you can then rename as you desire.

While the exceptions table gives you the information you need to quickly identify problem rows, it's still up to you to deal with those rows. In most cases, you'll want to delete them so that you can revalidate the constraints involved.

 For large tables, enabling and validating constraints can be a time-consuming process. The constraint validation process validates all rows, not just the new ones. In situations where you are adding a small number of rows to an extremely large table, this constraint validation can consume considerably more time than the actual loading of the data. In such a case, Oracle recommends using a conventional path load instead of a direct path load.

Direct Path Loads and Database Triggers

Database triggers are never executed during a direct path load. At the beginning of a direct path load, SQL*Loader disables all database triggers on the table or tables being loaded. SQL*Loader also writes a list of these disabled triggers to the log file. For example:

```
Trigger GNIS."WATERFALLS_BEFORE_UPDATE" was disabled before the load.
Trigger GNIS."WATERFALLS_BEFORE_INSERT" was disabled before the load.
Trigger GNIS."WATERFALLS_BEFORE_DELETE" was disabled before the load.
```

At the end of the load, all of the disabled triggers are automatically reenabled, and SQL*Loader again generates log entries. For example:

```
GNIS."WATERFALLS_BEFORE_UPDATE" was re-enabled.
GNIS."WATERFALLS_BEFORE_INSERT" was re-enabled.
GNIS."WATERFALLS_BEFORE_DELETE" was re-enabled.
```

Unlike the case with constraints, there isn't any REENABLE DISABLED_TRIGGERS clause. You have no such control over how SQL*Loader functions with regard to triggers during a direct path load.

Note that *all* triggers on *any* tables being loaded are disabled. Even though you would think only INSERT triggers would matter during a load, UPDATE and DELETE triggers are disabled as well. If you are loading a table that has triggers defined on it, you need to think through how you are going to deal with the fact that those triggers won't fire during a direct path load. Here are a few approaches to consider:

- If you use triggers to enforce data integrity, consider replacing your triggers with integrity constraints if it's at all possible to do that.

- Create an UPDATE trigger that duplicates the effect of the INSERT trigger, and execute an UPDATE statement modifing each of the new rows you loaded.

- Create a stored procedure that duplicates the effect of the INSERT trigger, and execute the stored procedure for the new rows loaded.

- Preprocess the data that you are loading to obviate the need for the triggers to fire in the first place.

If it's feasible, the last option is certainly the cleanest solution. If you are using triggers to validate data, then find some other way to validate the data that you are loading. If you are using triggers to replicate data, then you may be able to get around that by loading the data twice, once into each table.

Data Saves

A conventional path load commits data after a certain number of rows are loaded. You can even specify the COMMIT interval using the ROWS command-line option. If you set ROWS to 100, SQL*Loader will execute a COMMIT for every 100 rows loaded. This protects you from having to redo the entire load in the event that the load process fails. For direct path loads, SQL*Loader provides a similar protection mechanism referred to as a *data save*. The term "commit" doesn't apply to a direct path load, because the direct path bypasses all SQL processing. The term "save" is used instead. You still use the ROWS option to specify the interval. In the following example, a save interval of 5120 will cause SQL*Loader to save data every 5120 records:

```
sqlldr USER=smishra@testdb DIRECT=TRUE ROWS=5120 CONTROL=waterfalls.ctl
```

During a direct path load, when SQL*Loader performs data saves, you see messages such as the following:

```
Save data point reached - logical record count 5120.
Save data point reached - logical record count 10240.
Save data point reached - logical record count 15505.
Save data point reached - logical record count 20113.
```

A data save is very similar to a commit in the sense that it actually saves data that can't be rolled back, and the saved data is visible to other Oracle sessions and users. The difference between a commit and a data save is that after a commit, the indexes of the table are updated; in contrast, after a data save the indexes are not updated; they remain in an unusable state until the load completes.

 See Chapter 6, *Recovering from Failure*, for help on restarting a failed load.

If you don't specify ROWS, a direct path load saves only at the end of the load. Although data saves provide protection against failures, saving too frequently can slow down the load performance. When deciding on an interval, think in terms of how much time you want to lose in case you need to restart the load in the event of a failure. If you can afford the time to redo the entire load, you may not need to specify a save interval at all.

Loading Data Fields Greater than 64K

SQL*Loader can't load data with a physical record length greater than 64 KB (65536 bytes). In Oracle9*i*, this limit is increased to 20 MB. If you have a table with a LONG data type, or if you are loading a binary file into an Oracle table, you may run into problems, because in those cases it is likely that you will encounter physical records greater than 64 KB in size. For direct path loads, Oracle provides you with a mechanism for using more than one read buffer, thus circumventing this problem.

You can use the READBUFFERS keyword in the control file to specify the number of buffers to be used for a direct path load. For record lengths greater than 64 KB, you may need more than one buffer. The default value for READBUFFERS is 4. If the default value is not sufficient for the load you are performing, you will get an error message like the following:

```
ORA-02374: No more slots for read buffer queue.
```

This has got to rank as one of the least informative error messages. Don't get too hung up on the text of the error message. Maybe someday Oracle will replace it with something users can understand. If you receive the ORA-02374 error, you should increase the value for READBUFFERS in your control file. The READ-BUFFERS keyword comes after the INFILE clause, and precedes the INTO TABLE clause. The following example shows the READBUFFERS keyword being used to allocate a total of 10 buffers:

```
OPTIONS (DIRECT=TRUE)
LOAD DATA
    INFILE waterfalls.dat
    READBUFFERS 10
    INSERT INTO TABLE waterfalls
    ...
```

Keep increasing the value of READBUFFERS until you stop getting the ORA-02374 error. Oracle recommends that you should not specify (or increase) the value of READBUFFERS unless you get the ORA-02374 error, because higher values for READBUFFERS do not enhance load performance; they only increase memory requirements. There's no point in using more memory than you need.

 READBUFFERS is obsolete in Oracle9*i*.

UNRECOVERABLE Loads

By default, all data loads performed by SQL*Loader, whether conventional path or direct path, are recoverable. This means that the load operations are recorded in the redo log files of the database, and in the event of a media failure, standard Oracle recovery procedures can be used to recover any lost data.

When performing a direct path load, you have the option of performing an unre-coverable load. An *unrecoverable load* is one that will not be recorded in the data-base redo log files. The advantage is that you save redo log space and the time required to write the redo log data, thereby speeding up the load appreciably. The disadvantage is that data loaded in an unrecoverable load can't be recovered in the event of a media failure.

 Because data loaded via an unrecoverable load can't be recovered in the event of a media failure, we recommend that you take a backup after the load has finished. There is no need to take a full database backup unless you aren't running in ARCHIVELOG mode. As long as you *are* running in ARCHIVELOG mode, you can protect yourself by backing up only the data files affected by the load. If you can't take a backup immediately after the load, try to take a backup at the ear-liest possible opportunity.

To perform an unrecoverable load, you specify the keyword UNRECOVERABLE at the beginning of the LOAD statement in your control file. For example:

```
OPTIONS (DIRECT=TRUE)
UNRECOVERABLE LOAD DATA
    INFILE waterfalls.dat
    INSERT INTO TABLE waterfalls
    SORTED INDEXES (waterfalls_pk)
    SINGLEROW
    REENABLE DISABLED_CONSTRAINTS
FIELDS TERMINATED BY ','
    (falls_name, falls_county, falls_state)
```

There is also a RECOVERABLE keyword, but it's rarely used because recoverable loads represent the default behavior. However, if you need to make it explicit that you want a recoverable load to be done, specify RECOVERABLE LOAD in your control file. Remember that unrecoverable loads are possible only when you use the direct path. You can't use the UNRECOVERABLE keyword with conventional path loads.

Parallel Data Loading

With SQL*Loader you can execute multiple data loading sessions concurrently. These concurrent sessions can load data into different tables, into the same table, or into different partitions of one table. SQL*Loader supports three types of parallel data loading:

- Concurrent conventional path loads
- Concurrent direct path loads into multiple segments
- Concurrent direct path loads into a single segment

Multiple-CPU machines experience significant performance improvements as a result of parallel data loading. You can also perform parallel data loads on single-CPU machines; however, be aware that overloading a single-CPU machine with multiple concurrent load sessions may actually reduce your overall load performance.

Preparing for Parallel Data Loading

Performing a parallel data load requires some work on your part. SQL*Loader doesn't divide the work up automatically. In preparation for a parallel data load, you need to do the following:

1. Create multiple input data files.
2. Create a SQL*Loader control file for each input data file.

3. Initiate multiple SQL*Loader sessions, one for each control file and data file pair.

To initiate concurrent data loading sessions, you execute the *sqlldr* command multiple times. For example, the following commands could be used to initiate a load performed in parallel by four different sessions:

```
SQLLOAD scott/tiger CONTROL=part1.ctl
SQLLOAD scott/tiger CONTROL=part2.ctl
SQLLOAD scott/tiger CONTROL=part3.ctl
SQLLOAD scott/tiger CONTROL=part4.ctl
```

Note that the commands here should be executed from four different operating system sessions. The intent is to get four SQL*Loader sessions going at once, not to run four sessions one after another. For example, if you are using the Unix operating system, you could open four command-prompt windows, and execute one SQL*Loader command in each window.

Concurrent Conventional Path Loads

You can use multiple concurrent conventional path load sessions to load data into any of the following:

- One table
- Several different tables
- Several different partitions of the same table

The advantage of using concurrent conventional path loads rather than a single conventional path load is that you can reduce the total elapsed load time required for all the data to be loaded. However, given the same amount of data, concurrent conventional path loads may not be as fast as even a single direct path load. On the other hand, concurrent conventional path loads do have some advantages over a single direct path load:

- Integrity constraints are applied during the load, not just at the end.
- INSERT triggers are executed.
- Indexes are maintained during the load.

If you are using multiple load sessions to load the same table, you should specify the APPEND option in each of your control files. You can't specify the INSERT option, because only one of the loads will find the table empty to begin with. You can't specify DELETE or TRUNCATE, because you risk losing data as each of the loads truncates or deletes data loaded by the other.

Concurrent Direct Path Loads

Parallel direct path loads typically yield performance gains far above those you get from parallel conventional path loads. You can use multiple concurrent direct path load sessions to load data into the following:

* The same table

* The same partition of a partitioned table

* Different tables

* Different partitions of the same table

As long as each of your direct path load sessions is loading a different segment, you can invoke concurrent direct path loads in the same manner as you would invoke any other direct path load. If you have two or more direct path loads going against the same segment, then you need to make use of the PARALLEL keyword.

Loading multiple segments concurrently

A *segment* is a generic Oracle term that can refer either to an unpartitioned table or to one partition of a partitioned table. You can run many direct path loads in parallel, and as long as each load session is loading data into a different segment from the others, no special action on your part is required. You either specify DIRECT=TRUE in the OPTIONS clause of each control file, or you specify DIRECT=TRUE in the command line of each load session. For example:

```
SQLLOAD scott/tiger CONTROL=part1.ctl DIRECT=TRUE
SQLLOAD scott/tiger CONTROL=part2.ctl DIRECT=TRUE
SQLLOAD scott/tiger CONTROL=part3.ctl DIRECT=TRUE
SQLLOAD scott/tiger CONTROL=part4.ctl DIRECT=TRUE
```

If you are using multiple direct path load sessions to load data into multiple tables, you can consider each session to be independent of the others. If you are using multiple direct path load sessions to load data into multiple partitions of the same table, you can also consider each session to be independent of the others. In addition, you must use the APPEND option, and you should partition your input data such that the data in each data file corresponds to the partition into which it is being loaded. Otherwise, many records will be rejected, and performance will deteriorate. You must also use the PARTITION or SUBPARTITION keyword in your INTO TABLE clause.

In addition, if you are loading into multiple partitions of a table, you must do the following before you initiate any of the parallel load sessions:

* Disable all referential integrity constraints on the table.

* Disable all check constraints on the table.

- Disable all triggers defined for the table.

- Drop all global indexes of the table.

Once all the parallel load sessions are complete, you can reenable the constraints and triggers, and you can recreate any global indexes that you dropped. A direct path load on a partition of a table will maintain the local indexes for the partition, but not the global indexes on the table itself. Therefore, you must rebuild any global indexes after the load is complete.

Loading one segment concurrently

It's also possible to run multiple direct path loads that all load the same segment at the same time. This is commonly done when loading large amounts of decision support data into a data warehouse. You can have multiple direct path loads going against the same table, or against the same partition of a table. On a multiple-CPU machine, using such concurrent loads can significantly reduce the time needed to load a given amount of data.

Loading one segment from multiple, concurrent, direct path loads is a bit more involved than any of the previous cases we've discussed. You need to use the PARALLEL=TRUE option to invoke SQL*Loader's support for multiple direct path loads to the same segment. This is in addition to specifying DIRECT=TRUE. You can specify PARALLEL=TRUE in the OPTIONS clause of each control file, or in each SQL*Loader command line. The following four commands, each executed from a separate operating system session, will invoke four concurrent direct path loads against the same table:

```
SQLLOAD scott/tiger CONTROL=part1.ctl DIRECT=TRUE PARALLEL=TRUE
SQLLOAD scott/tiger CONTROL=part2.ctl DIRECT=TRUE PARALLEL=TRUE
SQLLOAD scott/tiger CONTROL=part3.ctl DIRECT=TRUE PARALLEL=TRUE
SQLLOAD scott/tiger CONTROL=part4.ctl DIRECT=TRUE PARALLEL=TRUE
```

This type of data loading, where multiple direct path loads run against the same segment, is referred to as a *parallel direct path load*.

How a parallel direct path load works

Because each parallel load session is a direct path load, it prepares data blocks from the input data and appends those blocks to the table. The extents allocated by the parallel load sessions are marked as TEMPORARY during the load process. Figure 10-3 depicts this.

After all the sessions finish, the last loaded extent from each parallel load session is trimmed to release any free space. These temporary extents are then merged together and added to the existing segment of the table or the partition. They are added above the high-water mark, which is then adjusted to reflect the additional data.

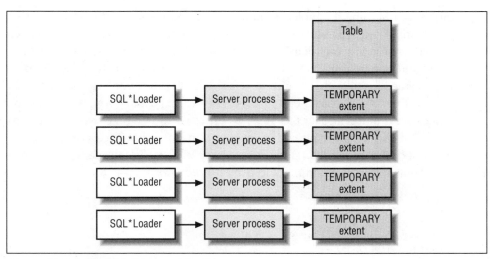

Figure 10-3. A parallel direct path load

Restrictions on parallel direct path loads

You must be aware of the following restriction and limitations when using parallel direct path loads. These restrictions are over and above the restrictions on direct path loads in general that we discussed earlier in this chapter:

- Parallel direct path loads do not maintain either global or local indexes. You need to rebuild all indexes on the table being loaded after the load is complete.

- You can only use the APPEND loading method with parallel direct path loads. You can't use the TRUNCATE, REPLACE, or INSERT options.

- You must disable all referential integrity and CHECK constraints on the table being loaded for the duration of the load.

- You must disable all triggers on the table being loaded for the duration of the load.

You must not specify the REENABLE DISABLED_CONSTRAINTS clause in any of the control files used to perform a parallel direct path load. If you do specify this clause, the first load session that finishes will attempt to reenable constraints while the other load sessions are still active. The result will be a failed load. You must manually reenable any disabled constraints after all the parallel sessions have completed.

Storage management with parallel direct path loads

When you use PARALLEL=TRUE to run a parallel direct path load, each parallel load session allocates its own extents while loading into the table or partition in question. Because of this, you have a great deal of flexibility in managing the storage for the load. Used well, this flexibility can lead to additional performance gains.

If the tablespace holding the table or partition that you are loading is spread across multiple datafiles on separate disks, you can achieve a significant performance improvement by forcing each load session to allocate extents in separate datafiles. To do this, you use the OPTIONS clause in your control file for the table or partition being loaded, and in that clause you use the FILE keyword to associate that control file with a specific datafile. As far as possible, make sure you associate each control file with a different data file. Also, when using the FILE keyword, you must make sure that the datafile you are specifying is in the tablespace containing the table or partition being loaded. Here is an example of a LOAD statement that will cause all extents to be allocated in a file named *data1.dbf*:

```
OPTIONS (DIRECT=TRUE, PARALLEL=TRUE)
LOAD DATA
    INFILE waterfalls.dat
    INSERT INTO TABLE waterfalls
    OPTIONS (FILE='/u02/oradata/TEST/data1.dbf'
...
```

In addition to specifying the name of the datafile to use, you can also control the size of the extents allocated by each load session. To do that, use the STORAGE keyword in the OPTIONS clause. You can specify values for INITIAL, NEXT, PCT-INCREASE, MINEXTENTS, and MAXEXTENTS. For example:

```
OPTIONS (DIRECT=TRUE, PARALLEL=TRUE)
LOAD DATA
    INFILE seller.dat
    INSERT INTO TABLE seller
    OPTIONS (FILE='/u02/oradata/TEST/data1.dbf',STORAGE=(INITIAL 10M NEXT 10M
        PCTINCREASE 0))
    . . .
```

 While you can specify values for MINEXTENTS and MAXEXTENTS using the STORAGE keyword, Oracle recommends against doing so. In addition, the *Oracle8i Utilities* manual points out that anything other than INITIAL, NEXT, and PCTINCREASE may be ignored in a future release. When specifying the STORAGE clause, we recommend that you use a value of 0 for PCTINCREASE; otherwise, you could have exponentially increasing extent sizes for your table, and this could cause problems in storage management.

If you don't use the STORAGE keyword, the storage parameters in the definition of the table or the partition being loaded are used for all extents allocated by all load sessions.

11

Loading Large Objects

The Oracle database supports large object (LOB) datatypes that allow you to store up to four gigabytes of text or binary data in a single database column. SQL*Loader allows you to load data into these LOB columns. As you might imagine, there are some specific issues that come into play when you load LOBs. First off, large objects are, well, *large*. It's not likely that you'll have one large data file containing LOB data for hundreds or thousands of records. The more likely scenario is that each LOB that you load will be in its own file. Thus you need a mechanism for pointing SQL*Loader to the appropriate file for each LOB value that you load. The other issue you'll encounter pertains to flexibility in terms of different input data formats. SQL*Loader is quite flexible when it comes to loading scalar data—you can deal with almost any imaginable file format. But when it comes to loading LOB data, you have a more limited set of options.

About Large Objects

In this section we'll examine what large objects are, explain the data used in the examples in this chapter, and show the options for loading LOB data.

What Are Large Objects?

Oracle uses the term *large object*, usually abbreviated to LOB, to describe a particular class of scalar datatypes that can be used to store large amounts of data in a single database column. A LOB can be one of the following four types:

CLOB
 A datatype that holds up to four gigabytes of character data.

NCLOB
 The national language version of a CLOB.

BLOB

> A datatype that holds up to four gigabytes of binary data.

BFILE

> A datatype that holds a pointer to an operating system file stored externally to the database.

Each of the types in this list can be used as the basis for a database column. The term LOB, on the other hand, does not represent a specific type. Rather it's a general way to refer to any and/or all of the types in this list. SQL*Loader can be used to load data into any type of LOB column.

This Chapter's Examples

All the examples in this chapter center around loading various types of LOB data for the following database table named *waterfalls*:

```
CREATE TABLE waterfalls (
    state CHAR(2),
    county VARCHAR2(60),
    falls_name VARCHAR2(80),
    falls_description CLOB,
    falls_photo BLOB,
    falls_directions CLOB,
    falls_web_page BFILE
);
```

This *waterfalls* table contains four LOB columns. The two CLOB columns contain character data. The BLOB column contains binary data, and the BFILE column contains pointers to LOBs stored outside the database itself. In this chapter, we'll use each of these columns to illustrate a different facet of loading LOB data.

Understanding Your Options

When it comes to loading LOB columns, you need to put more thought and effort into how you format the LOB data that you want to load. Fundamentally, you have the following scenarios at your disposal:

- Each large object is in its own file, separate from the file containing scalar data.

- Several large objects are combined into one file.

- Large object data is embedded in the same file that contains the scalar data.

The first scenario is probably the most likely. The type of data that you would typically load into a LOB column is also the type of data that you would typically store in a separate operating system file. Image data provides a good example. At the operating system level, images are typically stored in JPEG files, PNG files, or some other format where one file contains one image.

One object, one file

You can use the one object, one file scenario to load image files, sound files, or any other type of file into a database LOB column. The basic concept is simple, and is illustrated in Figure 11-1. You have a data file containing traditional scalar data. That file drives the load process. The logical records in the driving data file must then specify the operating system file containing the data to be loaded into each LOB column that you are loading.

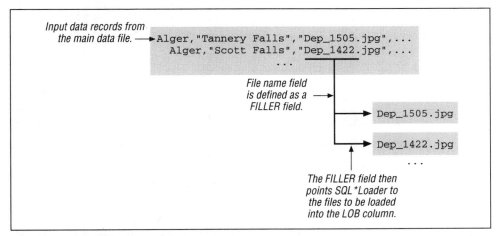

Figure 11-1. Loading LOBs from external data files

In SQL*Loader parlance, the external files shown in Figure 11-1 are referred to as LOBFILEs. A *LOBFILE* is simply an operating system file containing data to be loaded into a LOB column. Don't confuse LOBFILEs with secondary data files. Secondary data files are used when loading collection types such as varying arrays and nested tables, and are described in Chapter 12, *Loading Objects and Collections*.

The key to loading LOB columns from external LOBFILEs is to ensure that each record in the driving data file has a field containing the name of the LOB file to be loaded with that record. If you are loading multiple LOB columns per record, you'll need to specify multiple file names.

Many LOBS in one file

SQL*Loader can also load multiple LOBs from a single LOBFILE. This is illustrated in Figure 11-2. In order for this to work, you must have some way to distinguish where one LOB ends and another begins. To do that, you have several options, described in the section "Placing Multiple LOBs in One File," later in this chapter.

In addition to the scenario illustrated in Figure 11-2, SQL*Loader can switch from one LOBFILE to the next as the load progresses. You accomplish this feat by embedding the LOBFILE names in your main data records. You then have to

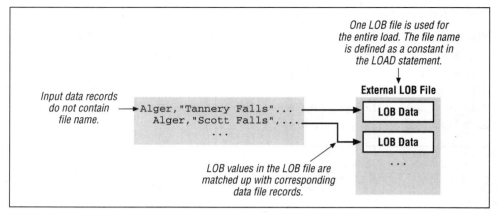

Figure 11-2. Loading multiple LOBs from one file

group together all records pointing to the same LOBFILE, and you must sort that group so that the order of those records in your data file matches the order of LOBs in the corresponding LOBFILE. You're not likely to succeed in all this unless you write custom programs to generate the data files and LOBFILEs from which you are going to load.

LOBS in your main data file

A final option is to simply embed LOB data in your main data file, thus dispensing with LOBFILEs altogether. Any character or binary data may be loaded into a LOB column of the appropriate type. For example, the following field description can be used to load delimited character data into a CLOB column:

```
falls_description CHAR TERMINATED BY ',' ENCLOSED BY '"'
```

This works fine if your LOB data doesn't contain any embedded newline characters. For example:

```
"Alger","Tannery Falls","One of three nice falls in a ..."
```

If you need to spread LOB data over several physical lines, you can take advantage of SQL*Loader's ability to define something other than the newline character as a physical record separator. The result is that a logical record can consist of more than one line of data. The line breaks are preserved, and that's what differentiates such a record from one that has been built up using continuation characters.

Considerations when Loading LOBs

There are two main considerations that you need to be aware of when dealing with LOBs. One consideration concerns size. LOBs are large, and you need to give some thought to how all that data is going to fit into memory. Another consideration concerns the behavior of the DEFAULTIF and NULLIF clauses.

Record and Field Sizes

Earlier in this book you learned that SQL*Loader reads physical records from a data file, assembles one or more physical records into a logical record, and then inserts data from that logical record into the database. That logical record must be able to fit in memory. This isn't normally an issue when you are loading scalar data. Even a home PC will have more than enough memory to accommodate pretty much any record format involving scalar data. The situation changes, however, when LOB data is involved.

When you are loading LOB data that is contained inline within your main data file, the "in memory" requirement still applies. SQL*Loader must be able to hold the entire logical record in memory. This can be a problem if some of your inline LOBs are gigabytes in size. For this reason, if you are loading truly large LOBs, it's probably best to stick with external LOBFILEs.

LOB data read from an external LOBFILE is not subject to the "in memory" requirement. SQL*Loader can read data from a LOBFILE, and write it into a LOB column, without ever having to construct an in-memory copy of the LOB.

One related issue that we have run across when loading LOB columns is the issue of field size. When you define a LOB column in the database, you don't specify a length. You only specify a type, such as BLOB or CLOB, and because the column is a LOB column, Oracle allows you to store up to four gigabytes of data. With SQL*Loader, we've found that if you are loading inline LOBs of any size, you will need to specify a maximum length in your field description. Otherwise, your LOB values will be truncated, and the associated records rejected. This only applies when dealing with inline LOBs. When you use external LOBFILEs, you don't need to specify a maximum length for the LOB.

DEFAULTIF and NULLIF

You can use SQL*Loader's DEFAULTIF and NULLIF clauses in field descriptions for LOB columns, but the following caveats and restrictions apply:

- When you write a NULLIF or DEFAULTIF clause, you can only refer to fields in your main data file. You can't refer to fields in secondary data files or LOBFILEs.

- The DEFAULTIF clause will initialize a LOB to an empty value rather than a null value.

This second item can be a bit confusing at first. To understand it, you must understand the difference between an empty LOB and a null LOB. Oracle manipulates

LOBs internally by way of a small structure referred to as a *LOB locator*. This structure contains the length of the LOB data, and a pointer to that data. LOB locators are small, and are easily passed around between procedures and functions. When you write code to select data from a LOB column, what you actually get is the LOB locator. You then use that locator to retrieve and manipulate the LOB data.

Now, here is the most important thing to understand about all of this. It is possible—common, even—to create a LOB locator that doesn't point to any LOB data. Such a locator is said to be empty, hence the term *empty LOB*. So with respect to LOBs, the difference between null and empty can be summed up as follows:

- A LOB column is *null* if it contains no locator.

- A LOB column is *empty* if it contains a locator that does not point to any data.

If you specify a DEFAULTIF clause for a LOB field, and the condition for that clause is satisfied, SQL*Loader creates an empty LOB. So make your choice between DEFAULTIF or NULLIF depending on whether you want empty LOBs or null LOB columns as a result.

Loading Inline LOBs

If your LOB values are relatively small in terms of size, you can load them from your data file just as you would load any scalar fields. The only difference would be that your destination column is defined as a LOB type. If you're dealing with stream data, you can also take advantage of SQL*Loader's ability to change the delimiter that separates physical records.

Treating a LOB Like Scalar Data

Consider the problem of loading the following data into the *waterfalls* table. The first two fields contain the county name and falls name. These end up being stored in VARCHAR2 columns. The third field is a description of each falls, and ends up being stored in the CLOB column named *falls_description*. Some descriptions are quite long, and the records here have been truncated to fit the printed page in this book:

```
"Alger","Tannery Falls","One of three nice falls in a nature sanctuary...
"Alger","Scott Falls","Scott Falls is a small, but very picturesque...
"Alger","Chapel Falls","The highest waterfall in the Pictured Rocks...
```

Even though the third field is being loaded into a CLOB column, you can define it in your SQL*Loader control file just as you would any other text field. For example:

```
LOAD DATA
    INFILE 'waterfalls_oneline.dat'
    REPLACE INTO TABLE WATERFALLS
    (
    state CONSTANT 'MI',
```

```
county CHAR TERMINATED BY ',' ENCLOSED BY '"',
falls_name CHAR TERMINATED BY ',' ENCLOSED BY '"',
falls_description CHAR(1000) TERMINATED BY ',' ENCLOSED BY '"'
)
```

One thing that's particularly important to notice about this example is the length specified for the *falls_description* field. We set it to 1000 in this case to allow for a maximum of that many characters. The default maximum length for CHAR fields is 255. Any records with field lengths exceeding the maximum will be thrown out and written to the bad file.

Changing the Stream Delimiter

The default record separator for stream files is the linefeed character, or the combination of carriage return/linefeed, depending on the specific platform you are using. Essentially, that means SQL*Loader sees the records the same way you do when you view the file in a text editor. You can change the record separator to something else by specifying an alternate value as an argument to the "str" file option. For example, the file option specified in the following INFILE statement will cause a string of three asterisks to be used as a record separator:

```
INFILE 'waterfalls.dat' "str '***'"
```

Using an alternate separator like this allows you to load data that contains embedded line breaks. The following data contains the same county name, falls name, and falls description as in the previous example, but this time the falls description has been entered on multiple lines:

```
Alger,"Tannery Falls","One of three nice falls in a nature
sanctuary located in Munising."
***
Alger,"Scott Falls","Scott Falls is a small, but very picturesque
waterfall that's easily seen from the road. It's easily seen
that is, as you travel east on M-28 out of Au Train. While
only 20-30 feet from the road, the falls face west. If you're
traveling west, you'll miss them unless you happen to look
in your rearview mirror at just the right moment. What you
won't miss is the Scott Falls Roadside Park—a scenic picnic
area on the shore of Lake Superior just across the road from
the falls."
***
Alger,"Chapel Falls","The highest waterfall in the Pictured
Rocks National Lakeshore. Chapel falls is where Section Creek
falls over a canyon wall towards Chapel Lake."
***
```

You can see that a string of three asterisks terminates each logical record. By using that string of three asterisks as a record separator, you can treat each series of lines as one logical record. If you're going to do something like this, you need to realize that the newline characters that terminate each line won't go away. Newline characters are platform-specific, but on Windows NT platforms, each line of aster-isks will be terminated by carriage return and linefeed characters. It's best to account for those characters when you define your record separator. Thus, under Windows NT, we would include the carriage return and linefeed characters in our separator string. For example:

```
LOAD DATA
   INFILE 'waterfalls.dat' "str X'2A2A2A0D0A'"
   REPLACE INTO TABLE WATERFALLS
   (
   state CONSTANT 'MI',
   county CHAR TERMINATED BY ',',
   falls_name CHAR TERMINATED BY ',' ENCLOSED BY '"',
   falls_description CHAR(1000) TERMINATED BY ',' ENCLOSED BY '"'
   )
```

The record separator in this case has been specified as a string of hexadecimal digits. X'2A' is the ASCII value for an asterisk. X'0D' is a carriage return, and X'0A' is a linefeed. Thus, the record separator of X'2A2A2A0D0A' causes all characters between each two records to be ignored.

Why is this important? Because if you specify a record separator of only three aster-isks, then the carriage return and linefeed characters that follow those asterisks will be treated as part of the next physical record. In our example, they will end up at the beginning of the county name field. Note that we constructed our example spe-cifically to illustrate this issue. The key is that we left the county name field unquoted. Try running it once using *str X'2A2A2A0D0A'*, and then run it again using *str '***'* Use SQL*Plus to query the data after each trial. When you use *str'***'*, you should see that the carriage return/linefeed characters become part of the county name. Quoting your strings insulates you from this problem, because SQL*Loader will skip over characters outside the enclosing characters you specify.

Loading LOBs from External Data Files

If you're truly dealing with large objects, chances are they won't be stored inline with any regular data that you might be loading. It's more likely that you'll be loading the entire contents of an operating system file into one LOB column. For example, you may need to load an image file or a sound file into a BLOB col-umn. SQL*Loader supports this. As we mentioned earlier, LOB files that are exter-nal to the main data file that you are loading with SQL*Loader are referred to as LOBFILEs. You can have a one-to-one correspondence between LOBFILEs and LOB columns, or you can read multiple LOB column values from one LOBFILE.

One aspect of SQL*Loader's behavior that you should keep in mind when loading LOBs from external files is the manner in which SQL*Loader reacts to LOBs that can't be loaded. If a LOB can't be loaded, the record containing the LOB won't be written to the bad file. Instead, the record will be loaded into the database, and the LOB column will be empty. Remember: an empty LOB means that a locator has been created, but that the locator doesn't point to any data.

Another thing worth knowing is that you may not need to specify a length for the LOB field. When we loaded LOB columns from our main data file, we needed to specify a maximum length in order for SQL*Loader to allocate enough memory. When we loaded from external LOBFILEs, we didn't need to worry about specifying any sort of length.

LOBFILE Clause Syntax

When you load LOB columns from external files, use SQL*Loader's LOBFILE clause in your field description in order to specify the file names. The following syntax diagram shows the syntax for a field specification that includes the LOB-FILE clause:

```
columnname LOBFILE ({fieldname | CONSTANT filename}
                    [CHARACTERSET charsetname])
```

The elements in the syntax are as follows:

columnname
> The name of a LOB column in the database table that you are loading.

fieldname
> The name of the field, usually a FILLER field, that contains the name of the external file containing the data that you want to load into the LOB column. The file name may include a directory path.

filename
> Specifies the name of a LOBFILE from which you are loading multiple LOBs. You may (and should) enclose the file name within either single or double quotes.

charsetname
> Identifies the character set used in the LOBFILE. This is only necessary if you are loading a character large object (CLOB) column.

Loading Entire Files

If you have a set of files that you want to load into a table such that the contents of each file becomes one LOB value, do the following:

1. Create a data file to drive the load. This data file must have one logical record per file to be loaded, and that logical record must specify the name of the file to be loaded into the LOB column.

2. Define the field containing the file name as a FILLER field.

3. Use the LOBFILE clause to load the contents of the file specified by the FILLER field into a LOB column.

This is actually simpler than it sounds, so let's walk through an example. To begin with, let's look at a slightly revised version of the waterfall data shown earlier in this chapter. This time, a fourth field has been added to each record. This new field is located in the third position and holds the name of a JPEG file with an image of each waterfall. For example:

```
Alger,"Tannery Falls","Dcp_1505.jpg","One of three nice falls in a nature
sanctuary located in Munising."
***
Alger,"Scott Falls","Dcp_1422.jpg","Scott Falls is a small, but very picturesque
waterfall that's easily seen from the road. It's easily seen
that is, as you travel east on M-28 out of Au Train. While
only 20-30 feet from the road, the falls face west. If you're
traveling west, you'll miss them unless you happen to look
in your rearview mirror at just the right moment. What you
won't miss is the Scott Falls Roadside Park—a scenic picnic
area on the shore of Lake Superior just across the road from
the falls."
***
Alger,"Chapel Falls","Dcp_1213.jpg","The highest waterfall in the Pictured
Rocks National Lakeshore. Chapel falls is where Section Creek
falls over a canyon wall towards Chapel Lake."
***
```

The first record that you see is for Tannery Falls. The third field in that record identifies *Dcp_1505.jpg* as the file that contains an image of those falls. In our *waterfalls* table, the *falls_photo* field is a BLOB. We don't want the file name in that column; we want to load the actual JPEG image data. The first step in doing that is to define the file name field as a FILLER field. The following LOAD statement does this:

```
LOAD DATA
    INFILE 'waterfalls_photos.dat' "str X'2A2A2A0D0A'"
    REPLACE INTO TABLE WATERFALLS
    (
    state CONSTANT 'MI',
    county CHAR TERMINATED BY ',',
    falls_name CHAR TERMINATED BY ',' ENCLOSED BY '"',
    falls_photo_file FILLER CHAR TERMINATED BY ',' ENCLOSED BY '"',
    falls_description CHAR(1000) TERMINATED BY ',' ENCLOSED BY '"'
    )
```

Defining *falls_photo_file* as a FILLER field doesn't get any data into the database. It just gives us access to the file name—remember, you can access the contents of a FILLER field from any expression in the control file. In this case, we want to define the *falls_photo* field as a RAW value, and use the LOBFILE clause to load the contents of the JPEG file named in the *falls_photo_file* field. We use the RAW type because an image is binary data, and we don't want SQL*Loader to perform any character set conversion on it. We simply want the raw binary data inserted into the *falls_photo* column. The following LOAD statement does this:

```
LOAD DATA
    INFILE 'waterfalls_photos.dat' "str X'2A2A2A0D0A'"
    REPLACE INTO TABLE WATERFALLS
    (
    state CONSTANT 'MI',
    county CHAR TERMINATED BY ',',
    falls_name CHAR TERMINATED BY ',' ENCLOSED BY '"',
    falls_photo_file FILLER CHAR TERMINATED BY ',' ENCLOSED BY '"',
    falls_photo LOBFILE(falls_photo_file) RAW TERMINATED BY EOF,
    falls_description CHAR(1000) TERMINATED BY ',' ENCLOSED BY '"'
    )
```

When you execute this load, SQL*Loader reads records from the data file and inserts them into the specified database table. For each record inserted, SQL*Loader also reads the contents of the file named in the LOBFILE clause. That data is stored in the *falls_photo* column. The TERMINATED BY EOF clause tells SQL*Loader to load the entire file into the one column.

You're not limited to loading just one LOB column per record. You can load as many LOB columns as you wish. All you have to do is extend the pattern that you see here to accommodate the number of LOBs that you want to load. You also aren't limited to loading the entire file. Rather than specify TERMINATED BY EOF, you can specify a specific sequence of characters as the terminator for a LOB. You can even specify enclosing characters. You'll read more about these options in the next section.

In the previous example, a multi-character delimiter of '***' was used in between each record. This was done to make the example easier to read. You'll get better performance if you use a single-character delimiter, even if that means using a nonprintable character like X'00'.

Placing Multiple LOBs in One File

You can load multiple LOB values from one file. To do this, you need to have a way of knowing when one LOB ends and another begins. There are at least three ways to know that:

- You can place a delimiter between each LOB value.

- You can create each LOB value with a fixed number of bytes.

- You can use a SQL*Loader type such as VARRAWC that allows you to embed the length of each LOB value in the first few bytes of its data.

Any of these approaches is likely to require custom programming on your part. It's highly unlikely that you would just stumble across a file containing large object data formatted in any of these three ways. You would have to write the program to generate such a file.

As an example, we'd like to extend the scenario in the previous section wherein a photo was loaded with each waterfall record. In this new scenario, we will also load a CLOB field with directions for reaching each waterfall. The CLOB field will be named *falls_directions*, and the data for that field will come from a single LOBFILE that is external to the main data file. Each value in that LOBFILE is terminated by a string of three asterisks (***), and is enclosed within double quotes. That LOBFILE data looks like this:

```
"To get to Tannery Falls, take Munising Avenue east out of
downtown Munising. Going east, Munising Avenue is the same
as H-58. You don't have to go far. Look for the the intersection
where Washington Street goes off to your left. Washington Street
takes you towards the hospital and the Munising Falls Visitor Center.
On your right, just before you get to Washington Street, you'll see a
stairway leading from the roadside up into the woods. You should see a
bridge as well, but the stairway is closer to town, and it's the stairway
that leads to these falls."
***
"Take M-28 west out of Munising. Drive through Christmas,
and begin watching for the Scott Falls Roadside Park on
your right. The falls are directly across the road
from the park, but you won't be able to see them when you
approach from the east."
***
"Drive 22 miles north-east of Munising via H-58 to a dirt road.
Turn north, and take the dirt road to the trailhead. After that
it's a 1.3 mile hike to the falls themselves."
***
```

There are two keys to loading this data. Each record in the main data file must have a corresponding set of directions in the LOBFILE. In addition, the order of values in the LOBFILE must correspond to the order of records in the main data file. The first set of directions is for Tannery Falls, so the first record in the data file must also be for Tannery Falls. The LOBFILE name stays constant for the entire load, so it's specified using the CONSTANT keyword in the LOBFILE clause. The field definition for the *falls_directions* field then looks like this:

```
falls_directions
    LOBFILE(CONSTANT 'waterfalls_directions.dat')
    TERMINATED BY X'2A2A2A0D0A' ENCLOSED BY '"',
```

Because the LOBFILE name is a constant, SQL*Loader will open the file at the beginning of the load, and keep it open for the duration of the load. The TERMINATED BY clause specifies the LOB delimiter as a string of three asterisks followed by carriage return and linefeed characters. The ENCLOSED BY clause specifies that each LOB value is enclosed within double quotes. These enclosing characters will be stripped off before the value is stored in the table. The entire LOAD statement to load the waterfall data with photos and directions looks like this:

```
LOAD DATA
    INFILE 'waterfalls_photos.dat' "str X'2A2A2A0D0A'"
    REPLACE INTO TABLE WATERFALLS
    (
    state CONSTANT 'MI',
    county CHAR TERMINATED BY ',',
    falls_name CHAR TERMINATED BY ',' ENCLOSED BY '"',
    falls_photo_file FILLER CHAR TERMINATED BY ',' ENCLOSED BY '"',
    falls_photo LOBFILE(falls_photo_file) RAW TERMINATED BY EOF,
    falls_directions
        LOBFILE(CONSTANT 'waterfalls_directions.dat')
        TERMINATED BY X'2A2A2A0D0A' ENCLOSED BY '"',
    falls_description CHAR(1000) TERMINATED BY ',' ENCLOSED BY '"'
    )
```

In this example, the LOB values were delimited. Remember, though, that you can also load from a file where each LOB is the same size, or from a file where the LOB values are in VARRAWC format.

Loading BFILEs

BFILE objects are rather strange beasts. A BFILE is a binary file that is stored externally to the database. In other words, a BFILE is an operating system file. BFILE database columns do not store data; instead, they store pointers to the operating system files in which the data is stored. You can use SQL*Loader to load BFILE columns, but what you are really loading is pointers to the files themselves. And to make all this even stranger, the files do not even need to exist for those pointers to be loaded.

Directory Objects

To create a pointer to a file and insert it into a BFILE column, you need to know two things: the name of the file and the directory that contains the file. Specifying the file name is easy; you just provide the operating system file name. Specifying the directory gets a bit tricky, because you do not use the operating system directory path. Instead, you need to supply the name of an Oracle directory alias. A *directory alias* is a name that you define in an Oracle database that takes the place of an operating system directory name. The idea is that if your code refers to such an alias, you can change the directory to which that alias points, and thus the directory used by your application, without having to modify any of your code. It's a good idea, but like anything else it has a downside.

You create directory aliases using the CREATE DIRECTORY statement. Directory aliases are not owned by any specific user. They affect all database users, and consequently they are usually created and managed only by the database administrator. The following statement creates a directory alias named *tannery_dir* that points to an operating system directory named *E:\web_sites\web_michigan_ waterfalls_dot_com\tannery_falls*:

```
CREATE DIRECTORY tannery_dir AS
    'E:\web_sites\web_michigan_waterfalls_dot_com\tannery_falls';
```

If you are going to load BFILE values into your database, you need to create a directory object for each operating system directory involved in the load. This is where we see a bit of a downside to the concept of using a directory alias. If your BFILEs are spread out over 100 directories, you will need to create 100 directory aliases.

BFILE Clause Syntax

When you write a field specification for a BFILE column, you need to use SQL*Loader's BFILE clause in the field description for the column that you are loading. This clause allows you to specify two values: the directory and the file name. You can specify either value as a constant, or you can refer to another field in your input record. Typically, this other field will be a FILLER field. The syntax for the BFILE clause is as follows:

```
columnname BFILE({dirfield | CONSTANT dirname},
                 {filefield | CONSTANT filename})
            [NULLIF condition [AND condition...]]
            [DEFAULTIF condition [AND condition...]]
```

The elements in the syntax are as follows:

columnname
> The name of a BFILE column in the database table that you are loading.

dirfield
> The name of a field, usually a FILLER field, that contains the name of the Oracle directory alias to use when loading the BFILE column.

dirname
> Alternatively, you can specify the directory alias name as a constant. This value may be enclosed within single or double quotes.

filefield
> The name of a field, usually a FILLER field, that contains the name of the operating system file to load into the BFILE column.

filename

Alternatively, you can specify the file name as a constant. You may enclose the file name within single or double quotes.

condition

A Boolean condition in either the NULLIF or DEFAULTIF clauses. The NULLIF clause causes SQL*Loader to store a null into the BFILE column when the specified conditions are met. The DEFAULTIF clause causes SQL*Loader to load an empty BFILE when the specified conditions are met. Chapter 4, *Loading from Fixed-Width Files*, and Chapter 5, *Loading Delimited Data*, both describe aspects of specifying NULLIF and DEFAULTIF conditions.

BFILE Field Specifications

The following data is a slightly modified version of the data used in the section "Loading LOBs from External Data Files," earlier in this chapter. Two fields have been added to the end of each record. The first field contains the name of an Oracle directory object, and the second field contains a file name. The ultimate goal is to populate a BFILE column with pointers to the specified files:

```
Alger,"Tannery Falls","Dcp_1505.jpg","One of three nice falls in a nature
sanctuary located in Munising.","tannery_dir","tannery_falls.shtml"
***
Alger,"Scott Falls","Dcp_1422.jpg","Scott Falls is a small, but very picturesque
waterfall that's easily seen from the road. It's easily seen
that is, as you travel east on M-28 out of Au Train. While
only 20-30 feet from the road, the falls face west. If you're
traveling west, you'll miss them unless you happen to look
in your rearview mirror at just the right moment. What you
won't miss is the Scott Falls Roadside Park—a scenic picnic
area on the shore of Lake Superior just across the road from
the falls.","scott_dir","scott_falls.shtml"
***
Alger,"Chapel Falls","Dcp_1213.jpg","The highest waterfall in the Pictured
Rocks National Lakeshore. Chapel falls is where Section Creek
falls over a canyon wall towards Chapel Lake.","chapel_dir","chapel_falls.shtml"
***
```

In the *waterfalls* table being used for the examples in this chapter, the *falls_web_page* column is a BFILE column. The first step to loading that column, using the data shown previously, is to define two FILLER fields that will contain the directory object and file names from the data file. In the following LOAD statement, the *falls_directory* and *falls_filename* fields serve this purpose:

```
LOAD DATA
    INFILE 'waterfalls_photos.dat' "str X'2A2A2A0D0A'"
    REPLACE INTO TABLE WATERFALLS
    (
    state CONSTANT 'MI',
```

```
county CHAR TERMINATED BY ',',
falls_name CHAR TERMINATED BY ',' ENCLOSED BY '"',
falls_photo_file FILLER CHAR TERMINATED BY ',' ENCLOSED BY '"',
falls_photo LOBFILE(falls_photo_file) RAW TERMINATED BY EOF,
falls_directions
    LOBFILE(CONSTANT 'waterfalls_directions.dat')
    TERMINATED BY X'2A2A2A0D0A' ENCLOSED BY '"',
falls_description CHAR(1000) TERMINATED BY ',' ENCLOSED BY '"',
falls_directory FILLER CHAR TERMINATED BY ',' ENCLOSED BY '"',
falls_filename FILLER CHAR TERMINATED BY ',' ENCLOSED BY '"',
falls_web_page BFILE(falls_directory, falls_filename)
)
```

The final field specification in this LOAD statement is for the BFILE column itself, and it's worth looking at more closely:

```
falls_web_page BFILE(falls_directory, falls_filename)
```

You can see here that the field is defined using the BFILE clause. This tells SQL*Loader that a BFILE column is being loaded. The first argument to the BFILE clause is the *falls_directory* field. As a result, SQL*Loader will read each record and obtain the directory object name from that field. Similarly, SQL*Loader will obtain the file name from the *falls_filename* field. These two pieces of data will be used to create a pointer that will then be stored in the *falls_web_page* column as a BFILE object.

It is not necessary for the files being loaded into a BFILE to even exist. SQL*Loader creates the pointers using the directory and file names. That's as far is it goes. Neither the operating system directory nor the file itself is needed.

12

Loading Objects and Collections

Oracle Corporation is continually adding new features to their database. Some of the more recent additions, which debuted with Oracle8, include support for objects and collections. To keep up with these database enhancements, SQL*Loader has also been enhanced. If you have object tables, or tables with object columns, you can populate them with data using SQL*Loader. SQL*Loader can also load data into columns containing data in the form of nested tables and varying arrays—the two collection types.

In Oracle8*i*, objects and collections can only be loaded via a conventional path load. In Oracle9*i*, under most circumstances, you'll also be able to load objects and collections in a direct path load.

Loading Object Tables and Columns

The release of Oracle8 saw the introduction of objects into the Oracle database. Support of objects was such a revolutionary event that Oracle Corporation started referring to their database as an *object-relational database*. You now have the ability to define an *object type*, which is the equivalent of what you would term a *class* in a Java or C++ environment, and to then create tables or columns based on that type. For example, the following SQL statement creates a simple object type named *feature_type*:

```
CREATE OR REPLACE TYPE feature_type AS OBJECT (
    feature_name VARCHAR2(60),
    feature_type VARCHAR2(12),
    feature_elevation NUMBER
    );
/
```

This type can now be used as the basis for creating objects in the Oracle database. Any objects that you create based on this type will then have three attributes: *feature_name*, *feature_type*, and *feature_elevation*. You can store these objects in an object table, or in an object column within a table.

Since tables and columns can now be based on object types, it follows that SQL*Loader should provide some support for bulk-loading object data. Happily, SQL*Loader does provide such support.

Loading Object Tables

An object table is a table that has a structure based on an object type. Each row in an object table represents one occurrence of an object of the table's underlying type. For example, the following statement creates an object table named *features* that is based on the previously shown type named *feature_type*:

```
CREATE TABLE features OF feature_type;
```

One interesting aspect of object tables is that they look and behave much like relational tables. If you describe an object table, it will look like any other Oracle table. For example:

```
SQL> DESCRIBE features
 Name                                       Null?    Type
 ---------------------------------------- -------- --------------
     FEATURE_NAME                                   VARCHAR2(60)
     FEATURE_TYPE                                   VARCHAR2(12)
     FEATURE_ELEVATION                              NUMBER
```

The *features* table shown here is an object table based on an object with three attributes, but it's also a relational table consisting of three columns. Because of this characteristic, you can use the table as the target of standard SQL statements such as INSERT, UPDATE, and DELETE. As a consequence, when you need to bulk-load data into an object table using SQL*Loader, you can handle that task the same as you would any other table loading task. No special SQL*Loader control file syntax is required. You write your LOAD statement the same way you would if you were loading a standard, relational table.

Loading Object Columns

Things get more interesting when you need to load data into a table containing an object column. An object column is one that is based on an object type. Object types can have many attributes, and while an object column can only have one value—that of the object stored in the column—that object can itself contain many values. Figure 12-1 illustrates this situation.

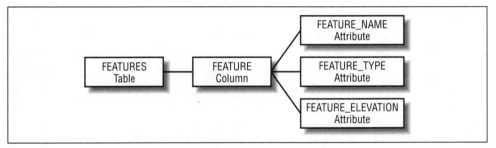

Figure 12-1. One object in an object column may have many attributes

The issue that arises when loading object columns is that you'll have multiple input fields that all need to be loaded as attributes of one column object. You need a mechanism by which you can define that to SQL*Loader. SQL*Loader provides this mechanism in the form of the COLUMN OBJECT clause, which you can include in your LOAD statement.

Creating an object column

This example shows a relational table being created that has one object column:

```
SQL> CREATE TABLE features (
  2      feature_id NUMBER,
  3      feature feature_type,
  4      modification_date DATE
  5      );

Table created.

SQL> DESCRIBE features
 Name                                        Null?    Type
 ------------------------------------------ -------- --------------------
 FEATURE_ID                                          NUMBER
 FEATURE                                             FEATURE_TYPE
 MODIFICATION_DATE                                   DATE
```

The object type named *feature_type* serves as a user-defined datatype for the *feature* column. When you load data into such a column, you need to describe the attributes being loaded in the same way that you describe the columns that you load into a table. You do this using the COLUMN OBJECT clause, which allows you to embed a nested field list within the definition of an object column.

 Object columns may be nested. An object column in a table can have an attribute that is an object type. That object type can further have an attribute that is an object type, and so forth. SQL*Loader's COLUMN OBJECT syntax can be nested in order to accommodate such nested objects.

The COLUMN OBJECT clause

To load data into a table with an object column, you must write a field list that describes the columns being loaded. You aleady know how to do this for columns based on scalar datatypes. When you describe an object column, you must also describe specific attributes that you are loading into that column. Let's assume that we want to load the following data into the *feature* object column of the *features* table. Let's further decide to generate the *feature_id* and *modification_date* values automatically during the load:

```
Trappers Lake                624 lake
Chapel Rock                      pillar
Bay Furnace Recreation Area  610 locale
Cedar Bog Lake                   lake
Wetmore Lookout             1003 Tower
Anna Marsh                       lake
```

The following LOAD statement shows how the COLUMN OBJECT clause can be used to describe the object column named *feature*. Notice in particular that the object column has its own field list:

```
LOAD DATA
INFILE 'coll_obj.dat'
TRUNCATE INTO TABLE features
    (
    feature_id SEQUENCE (COUNT,1),
    feature COLUMN OBJECT
        (
        feature_name POSITION (1:27) CHAR,
        feature_elevation POSITION (29:32) INTEGER EXTERNAL,
        feature_type POSITION (34:39) CHAR
        ),
    modification_date SYSDATE
    )
```

The field list for the object column describes the fields in the input file that correspond to attributes of the object. Any valid field description may appear in this list. If you use clauses such as NULLIF or DEFAULTIF, you may need to use dot notation to qualify your field names. See the section "Using NULLIF and DEFAULTIF with an Object or a Collection," later in this chapter.

It is not necessary to load all attributes of an object, nor must they be loaded in any particular order. With respect to the example shown here, there's no reason why the *feature_elevation* field could not have been listed first, prior to the *feature_name* field, in the COLUMN OBJECT clause.

Loading Collections

In Oracle-speak, the term *collection* is used to refer, generically, to either a nested table or a varying array (VARRAY). Both structures represent a collection of like objects. Semantically, the difference between these two collection types boils down to the following two points:

- Whether the order of elements is preserved when the data is stored in the database

- Whether there is a fixed upper limit on the number of elements

Nested tables are just like regular database tables in that there is no inherent ordering to the rows. When you query a nested table, you get the rows back in whatever order Oracle encounters them in the database datafiles. A varying array, on the other hand, always maintains the order of its elements. Array element number 2 will always be number 2 unless you explicitly move it somewhere else.

Nested tables are also like regular database tables in that they have no inherent upper limit on the number of rows that they can contain. You're only limited by disk space. VARRAYs, on the other hand, have an upper limit that you set when you create the VARRAY type.

For purposes of using SQL*Loader to load data into a collection, it doesn't much matter whether that collection is a nested table or a varying array. From the standpoint of SQL*Loader, you treat both collection types identically.

When you load data into a table, and that table has one or more collection columns, the data for those columns must come from somewhere. With SQL*Loader, you have the following two choices:

- You can place your collection data in your main data record.

- You can place your collection data in one or more secondary data files.

With either approach, there are some fairly specific requirements as to how you format and describe the collection data. You'll need to specifically generate your input data files around these requirements. Given a random file that someone hands you, it's unlikely that you would be able to use it to load either type of collection.

Memory Implications

There is one difference between SQL*Loader's handling of VARRAYs and nested tables. When you load data into a VARRAY column, SQL*Loader must build the entire array in memory before passing it to the Oracle server software. That is not the case when loading nested tables. The memory used for loading VARRAY columns is allocated in the bind array. However, when calculating the number of rows that can fit into the bind array, SQL*Loader has no way of knowing in advance how large your VARRAY objects will be. Thus, there's a real chance that SQL*Loader will compute a value for ROWS that is too high, and that will result in out-of-memory errors when you run the load. Consider the following command:

```
sqlldr system/manager bindsize=10000000 control=feature_names.ctl
```

This command specifies a bind array size of 10,000,000 bytes. SQL*Loader will use that size to compute a value for the number of rows in the bind array. If your VARRAY objects contain a large number of elements, the value calculated by SQL*Loader may prove to be too high. If this is the case, you can look in your log file, find the value for ROWS that SQL*Loader is computing, and then use the ROWS command-line option to supply a smaller value. For example, if the previously shown 10,000,000-byte bind array size resulted in a bind array of 1000 rows, and that further resulted in an out-of-memory error, you might cut the number of rows in half and rerun the load:

```
sqlldr system/manager bindsize=10000000 rows=500 control=feature_names.ctl
```

In this case, the bind array size would still be 10,000,000, but the number of rows in that bind array would only be 500. The reduced number of rows leaves more room for your VARRAY data.

Loading Collections from Inline Data

When you load a VARRAY or nested table column using data from your main data file, you need to place the collection data in each record as a series of repeating elements. Each logical record in your input file thus represents one row to be loaded into your database. There are three different approaches that you can take when representing collection data inline:

- You can have a fixed number of elements that is the same in each record.
- You can have a variable number of delimited elements.
- You can have a variable number of elements, where the occurrence count is specified by a numeric field that precedes the array data in the record.

The following data illustrates a simple case where each input record has exactly two array elements. Each array element consists of a feature type together with an occurrence count for that feature in the specified county:

```
"Alger",lake:213:stream:88,MI
"Marquette",lake:293:stream:145,MI
"Keweenaw",lake:86:falls:1,MI
```

From this data, you can see that Alger County contains 213 lakes, Marquette County 293 lakes, and Keweenaw County only 86 lakes. The first and last fields in these records are the county name and state code, respectively. When the number of elements is the same in each record, you specify the occurrence count as a constant in your SQL*Loader control file.

If you're loading delimited data, you can deal with a variable number of collection elements as long as your outer and inner delimiters are different. You need a delimiter by which SQL*Loader can recognize the end of the repeating data. For example:

```
"Alger",lake:213:stream:88:falls:18:bay:11:island:5,MI
```

In this example, all the data is delimited, and one of the key things you should notice is that the delimiter used for the VARRAY data is different from that used for the other fields in the record. One way to look at this conceptually is to consider all of the following data to represent one field:

```
lake:213:stream:88:falls:18:bay:11:island:5
```

In a sense, all of this data does belong to one field—the VARRAY field. The colon (:) is then used to separate the individual data elements so that SQL*Loader can parse the data and load it into different elements of the array. When you load repeating delimited data like this, you do not need to specify an occurrence count in your control file. SQL*Loader can determine the end of the collection data by the delimiter.

The final approach to representing collection data is to include an occurrence count with each record. For example:

```
"Alger",5,lake,213,stream,88,falls,18,bay,11,island,5,MI
"Marquette",6,lake,293,stream,145,falls,5,bay,8,island,5,summit,23,MI
"Keweenaw",3,lake,86,falls,1,summit,16,MI
```

In this example, all fields are delimited by commas, and consequently SQL*Loader has no way to determine the end of the collection data based on the delimiter alone. Because of this fact, an additional numeric field has been added to each record immediately following the county name. This field specifies the number of elements in the collection that follows. When you use this approach, it's important that your occurrence count field precede your collection field.

Specifying an inline collection

The syntax for specifying a collection field in your control file, when the data for that field is stored inline, is as follows:

```
column_name {VARRAY | NESTED TABLE} {COUNT(fieldname)
                                    | COUNT(CONSTANT integer)
                                    | termination
                                    | enclosure
```

```
                    [NULLIF field_condition [AND field_condition...]]
                    [DEFAULTIF field_condition [AND field_condition...]]
                    (field_list)

    termination := TERMINATED BY
                        WHITESPACE | X'hex_digits' | 'string'}
                        [OPTIONALLY] ENCLOSED [BY] {'string' | X'hex_digits'}
                                    [AND {'string' | X'hex_digits'}]

    enclosure := ENCLOSED [BY] {'string' | X'hex_digits'}
                            [AND {'string' | X'hex_digits'}]
```

The elements in the syntax are as follows:

column_name

The name of a nested table or VARRAY database column.

VARRAY

Indicates that you are loading a VARRAY column.

NESTED TABLE

Indicates that you are loading a nested table column.

COUNT(fieldname)

Specifies the name of the field that represents the number of items that are in the collection.

CONSTANT integer

Specifies one value for the number of items in the collection. This value will apply to each input record.

termination

Identifies terminating and, optionally, enclosing characters for the collection field. These are characters used to terminate or enclose the collection as a whole, and not the individual elements within the collection.

enclosure

Specifies enclosing characters for the collection field.

field_condition

A field condition. The use of field conditions with DEFAULTIF and NULLIF is described in Chapter 4, *Loading from Fixed-Width Files*.

field_list

A field list that describes the fields within the collection. Use the same syntax for this field list as you do for the field list describing an input record. Think of this field list as being a nested field list.

OPTIONALLY

When used in the enclosure clause, indicates that the enclosing characters are optional. SQL*Loader won't require them to be present, but will recognize them if they are present. This keyword may only be used for an enclosure clause that is part of a TERMINATED BY clause.

AND

When used in an enclosure clause, allows you to specify a second enclosing string. If you do this, the first string that you specify marks the beginning of the field value, while the second string marks the end of the field value.

WHITESPACE

Any whitespace character, or string of whitespace characters, will end the field. Both space characters and tab characters count as whitespace. This is a good option to use if you have a varying number of spaces or tabs between fields. However, be sure that you enclose your data, or that your data fields do not include space or tab characters.

hex_digits

Allows you to specify a termination character using hexadecimal digits. Each two hexadecimal digits represents one byte. On an ASCII system, specifying X'2C' is the same as specifying a comma (,). Use hex digits when you are dealing with binary data, or when your delimiters aren't printable characters. C strings, for example, are terminated by X'00' characters.

string

A single character, or string of characters, that marks the end of the field.

At first glance, this syntax may look complicated and intimidating. Realize though, that you are already familiar with most of these clauses.

Example: Loading inline, delimited data

In this example, we're going to walk you through the process of loading some inline, delimited data into a VARRAY column. Each input record will contain a different number of array elements, so we'll have to depend on the delimiters to determine the number of elements to load for each record. The destination table contains one VARRAY column named *feature_count*. The *feature_count* column is an array of up to ten instances of the object type named *feature_count_type*. The following DDL statements can be used to create the necessary types and then the destination table:

```
CREATE OR REPLACE TYPE feature_count_type AS OBJECT (
    feature_type VARCHAR2(60),
    occurs INTEGER
    );
/

CREATE OR REPLACE TYPE feature_count_array
    AS VARRAY(10) of feature_count_type;
/
```

```
CREATE TABLE feature_counts (
   state VARCHAR2(2),
   county VARCHAR2(20),
   feature_count feature_count_array
   );
```

The data being loaded into the table is comma-delimited, and looks like this:

```
"Alger",lake:213:stream:88:falls:18:bay:11:island:5,MI
"Marquette",lake:293:stream:145:falls:5:bay:8:island:5:summit:23,MI
"Keweenaw",lake:86:falls:1:summit:16,MI
```

There are three columns in the table, and if you use the comma as a delimiter, you'll get three fields from each of the data records shown here. We can begin to write our LOAD statement as follows:

```
LOAD DATA
INFILE 'coll_inline.dat'
TRUNCATE INTO TABLE feature_counts
   (
   county CHAR TERMINATED BY ',' ENCLOSED BY '"',
   feature_count VARRAY TERMINATED BY ','
      (
      ...
      ),
   state CHAR TERMINATED BY ','
   )
```

The *feature_count* field is a VARRAY, so we have to complete the field definition by adding a field list. This is where things can get a bit confusing. If you look closely at the DDL shown earlier, you'll see that the *feature_count* column in the table is an array of 10 objects. Our field list for the *feature_count* field in the SQL*Loader control file must define the underlying object type to SQL*Loader. That's done by nesting a column object definition within the field list of the *feature_count* field. For example:

```
feature_count VARRAY TERMINATED BY ','
   (
   dummy_name COLUMN OBJECT
      (
      ...
      )
   ),
```

The name that you give the column object doesn't matter, and in this example we chose to use *dummy_name*. The important thing is that the column object definition must itself include a field list that defines the fields defined for the object. In our example, the VARRAY is an array of *feature_count_type* objects, so the field list for our column object must define the two fields that make up that type. Here is the final version of the LOAD statement showing the complete definition for the *feature_count* column:

```
LOAD DATA
INFILE 'coll_inline.dat'
TRUNCATE INTO TABLE feature_counts
   (
   county CHAR TERMINATED BY ',' ENCLOSED BY '"',
   feature_count VARRAY TERMINATED BY ','
      (
      dummy_name COLUMN OBJECT
         (
         feature_type CHAR TERMINATED BY ':',
         occurs INTEGER EXTERNAL TERMINATED BY ':'
         )
      ),
   state CHAR TERMINATED BY ','
   )
```

This gets somewhat confusing because of the nested field lists, but it does make sense as you think about it. The outermost name in the VARRAY field definition is *feature_count*, and that identifies the name of the VARRAY column in the table that you are loading. The VARRAY column is an array of objects, and the first name nested underneath *feature_count* is an arbitrary name for the column object definition. The field names in the column object definition, in this case *feature_type* and *occurs*, must match those in the underlying type definition.

A very important aspect of this LOAD statement that you should pay particular attention to is the delimiter specified for the column object's fields, as opposed to the delimiter specified for the VARRAY field as whole. The entire VARRAY field is terminated by a comma (,), and in the Alger County record you'll see the following field data:

```
lake:213:stream:88:falls:18:bay:11:island:5
```

The individual elements within this repeating sequence of values are each terminated by a colon (:). If you look at the field list for the column object, you'll see that the colon has also been specified as the termination character for each of the column object fields. When SQL*Loader processes these input records, it first parses the entire VARRAY field using the comma as a delimiter. It then uses the colon to parse the individual values within that field, with each value used to create one object in the array.

When you load delimited data like this, you don't need to specify up front the number of array elements within each record. SQL*Loader determines that as it parses the individual elements within each VARRAY field.

Example: Specifying an occurrence count

The approach to loading nested tables is exactly the same as that shown in the previous section for loading a VARRAY field. The example in this section loads a nested table, and demonstrates the use of an occurrence count in the input record.

Rather than determine the number of nested table entries by parsing delimited values, SQL*Loader will look at the occurrence count stored in each record.

The following DDL statements create the destination table and the necessary types. These objects are similar to those created for the previous example; the only difference is that the type used for the *feature_count* column is defined as a table type rather than as a VARRAY:

```
CREATE OR REPLACE TYPE feature_count_type AS OBJECT (
    feature_type VARCHAR2(60),
    occurs INTEGER
    );
/

CREATE OR REPLACE TYPE feature_count_ntbl
    AS TABLE OF feature_count_type;
/

CREATE TABLE feature_counts_n (
    state VARCHAR2(2),
    county VARCHAR2(20),
    feature_count feature_count_ntbl
    ) NESTED TABLE feature_count
        STORE AS nested_feature_count_table;
```

The data to be loaded is also similar to that loaded in the previous example, but with two critical differences. First, all the fields are terminated by commas, so you can't rely on a delimiter to indicate the end of the repeating data. Second, a new field has been added to each record to indicate the number of repeating elements. This new field is an integer, and it's the second field in the record. Remember: it's important that this occurrence count precede the repeating data to which it refers. Following is an example of this data:

```
"Alger",5,lake,213,stream,88,falls,18,bay,11,island,5,MI
"Marquette",6,lake,293,stream,145,falls,5,bay,8,island,5,summit,23,MI
"Keweenaw",3,lake,86,falls,1,summit,16,MI
```

In this example, you'll see that Alger County has five repetitions of the feature name and count. Consequently, the occurrence count in the second field of the record is a 5. You tell SQL*Loader to use this count by referring to this field in a COUNT clause. The following LOAD statement will load the data shown here:

```
LOAD DATA
INFILE 'coll_inline_n.dat'
TRUNCATE INTO TABLE feature_counts_n
    (
    county CHAR TERMINATED BY ',' ENCLOSED BY '"',
    element_count FILLER INTEGER EXTERNAL TERMINATED BY ',',
    feature_count NESTED TABLE COUNT(element_count)
      (
      dummy_name COLUMN OBJECT
```

```
          (
          feature_type CHAR TERMINATED BY ',',
          occurs INTEGER EXTERNAL TERMINATED BY ','
          )
       ),
    state CHAR TERMINATED BY ','
    )
```

Note the following differences between this LOAD statement and the one used for the previous example:

- The second field is the new element count that was added to the record. We defined it as a FILLER field, because we didn't want to load this count into the destination table.

- The *feature_count* field is defined as a NESTED TABLE rather than a VARRAY.

- No termination character is specified for the *feature_count* field. Instead, the COUNT clause is used to cause SQL*Loader to load the number of occurrences specified by the *element_count* field.

- All fields, including the repeating fields, are terminated by commas. Because of this, it's important that the element count for each record be correct. If the element count doesn't match the number of repeating fields, SQL*Loader will lose its place in the record.

In this example, we defined the *element_count* field as a FILLER field because we didn't want to load that value into our destination table. It's not a requirement, though, for that field to be a FILLER field. If you wanted to load the element count, you could define it as a non-FILLER field, and you would still be able to reference it from the COUNT clause.

 It's also possible to specify a constant value in the COUNT clause. For example, if all your input records contain precisely five elements, you could use COUNT (CONSTANT 5). The CONSTANT keyword must be used when specifying a constant value.

Loading Collections from Secondary Data Files

The previous section talked about loading collections when the collection data was stored inline with the records that you were loading. If you are dealing with large amounts of repeating data, or if you just don't want the confusion of placing repeating data in your main input records, you can load collection data from one or more secondary data files. A *secondary data file* is one from which SQL*Loader reads additional data related to each input record. When using secondary data files, you can use either of the following two approaches:

- You can specify one secondary data file that is the same for all input records.

- You can embed the name of the appropriate secondary data file in each input record.

The first approach, that of using the same secondary data file for all input records, does not require that the secondary data file name appear in your input data. You can specify that file name as a constant in your control file.

If you choose to embed a secondary data file name in each input record, you can use a unique file for each record, or you can have multiple records point to the same file. If you point multiple input records to the same secondary data file, you must group input records together on that basis, and you must ensure that the order of input records in your main data file matches the order in which the data appears in your secondary data file. Figure 12-2 illustrates why this is important.

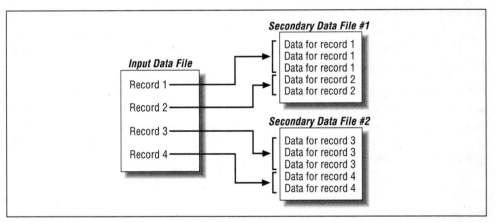

Figure 12-2. Multiple input records can share one secondary data file

As Figure 12-2 illustrates, each time SQL*Loader encounters a new secondary file name, it opens that file. It keeps that file open, and continues to read from it, until it encounters a new secondary file name, at which point SQL*Loader switches to the new file. If your input records aren't properly grouped, SQL*Loader will end up opening the same file twice. If that happens, SQL*Loader will reread from the beginning of the file, and you'll get the same secondary data loaded for two or more input records.

When you load data from a secondary data file, you must specify a count for the number of variable elements in each collection field that you load. SQL*Loader does not support the use of delimiters for the purpose of separating one collection from another when a secondary data file is used.

Specifying a secondary data file

The syntax you use to load collection data from a secondary data file is similar to that shown earlier. The difference is that you must include additional syntax to specify the secondary data file to use for each record. The following diagram shows this syntax in context with the rest of the field definition:

```
column_name {VARRAY | NESTED TABLE} secondary_data_file_clause
                              {COUNT(fieldname1)
                              | COUNT(CONSTANT integer)}
             [NULLIF field_condition [AND field_condition...]]
             [DEFAULTIF field_condition [AND field_condition...]]
             (field_list)

secondary_data_file_clause :=
    SDF({fieldname1|CONSTANT 'file_name'}) os_specific_options
        [MAXRECORDSIZE bytes] [CHARACTERSET 'charsetname']
        [termination | enclosure]

termination := TERMINATED BY
                   {WHITESPACE | X'hex_digits' | 'string'}
                   [OPTIONALLY] ENCLOSED [BY] {'string' | X'hex_digits'}
                                    [AND {'string' | X'hex_digits'}]

enclosure := ENCLOSED [BY] {'string' | X'hex_digits'}
                           [AND {'string' | X'hex_digits'}]
```

The elements in the syntax are as follows:

column_name
    The name of a nested table or VARRAY database column.

VARRAY
    Indicates that you are loading a VARRAY column.

NESTED TABLE
    Indicates that you are loading a nested table column.

COUNT(fieldname)
    Specifies the name of the field that represents the number of items that are in the collection.

secondary_data_file_clause
    Specifies the name and characteristics of the secondary data file(s) to use.

CONSTANT integer
    Specifies one value for the number of items in the collection. This value will apply to each input record.

fieldname1
    The name of a field in the data record that contains a secondary file name.

CONSTANT 'file_name'

Specifies one value for a secondary file name that will be used for all input records.

os_specific_options

A quoted string containing operating system–specific file options. The valid options for Sun Solaris, Windows NT, Linux, AIX, HP-UX, and Digital Unix are as follows:

" "

A null string, or no option string at all, causes SQL*Loader to use a stream record format in which each line is terminated by a newline character. This is usually appropriate when loading text files.

"FIX rec_len"

Causes SQL*Loader to use a fixed-length record format in which each record is exactly *rec_len* bytes long.

"VAR est_bytes"

Causes SQL*Loader to use a variable-length record format in which each record is prefaced by a 5-byte number that gives the length of the record in bytes. Use the *est_bytes* value to provide SQL*Loader with an estimated record size so that it can allocate buffers efficiently.

bytes

An integer representing the maximum number of bytes in a record in the secondary data file(s).

charsetname

A valid character set name identifying the character set used in the secondary data file(s).

termination

Identifies default terminating, and optionally enclosing, characters for the fields in the secondary data file.

enclosure

Specifies default enclosing characters for the fields in the secondary data file.

field_condition

A field condition. The use of field conditions with DEFAULTIF and NULLIF is described in Chapter 4.

field_list

A field list that describes the fields within the collection. Use the same syntax for this field list as you do for the field list describing an input record. Think of this field list as being a nested field list.

OPTIONALLY

When used in the enclosure clause, this keyword indicates that the enclosing characters are optional. SQL*Loader won't require them to be present, but will recognize them if they are present. This keyword may only be used for an enclosure clause that is part of a TERMINATED BY clause.

AND

When used in an enclosure clause, allows you to specify a second enclosing string. If you do this, the first string that you specify marks the beginning of the field value, while the second string marks the end of the field value.

WHITESPACE

Any whitespace character, or string of whitespace characters, will end the field. Both space characters and tab characters count as whitespace. This is a good option to use if you have a varying number of spaces or tabs between fields. However, be sure that you either enclose your data, or that your data does not include space or tab characters.

hex_digits

Allows you to specify a termination character using hexadecimal digits. Each two hexadecimal digits represents one byte. On an ASCII system, specifying X'2C' is the same as specifying a comma (,). Use hex digits when you are dealing with binary data, or when your delimiters aren't printable characters. C strings, for example, are terminated by X'00' characters.

string

A single character, or string of characters, that marks the end of the field.

Example: Loading a collection from a secondary data file

In this example, we are going to walk you through the process of loading collection data from multiple secondary data files. The destination table is the same one used earlier for the example involving inline VARRAY data. The data in the main input file is comma-delimited, and appears as follows:

```
"Alger",5,coll_nest_sdf2a.dat,MI
"Marquette",6,coll_nest_sdf2a.dat,MI
"Keweenaw",3,coll_nest_sdf2b.dat,MI
```

The second field in each input record is an integer representing the number of VARRAY elements to read from the secondary data file. The third field specifies the name of the secondary data file to use. Notice that the VARRAY elements for the first two records are both in the same secondary data file. Those records must be grouped together; the relative order of the VARRAY elements in the secondary data file must correspond to the relative order of the parent records in the main data file. The two secondary data files used for this example contain the data shown in Table 12-1.

Table 12-1. Example Secondary Data Files

coll_nest_sdf2a.dat Data	coll_nest_sdf2b.dat Data
lake:213	lake:86
stream:88	falls:1
falls:18	summit:16
bay:11	
island:5	
lake:293	
stream:145	
falls:5	
bay:8	
island:5	
summit:23	

As the main data records indicate, the first five records from the secondary data file named *coll_nest_sdf2a.dat* are associated with Alger County. The next six records go with Marquette County. The three records in the file named *coll_nest_sdf2b.dat* all belong to Keweenaw County.

To begin with, let's get the easy part out of the way and begin our LOAD statement as follows:

```
LOAD DATA
INFILE 'coll_nest2.dat'
TRUNCATE INTO TABLE feature_counts
    (
    county CHAR TERMINATED BY ',' ENCLOSED BY '"',
    array_count FILLER INTEGER EXTERNAL TERMINATED BY ',',
    array_file FILLER CHAR TERMINATED BY ',',
    feature_count VARRAY
    ...,
    state CHAR TERMINATED BY ','
    )
```

Notice the following key items in this statement:

- The *array_count* field is defined as a FILLER field. This gives us access to the integer value representing the number of VARRAY elements for each row being loaded.

- The *array_file* field is also defined as a FILLER field. This gives us access to the name of the secondary data file for each input record.

The *feature_count* description is not complete in the LOAD statement just shown. We need to add a secondary data file clause to it to identify the file containing the array data. This clause will reference the *array_file* field in the input record. We also need to add a COUNT clause to specify the number of array elements to read from that secondary data file. The COUNT clause will reference the *array_count* field. The description of the *feature_count* field will then look like this:

```
feature_count VARRAY
    SDF (array_file) COUNT(array_count)
...,
```

The *feature_count* description is not quite complete. We still need to add the field descriptions for the column object and the array type. Those are the same as you saw earlier in the inline example. The final *feature_count* description now is as follows:

```
feature_count VARRAY
    SDF (array_file) COUNT(array_count)
    (
    dummy_name COLUMN OBJECT
        (
        feature_type CHAR TERMINATED BY ':',
        occurs INTEGER EXTERNAL TERMINATED BY ':'
        )
    ),
```

Plug this field description into the LOAD statement shown at the beginning of this example, and the final result is as follows:

```
LOAD DATA
INFILE 'coll_nest2.dat'
TRUNCATE INTO TABLE feature_counts
    (
    county CHAR TERMINATED BY ',' ENCLOSED BY '"',
    array_count FILLER INTEGER EXTERNAL TERMINATED BY ',',
    array_file FILLER CHAR TERMINATED BY ',',
    feature_count VARRAY
        SDF (array_file) COUNT(array_count)
        (
        dummy_name COLUMN OBJECT
            (
            feature_type CHAR TERMINATED BY ':',
            occurs INTEGER EXTERNAL TERMINATED BY ':'
            )
        ),
    state CHAR TERMINATED BY ','
    )
```

If you run this load, SQL*Loader will read each record from the input file, determine the number of array elements that go with that record for the *feature_count* field, and load those array elements from the specified secondary data file. As long as the secondary data file remains the same between two input records, SQL*Loader will keep the file open. When the secondary data file name changes, SQL*Loader will close the old file and open the new one.

Using NULLIF and DEFAULTIF with an Object or a Collection

You can use the NULLIF and DEFAULTIF clauses when you are loading collection data. There are two different reasons you might do this:

- You can apply either clause to the collection as a whole.

- You can apply either clause to the individual fields within a collection.

The next two sections discuss these reasons.

Applying NULLIF or DEFAULTIF to an Object or a Collection as a Whole

The NULLIF and DEFAULTIF clauses can each be applied to a collection as a whole. You might do this to set the collection column to null when there are no elements to be loaded. For example, if your array count is zero, SQL*Loader's default behavior is to create an empty collection. An empty collection is not the same as a null collection. If you want an array count of zero to result in a null value for the collection column, you can use NULLIF as shown in the following LOAD statement:

```
LOAD DATA
INFILE 'coll_nest2.dat'
TRUNCATE INTO TABLE feature_counts
   (
   county CHAR TERMINATED BY ',' ENCLOSED BY '"',
   array_count FILLER INTEGER EXTERNAL TERMINATED BY ',',
   array_file FILLER CHAR TERMINATED BY ',',
   feature_count VARRAY
      SDF (array_file) COUNT(array_count)
      NULLIF array_count='0'
      (
      dummy_name COLUMN OBJECT
         (
         feature_type CHAR TERMINATED BY ':',
         occurs INTEGER EXTERNAL TERMINATED BY ':'
         )
      ),
   state CHAR TERMINATED BY ','
   )
```

The NULLIF clause that you see in this LOAD statement is attached to the *feature_count* field, which corresponds to the VARRAY column of the same name in the destination table. As a result, whenever the *array_count* field contains a "0", SQL*Loader will set the *feature_count* column to null. It may seem strange to compare a numeric value to the character "0", but you have to do that because you are really dealing with a character field. Recall from Chapter 3, *Fields and Datatypes*, that numeric external types such as INTEGER EXTERNAL are really considered to be character types.

Applying NULLIF or DEFAULTIF to a Field Within an Object or a Collection

The NULLIF and DEFAULTIF clauses may be applied to fields within a collection. From those clauses, you can reference a field in the table being loaded, or you can reference another field in the collection. When you reference another field in the collection, you need to use dot notation to fully qualify the field name. In other words, you need to qualify the field name in terms of the COLUMN OBJECT name and the field name that you use in your SQL*Loader control file. In the following LOAD statement, you'll see a NULLIF clause on the *feature_type* collection field. That clause causes the *feature_type* field to be set to null whenever a county has no occurrences of that particular feature:

```
LOAD DATA
INFILE 'coll_nest2.dat'
TRUNCATE INTO TABLE feature_counts
    (
    county CHAR TERMINATED BY ',' ENCLOSED BY '"',
    array_count FILLER INTEGER EXTERNAL TERMINATED BY ',',
    array_file FILLER CHAR TERMINATED BY ',',
    feature_count VARRAY
        SDF (array_file) COUNT(array_count)
        NULLIF array_count='0'
        (
        dummy_name COLUMN OBJECT
            (
            feature_type CHAR TERMINATED BY ':'
                NULLIF feature_count.dummy_name.occurs='0',
            occurs INTEGER EXTERNAL TERMINATED BY ':'
            )
        ),
    state CHAR TERMINATED BY ','
    )
```

Notice that the NULLIF clause uses the fully qualified name *feature_count. dummy_name.occurs* to refer to the occurs field in the collection. Figure 12-3 shows how this fully qualified name is derived.

When you use NULLIF or DEFAULTIF for a field in a collection, and you refer to another field in the same collection, SQL*Loader looks at, and then operates on, the two fields in the context of a single entry in the collection. With respect to the

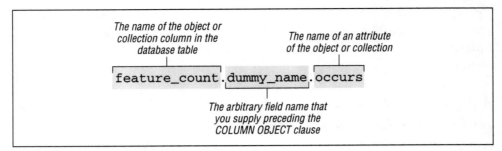

Figure 12-3. Deriving a fully qualified name

current example, a VARRAY might contain three elements. Any NULLIF or DEFAULTIF clauses will be applied to each of those three elements independently of the others. An OCCURS value of "0" in the first element will result in only the first element's *feature_type* field being set to null. When it comes to evaluating the NULLIF clause for the second element, SQL*Loader will look at the *occurs* field for that element, and the outcome will affect only the *feature_type* field for that same array element.

Index

Symbols

( ) (parentheses), 47
* (asterisk), 49, 50
\ (backslash), 20
: (colon), 227
    in SQL expressions, 153
= (equals sign), 124
    SILENT parameter, 18
<> (not-equal-to operators), 102, 124
. (period), 33
" (quotes), 87
    doubled, 110
    and SQL, 153
/ (forward-slash), 15

A

absolute positions, 50
ALTER ROLLBACK SEGMENT, 175
APPEND, 7, 30, 134
    concurrent conventional path loads, 200
    concurrent direct path loads, 201
    parallel direct path loads, 203
    for recovery, failed direct path loads, 139
    table loading method, 36
assumed decimal points, 70
    in columnar numeric data, 72

B

backup after unrecoverable loads, 198
BAD, 15
.bad filename extension, 15
bad files, 3, 4, 141
    creation, 142
    data written to, 141
    edited data, loading from, 144
    naming, 33, 142
BADFILE, 142
badfile_name element, INFILE clause, 32
BCD (binary-coded decimal data), 73
BFILE clauses, syntax, 218
BFILEs, 206
    field specifications, 219
    objects, 217
binary data, loading, 74
binary file datatypes, 69
bind arrays, 12, 168
    BINDSIZE and ROWS parameters, 17
    command-line parameters, 168
    and commit frequency, 172
    determining size, 177
    maximum size, setting, 170
    memory allocation, 170
        for VARRAYs, 225
    and rollback segments, 175
    row numbers, setting, 171
    size and load performance, 173, 179

We'd like to hear your suggestions for improving our indexes. Send email to *index@oreilly.com*.

About the Authors

Jonathan Gennick is a writer and editor. His writing career began in 1997 when he coauthored *Teach Yourself PL/SQL in 21 Days*. Since then, he has written several O'Reilly books, including *Oracle SQL*Plus: The Definitive Guide*, *Oracle SQL*Plus Pocket Reference*, and *Oracle Net8 Configuration and Troubleshooting*. He has also edited a number of books for O'Reilly and other publishers, and he recently joined O'Reilly as an associate editor, specializing in Oracle books. Jonathan was formerly a manager in KPMG's Public Services Systems Integration practice, where he was also the lead database administrator for the utilities group working out of KPMG's Detroit office. He has more than a decade of experience with relational databases.

Jonathan is a member of MENSA, and he holds a Bachelor of Arts degree in Information and Computer Science from Andrews University in Berrien Springs, Michigan. He currently resides in Munising, Michigan, with his wife Donna and their two children: twelve-year-old Jenny, who often wishes her father wouldn't spend quite so much time writing, and five-year-old Jeff, who has never seen it any other way. You can reach Jonathan by email at *jonathan@gennick.com*. You can also visit Jonathan's web site at *http://gennick.com*.

Sanjay Mishra is a certified Oracle database administrator with more than nine years of IT experience. For the past six years, he has been involved in the design, architecture, and implementation of many mission-critical and decision support databases. He has worked extensively in the areas of database architecture, database management, backup/recovery, disaster planning, performance tuning, Oracle Parallel Server, and parallel execution. He has a Bachelor of Science degree in Electrical Engineering and a Master of Engineering degree in Systems Science and Automation. He is the coauthor of *Oracle Parallel Processing* (O'Reilly & Associates) and can be reached at *sanjay_mishra@i2.com*.

Colophon

Our look is the result of reader comments, our own experimentation, and feedback from distribution channels. Distinctive covers complement our distinctive approach to technical topics, breathing personality and life into potentially dry subjects.

The animal on the cover of *Oracle SQL*Loader: The Definitive Guide* is a scarab beetle. There are nearly 30,000 members of the scarab beetle family, and over 1,200 in North America alone. This large, heavy-bodied beetle is classified in the order *Coleoptera*, family *Scarabaeidae*. Many scarab beetles are brightly colored, and some are iridescent. In North America, the largest scarabs are the Hercules beetle and the closely related elephant and rhinoceros beetles. The males of these species have prominent horns.

Many scarabs are scavengers, living on decaying vegetation and animal dung. They are consider efficient recyclers and valuable for reducing disease-breeding waste. Some of the scavengers of the scarab family use their front legs to gather dung and roll it into a ball. They carry the ball underground and use it as food and a place to lay their eggs. The Mediterranean black scarab's apparently magical ability to reproduce from mud and decaying organic materials led the ancient Egyptians to associate the scarab with resurrection and immortality. The beetles were considered sacred, and representations in stone and metal were buried with mummies.

A member of the North American scarab family plays a key role in Edgar Allen Poe's story "The Gold-Bug." In his search of Sullivan's Island, South Carolina, a scarab beetle is William Legrand's mysterious guide to the buried treasure of Captian Kidd.

Colleen Gorman was the production editor and the copyeditor for *Oracle SQL*Loader: The Definitive Guide*. Sarah Jane Shangraw and Linley Dolby provided quality control, and Leanne Soylemez was the proofreader. John Bickelhaupt wrote the index.

Ellie Volckhausen designed the cover of this book, based on a series design by Edie Freedman. The cover image is from *Cuvier's Animals*. Emma Colby produced the cover layout with QuarkXPress 4.1 using Adobe's ITC Garamond font.

Melanie Wang designed the interior layout based on a series design by Nancy Priest. Anne-Marie Vaduva converted the files from Microsoft Word to FrameMaker 5.5.6 using tools created by Mike Sierra. The text and heading fonts are ITC Garamond Light and Garamond Book; the code font is Constant Willison. The illustrations that appear in the book were produced by Robert Romano and Jessamyn Read using Macromedia FreeHand 9 and Adobe Photoshop 6. This colophon was written by Colleen Gorman.

Whenever possible, our books use a durable and flexible lay-flat binding. If the page count exceeds this binding's limit, perfect binding is used.